A Minimally Good Life

*What We Owe to Others and What
We Can Justifiably Demand*

NICOLE HASSOUN

OXFORD
UNIVERSITY PRESS

Great Clarendon Street, Oxford, OX2 6DP,
United Kingdom

Oxford University Press is a department of the University of Oxford.
It furthers the University's objective of excellence in research, scholarship,
and education by publishing worldwide. Oxford is a registered trade mark of
Oxford University Press in the UK and in certain other countries

© Nicole Hassoun 2024

The moral rights of the author have been asserted

All rights reserved. No part of this publication may be reproduced, stored in
a retrieval system, or transmitted, in any form or by any means, without the
prior permission in writing of Oxford University Press, or as expressly permitted
by law, by licence or under terms agreed with the appropriate reprographics
rights organization. Enquiries concerning reproduction outside the scope of the
above should be sent to the Rights Department, Oxford University Press, at the
address above

You must not circulate this work in any other form
and you must impose this same condition on any acquirer

Published in the United States of America by Oxford University Press
198 Madison Avenue, New York, NY 10016, United States of America

British Library Cataloguing in Publication Data
Data available

Library of Congress Control Number: 2024935233

ISBN 9780192856159

DOI: 10.1093/9780191946455.001.0001

Printed and bound in the UK by
Clays Ltd, Elcograf S.p.A.

Links to third party websites are provided by Oxford in good faith and
for information only. Oxford disclaims any responsibility for the materials
contained in any third party website referenced in this work.

To my dad and mom, for everything. Thank you for making sure we always had enough and for teaching us the importance of helping others live well enough too.

Contents

Acknowledgments ix

    Introduction—A Minimally Good Life: What We Owe to Others and What We Can Justifiably Demand   1

1. The Account of the Minimally Good Life   10
2. Good Enough? Other Accounts of the Minimally Good Life   34
3. The Minimally Good Life and Basic Justice   58
4. Advantages of the Minimally Good Life Account   80
5. Helping People Live Minimally Well in Present and Future Generations   99
6. Hope and the Virtue of Creative Resolve   123

    Conclusion—Beyond a Basic Minimum: Is A Minimally Good Life Really Good Enough?   142

Appendix I   149
Appendix II   151
Appendix III   153

References   159
Index   173

Acknowledgments

I am grateful for comments from audiences at Stockholm University, Trinity College Dublin, University of Lisbon, University of Gothenburg, Vanderbilt University, University of Helsinki, CUNY, the Institute for Future Studies, Bowling Green, Goethe University, Colgate College, Ithaca College, International Conference on Global Human Rights, Bled Philosophical Conference, Free University of Berlin, Philosophy, Politics and Economics Society Meeting Hope and Optimism Conference, Concordia University, University of Massachusetts Boston, University of California San Diego, St. Louis University, Eastern and Pacific Divisions of the American Philosophical Association, University of Connecticut, Middlebury College, International Colloquium on Justice, Democracy and Political Emotions in Transnational Perspective, Hungarian Academy of Sciences, and the Hope and Optimism and Happiness & Wellbeing midpoint and capstone conferences.

I would like to thank Dan Haybron, Andrew Chignell, Liam Shields, Ben Nelson, Chris Armstrong, Anders Herlitz, Avi Appel, David Miller, Dale Dorsey, Antti Kauppinen, Matthew Liao, Garrett Cullity, Nicholas Smith, Gillian Brock, Darrel Moellendorf, Thomas Pölzler, Adam Etinson, Caesar Atuire, Christine Straehle, Tony Reeves, Carl Knight, Andreas Albertsen, Luc Bovens, Johnathan Wolff, Richard Miller, Charles Goodman, Ernest Wang, Alex Esposito, Anja Karnein, Sarah Wright, Bradley Monton, Katie Stockdale, Michael Milona, Govind Persad, Julian Culp, Christian Barry, Michael Da Silva, Andreas Albertsen, Iwao Hirose, David Miller, Daniel Hausman, Brian Berkey, Tim Campbell, Yukiko Asada, Johnathan Wolff, and Judith Lichtenberg for particularly extensive comments and discussion of the minimally good life and creative resolve. I would also like to thank all of my students and colleagues at Binghamton University and Cornell University who read earlier versions of this work and the Global Health Impact team (global-health-impact.org/new) especially Diana Dedi, Xiaoshun Li, Milan Patel, Jaden Iskeiv, Ainsley Garipoli, Noa Mizrachi, Ariana Rodriguez, and Caroline Tuczinski for research assistance. I apologize for leaving this list vastly incomplete.

I am incredibly grateful for support from Binghamton University and the Collegium for Advanced Studies at the University of Helsinki for the time necessary to complete this project. Early research and papers laying the basis for the book were made possible through the support of a grant from the John Templeton Foundation (through the https://www.happinessandwellbeing.org/ and http://hopeoptimism.com/ projects). The opinions expressed in this publication are those of the author and do not necessarily reflect the views of the John Templeton Foundation.

Introduction—A Minimally Good Life

What We Owe to Others and What We Can Justifiably Demand

1. Common Humanity and the Basic Minimum

At the start of the Coronavirus pandemic the *New York Times* ran several editorials talking about social safety nets. One read: "This will be the true legacy of our Gilded Age, suddenly behind us: that when our country could have afforded to mend our national safety net, we shredded it instead. And after the dead have been counted, after the masks and gloves are discarded or packed away until the next pandemic, it is our failure to shore up the safety net in our years of prosperity past that will destroy far more lives than the coronavirus itself" (Sandler, 2020). Another said: "the best way to break this cycle of fear and further contagion is to dispense with zero-sum thinking and stitch together a safety net big enough, and strong enough, for everyone" (*New York Times* Editorial Board, 2020).

Still, in the Coronavirus pandemic's wake and as international conflict and inflation surge, one can almost hear the desperate call for greater social security and stronger safety nets around the world. Existing safety nets in many countries have obvious problems: most reasonable people agree that children should not go hungry and everyone should have access to emergency medical care. But how can we determine what kind of social safety net will suffice?

What do we owe to each other, and what can we claim, out of respect for our common humanity? The United Nations' Sustainable Development Goals, the Universal Declaration of Human Rights, and many states' constitutions embody different answers to this question. The philosophical literature also contains many potential accounts of what this respect requires (Tan, 2004; Risse, 2012; Hassoun, 2013; Hassoun, 2016; Hassoun, 2020a).

A Minimally Good Life: What We Owe to Others and What We Can Justifiably Demand argues that *respect for our common humanity* at least requires helping others live minimally good lives when doing so does not entail sacrificing our own ability to live well enough. This, it suggests, provides a unified answer to the question of what we must give to, and can demand from, others as a basic minimum.

A Minimally Good Life's first part just defends a mechanism for arriving at its account of the basic minimum. It argues that everyone must obtain what helps them secure the relationships, pleasures, knowledge, appreciation, worthwhile activities, and other life-improving goods they need to live minimally good lives. We can figure out exactly what someone needs to live well enough by considering what a reasonable, caring, and free person would need to contently live that person's life. *A Minimally Good Life*'s first part explains at length exactly what this requires, but the basic idea is simple: As reasonable, caring, free, people we should put ourselves into each other's shoes and think about what we would need to live well enough *if we were that person*. Moreover, *A Minimally Good Life*'s first part argues that alternative accounts of what the basic minimum require fail to attend carefully enough to what different people need.

A Minimally Good Life's second part argues that respect for common humanity requires helping others live minimally good, or dignified, lives. It contends that our common humanity lies, in part, in the fact that we are needy, vulnerable creatures standing in important relationships of care and concern to others. These relationships have value. We need these relationships to survive and flourish as free, but constrained, human agents in light of our vulnerability to the radical contingency that shapes our lives. Respect for common humanity demands that we each do our part to foster and sustain these relationships. They partly constitute our distinctively human forms of life. This account may inform theories about what we owe to others in our personal, as well as political, lives. *A Minimally Good Life* argues that competing accounts of what respect for common humanity requires demand either too much or too little.

In explaining how its unified account of what we owe to others and can demand as a basic minimum can play important roles in both our ethical and political lives, *A Minimally Good Life* addresses several pressing questions in moral and political theory: What, if any, basic minimum must legitimate states provide for their subjects? Do we owe people a basic minimum as individuals irrespective of our specific attachments? What, if any, basic minimum must societies help their subjects secure? Does the basic minimum differ when we consider what we owe to people in other societies out of concern for global justice or respect for human rights? What exactly is good enough?

2. What Sufficiency Really Requires

A Minimally Good Life provides a philosophically robust account of the basic minimum. Its account of the minimally good life should engage readers interested in sufficiency theory as well as legitimacy, beneficence, global justice, and human rights. Many argue that social, or global, justice requires helping everyone live at least minimally good lives (Dorsey, 2012; Hassoun, 2013; Liao, 2015; Hassoun, 2016). Others suggest that people have human rights to whatever protects their ability to live such lives (Nickel, 2007; Hassoun, 2020a;). To date, however, most sufficiency theorists have tried to stay relatively neutral about exactly what people need to rise above the threshold (Benbaji, 2005; Crisp, 2006; Huseby, 2010; Shields, 2016; Huseby, 2020; Shields, 2020).[1,2]

To understand what we owe to people as a basic minimum and why the threshold is special, we need a detailed, and much more fully developed, account of what people require for a basic minimum and an explanation of why they need so much. Often sufficiency theories just define the threshold as what we should be content to attain or as the level at which compassion gives out, but do not explain where that level lies or how to think about compassion or contentment (Crisp, 2006; Huseby, 2010; Huseby, 2020). Roger Crisp asserts, for instance, that a compassionate impartial spectator would have special concern for those who fare poorly and cannot live sufficiently good lives. He says compassionate people would aim to help a greater number of those who are worse-off below this threshold. However, it is not clear what people need to live sufficiently good lives nor how we should help those below the threshold on Crisp's account (Crisp, 2006, 252; Crisp, 2008).[3] Few of even

---

[1] Even theories appealing to the idea that concern for individuals' ability to live minimally good lives at least partly grounds human rights have often remained relatively silent on the exact content of this life (Nickel, 2007; Buchanan, 2013). I do not offer a full account of what appropriate concern for common humanity itself requires, but see Chapter 3 for discussion.

[2] Robert Huseby's account in "Sufficiency: Restated and Defended" is particularly implausible. He says that everyone should be content with their level of welfare but since some have expensive tastes, in practice, we should only ensure that there is some reasonable chance that people can rest content (Huseby, 2010). He does not provide an account of what contentment requires. In "Sufficiency and the Threshold Question," Huseby much more plausibly says that what matters is that people have good lives understood to include subjective and objective elements and that one should endorse one's life for good reasons (Huseby, 2020). However, he does not say much more than this. Instead, he focuses on how much priority to give to helping those below this threshold and a higher one at which he thinks distributive concerns are simply irrelevant. I believe we need an account of what people require to live good (enough) lives to justify any view about what kind of priority applies and even to explain what constitutes sufficiency itself.

[3] Although Crisp has some interesting things to say about compassion, different accounts of the compassionate ideal observer might provide more or less support for each of Crisp's claims (Crisp, 2008).

the best worked out accounts have gone beyond specifying more than a currency of justice (but see Frankfurt (1988, 104–116) and Axelsen and Nielsen (2016), which I discuss at some length in Chapter 2, and Nielsen (2016) for an explanation of contentment—on which I draw in Chapter 1).[4] Sufficiency theorists might, most plausibly, adopt welfare or capability accounts of what we owe to each other as a basic minimum (Benbaji, 2006; Huseby, 2010; Axelsen and Nielsen, 2016). After all, few contemporary theorists endorse pure resource theories of the basic minimum.[5] *A Minimally Good Life* argues, however, that the best available welfare capability accounts often focus on the wrong things demanding either too much or not enough (and sometimes both).

Rather, *A Minimally Good Life* draws on, but goes well beyond, canonical sufficiency theories in defending a novel, quasi-contractualist, mechanism to arrive at a broad, pluralistic account of the minimally good life that provides a plausible threshold. *A Minimally Good Life* does not rest its argument on the simple assertion that we should demonstrate appropriate impartiality and compassion, though it develops some ideas similar to those in Frankfurt (1987) and Crisp (2006).[6] It explains what kind of compassion we must employ and why there is a significant shift in the reasons we have for helping people above and below the threshold at which we should rest content as well as what gives the threshold its non-instrumental importance. *A Minimally Good Life* argues that we must empathize with people appropriately in arriving at the judgment that there are no serious reasons to doubt their lives can be well lived. That is, it provides a conception of what reasonable, free, care demands to argue that we should help everyone live minimally well and explains at length what people need to live such lives. On *A Minimally Good Life*'s account, minimally good lives require sufficient capabilities, autonomy, resources, opportunities, and other life-enhancing goods. It, thus, bridges the divide between welfare, capability, and other (e.g. resource/institutional) theories. That is, *A Minimally Good Life* provides a broadly pluralistic account

---

[4] Axelsen and Nielsen (2015 and 2016) provide what is perhaps the best worked out alternative grounded in a conception of capabilities. On their account, central capabilities include those relevant for satisfying biological and physical needs, fundamental interests in agency, and social interests. Moreover, they say that individuals should have some influence over the process of selecting central capabilities since personal choice is so important, but they do not further characterize the method for arriving at reasonable agreement that they endorse (Axelsen and Nielsen, 2016, 22). See Chapter 2 for further discussion.

[5] John Rawls is concerned with more than resources. Even his difference principle focuses on primary goods including rights, liberties, powers, freedoms, and the social basis of self-respect (Rawls, 1971), but see Pogge (2002) for defense.

[6] It is notable, however, that they both aim to explain at what point distributive concerns should disappear. Unlike these canonical sufficiency theorists, I want to identify the basic minimum.

on which people need different amounts of many different things to live minimally good lives. Below I outline the arguments in each of this book's chapters in turn.

3. Outline

To arrive at a plausible account of the basic minimum, the first chapter argues that, as reasonable, caring, free people we should consider whether *we* would contentedly live the lives that the least fortunate actually live. We should put ourselves into each other's shoes and think about what each person needs to live well enough. We should ask what *we* would need to contentedly live others' lives. We should not directly ask each person what they need. People often make mistakes about what they need and politically contest needs (Fraser, 1989; Hassoun, 2016). Some adapt to poor conditions and do not strive to improve them (Nussbaum, 2000b). Deprivation can also undermine individuals' ability to understand the poverty of their conditions. If we get some critical distance from others' experience, we can see whether they require everything they think they need to live well enough. We may find that people need resources, capabilities, institutions, or other things that they do not believe they need. Not everyone will agree on what someone needs to live a minimally good life, but I argue that free, reasonable, and caring people should agree on many things.[7] However, I intend the mechanism to be useful in the real world where even free, reasonable, and caring people may lack the requisite information to arrive at good judgments or make mistakes in some cases. Deliberation can help resolve remaining disagreements and put the proposal into practice.[8]

People need many of the same things, but the differences between people also matter immensely. Everyone must meet their basic needs for food, water, shelter, and so forth. Moreover, to live at least minimally well, the good things in each person's life (such as relationships, pleasures, knowledge, appreciation, and worthwhile activities) must compensate for their difficulties, pains,

---

[7] I argue that this follows from what it means to be reasonable, caring, and free (supposing people have all of the relevant information).
[8] There is, of course, some tension between providing a theory that is useful for actual decision makers and providing one that can offer determinate answers that are not vague or poorly defined. Still, I hope to provide a more fully fleshed out theory than many of the alternatives and one that is useful in the real world.

losses, and frustrations.[9] Everyone also needs decent opportunities and the capabilities to realize them. At the same time, our differences explain why we need different things. Pregnant women, for instance, need more food than most other women. Those who cannot walk often need help to get around. In some cases, we have to consider cultural and religious differences just to ensure that everyone secures proper nourishment. My account better recognizes both similarities and differences in individuals' needs than many alternatives.

The second chapter argues that the minimally good life account of the basic minimum has some advantages over the main competing accounts. It argues that we need a broad, pluralistic account of what, at a minimum, we owe to others that includes many of the things on the common lists of what makes lives minimally good. This chapter suggests that the account attunes better to differences between individuals than many welfare and capability theories. It better protects *everyone's* ability to secure *everything* they require to reach a basic minimum without suggesting people need things they do not.

The third chapter considers how the minimally good life account can yield a standard for *basic justice*—what we must provide for people *simply out of respect for our common humanity*.[10] I, first, argue that we must help each other live minimally good lives when that does not require sacrificing our own ability to do likewise to respect each other's common humanity. No one deserves their basic freedom and constraint. Everyone has needs and vulnerabilities, and we are all interdependent. So, we have reasons to respond to each other's needs and claims to decent treatment: Each person's ability to live at least a minimally good life matters a lot to that person and their important relationships with one another. And, I believe no one should have to sacrifice their ability to live such a life to help others for the same reason. Neither borders nor politics limit these claims. They amount to human rights obligations that play an important role in a full theory of global justice. Moreover, I argue that we must help everyone secure whatever will let them live minimally well in

---

[9] Some worry about incommensurability between disparate goods on objective list theories as well as interpersonal comparability on utility-based views. Yet few will reject the idea that we can arrive at well-founded overall judgments about individuals' quality of life in practice. Subsequent chapters propose a mechanism for arriving at that kind of judgment.

[10] Basic justice, on my account, includes individual obligations to respect, protect, and fulfill human rights. Moreover, I believe that it properly incorporates obligations of beneficence at issue in our personal lives (these extend beyond political ties). However, readers who do not think we can incorporate obligations of beneficence under the title "basic justice" can simply omit the phrase. They can talk directly about obligations of beneficence grounded in appropriate concern for common humanity.

our personal as well as political lives.[11] Finally, I argue that even critics who deny all of this should agree that members of political societies (if not the global community) should help those they subject to coercive rules live minimally good lives when that does not require sacrificing their own ability to do so.

The fourth chapter argues that many alternative accounts of what basic justice requires demand either too much or not enough (and sometimes both). I argue that the minimally good life account has several advantages over many of the main competitors: First, it leaves significant room for altruism. At the same time, it recognizes the importance of freedom, rights, and responsibility. The proposed standard often requires us to give significantly to help others; we must sacrifice anything others need to live minimally good lives that we do not similarly need. That said, it does not require we give to others everything from which they might benefit (though there may be other reasons we should help people beyond the basic minimum). Second, it treats people equally in demanding that everyone—at least as members of society, if not the global community—help provide for others a basic minimum when they can without sacrificing their own ability to secure this minimum. So, it reconciles the perspectives of those who must give with those who require aid. While this generates significant demands, it also limits these demands significantly.

The fifth chapter considers how we should help people live minimally good lives in present and future generations when doing so does not require sacrificing our own ability to live well enough. In present generations, it argues that we should prioritize the least well-off and consider how many people we can help. However, in future generations, we should ensure that whoever comes into existence is already at the threshold for a minimally good life because otherwise those in the future will preventably be below the threshold for some time and this will violate their rights to a basic minimum. Moreover, acknowledging the rights of people in future generations to a basic minimum—whenever they come into existence—arguably entails that we should not generally bring people into existence who will not secure such a minimum (barring tragic choices). This, I suggest, provides the basis for a new reply to the repugnant conclusion (which strangely ends up being better to bring into existence as many very poorly-off people as possible). Finally,

---

[11] This is so even if more than life quality matters for basic justice. Moreover, I set aside questions about environmental justice and ethics here, though see Hassoun (2011a) for some relevant discussion.

contra so-called "longtermists," I argue that we should not prioritize preventing tragedies that could afflict many generations in the far future who need not come into existence at great cost to those in present and near-future generations (e.g. if doing so requires allowing mass starvation, devastation due to climate change, etc.). Rather, barring tragic conflicts, I argue that we should both aid the global poor now and ensure everyone who comes into existence in the future has a basic minimum.[12]

The final chapter considers how we can help people live minimally good lives in our imperfect world where it seems impossible to help everyone. It defends a new virtue that I call *creative resolve* that can help us when we face apparent tragedy (Hassoun, 2020a; Hassoun, 2024). In a phrase, creative resolve disposes us to commit, imagine, and act to help people secure the things they need to live well enough insofar as necessary, possible, and otherwise permissible. It can also help us secure other significant moral goods even when it seems we face a tragic dilemma. Those who have the virtue (1) question limits to the possibility of helping people live minimally well (and securing other significant moral goods); (2) seek out creative ways of securing (or better securing) these goods; and (3) try to secure them. I believe that this virtue can help us transform political systems to ensure that they help everyone live minimally good lives. So, I outline some concrete ways the virtue can help us make progress towards this end.

A Minimally Good Life's conclusion explains how its account of the minimally good life works in practice as well as theory. Our world appears terribly tragic with many people languishing below the threshold for a minimally good life. Yet we need to know what we must do for people; what ideal theory in our very non-ideal circumstances demands.[13] *A Minimally Good Life* aims to give a philosophically rich and deep account of how we can figure out what basic minimum we owe to each other in our world; what every person needs and can demand. Moreover, it attends carefully to differences between individuals so that we do not neglect some in setting a basic minimum that will suffice for others. Even the most severely disadvantaged and disabled have

---

[12] The chapter also considers how to measure life quality and suggests that to develop concrete indicators of whether people can live well enough, it may sometimes suffice to ask people what kinds of lives they would contently live.

[13] I do not suppose here that ideal theory requires full compliance. Our moral obligations are not limited by failures of human motivation nor other things that are under our control. Moreover, I do not suppose that the ideal must be achievable (though that may be so). That said, what ideal theory requires can vary with circumstances. So, ideally, everyone might cooperate, but where people are not cooperating, *A Minimally Good Life* suggests that ideal theory requires those who are willing, and able, to take up some of the slack.

rights to live at least minimally well on this book's account. Despite our idiosyncrasies, employing the mechanism the book provides makes it clear that people need many of the same things to live well enough.[14]

4. Theory and Practice

COVID-19 disrupted life on every continent and its economic effects threatened to swamp its health consequences. It cost the global economy trillions of dollars (Cutler and Summers, 2020). People around the world lost their jobs and livelihoods. So, we must answer questions about what we owe to others as a basic minimum. These answers can inform our judgments about our own societies' provisions for basic welfare and our social safety nets' adequacy. Respect for common humanity should inform our global response to pandemics. It can also help us respond to other major disasters that, with climate change, will more frequently come our way. Global justice and respect for human rights, I will argue, require the global community to take proactive steps to help people everywhere live well enough. States and international organizations have to do much more to provide for all a sufficient basic minimum. Individuals must help others live well enough in their personal, as well as political, lives. And, where states and international organizations fail, and we can do so without sacrificing our ability to live a minimally good life, each of us must exercise creative resolve to ensure that everyone can flourish.

---

[14] Although I do not offer a full account of what contentment amounts to, I explain how we should evaluate the quality of an individual's life at some length in subsequent chapters. Moreover, I suggest that contentment is a judgment informed by feeling or affect—where the discontent feel averse to a situation and judge it to be unacceptable. The mechanism I propose for arriving at the judgment aims to ensure that it is non-comparative, relatively free of framing effects and bias, reasonable, and compassionate. Finally, the mechanism should give one some critical distance from previous experience, socialization, realistic, and desirable options.

1
The Account of the Minimally Good Life

1. Introduction

What, if anything, do we owe others as a basic minimum? Sufficiency theorists claim that we must provide everyone with enough—but, to date, few well-worked-out accounts of the sufficiency threshold exist.[*] We need a well-specified, more fully developed, account of the threshold to decide what, if any, basic minimum people can claim. There are many possible accounts in the literature (Frankfurt, 1988b; Benbaji, 2006; Crisp, 2006; Brock, 2009; Huseby, 2010; Nussbaum, 2011; Segall, 2014; Axelsen and Nielsen, 2015; Axelsen and Nielsen, 2016; Huseby, 2020).[1] The next chapter considers some of main competitors and argues that they do not provide adequate accounts of the specific things people require for a basic minimum (Frankfurt, 1988, 90–116; Nussbaum, 2007; Dorsey, 2012; Liao, 2015; Axelsen and Nielsen, 2016). If we endorse sufficiency theory's positive thesis, if (basic) justice requires helping everyone secure a basic minimum, what does that require? This chapter outlines a contractualist—or, better, discursive—account of the minimally good life that might inform theories about what members of just

---

[*] This chapter draws heavily on: Hassoun, Nicole. 2021. "Sufficiency and the Minimally Good Life." *Utilitas*, 33 (3): 321–336. It also draws on Hassoun, Nicole. 2021a. "Good Enough? The Minimally Good Life Account of the Basic Minimum." *Australasian Journal of Philosophy* 100 (2): 330–341. Also see Hassoun, Nicole. 2017. "The Evolution of Wealth; Democracy or Revolution?" In *Wealth: NOMOS LVIII*, ed. Jack Knight and Melissa Schwartzberg, 125–145. New York: New York University Press and Hassoun, Nicole. 2020b. "What Is a Minimally Good Life and Are You Prepared to Live It?" *PSYCHE Newsletter*. September 21, 2020. https://psyche.co/ideas/what-is-a-minimally-good-life-and-are-you-prepared-to-live-it. For some preliminary work on this topic and discussion of these ideas.

[1] Some sufficientarians dismiss the need for a philosophically robust, determinate, policy-relevant threshold. Using the example of the $1/day poverty line, Edward Page says, for instance, that "in the sense that they are widely understood, and provide practical assistance for the application of moral principles, such thresholds are far from arbitrary" even if they are vague (Page, 2007, 17). However, what specifically sufficiency requires hangs on exactly how we understand this threshold. Grounding sufficiency theory in basic needs and respect for autonomy (as he proposes) will, for instance, have very different implications for what we owe to people than grounding the theory in a conception of capabilities, welfare, or what resources people are due (even if these resources are much more robust than what is necessary to avoid such extreme poverty).

societies, if not the international community, owe to each other as a basic minimum.[2]

This chapter does *not* argue that we *should* help people live even minimally well nor does it explain exactly how we should do so. One does not have to agree that we owe people this (or any) basic minimum to accept this chapter's account of what a minimally good life requires. Nor do I argue that we must only help people secure a basic minimum—sufficiency theory's negative thesis (because I think we often owe people more than this).[3] Rather, I outline an account of what the basic minimum requires that proponents of many different theories of social justice might endorse. The next chapter defends this book's account of the minimally good life. It is not until Chapters 3 and 4 that I argue that we owe people this much.

2. The Minimally Good Life

To live minimally good lives, people need an adequate range of the fundamental conditions for securing meaningful pursuits, relationships, pleasures, knowledge, appreciation, worthwhile activities, and other life-improving goods. Specifically, people must secure those goods a reasonable, free, caring person would (in conversation with others) set as a minimal standard of justifiable aspiration/basic right.[4] Deliberation and debate can help us resolve disagreements that may persist even among reasonable, free, caring people with all the relevant information. I will refer to the relationships, pleasures, knowledge, appreciation, worthwhile activities, and other life-enhancing goods a reasonable, caring, free person would set as a minimal standard of justifiable aspiration/basic right as *the things that make lives minimally good*. To live a minimally good life, I will argue that one must secure these things as well as an adequate range of prerequisite conditions. At least, people can *justifiably aspire* to this much *as a matter of basic right*.

---

[2] I do not try to establish procedurally that we must help people secure what they need to live well enough. Rather, I provide a substantive argument for using this mechanism. Subsequent chapters extend this argument and defend the conclusion that we must help others live minimally well when we can do so at reasonable cost.

[3] Of course, if respect for common humanity requires helping people secure more than a basic minimum, it may demand a lot. See subsequent chapters' discussion of demandingness.

[4] Note that some oppressed people can arrive at good judgments about what others need to live minimally well, the claim is only that people should be free from oppression that undermines this judgment, not that we should exclude the oppressed from discussion and deliberation about this standard. Moreover, as I will explain below, the range of fundamental conditions is set in conjunction with the list as different people likely need different kinds, and amounts, of these goods.

It is important to articulate both the conditions and things necessary for minimally good lives to give the account enough content for policymakers and others concerned to help people live well enough. *A Minimally Good Life* tries to establish a basic right to both secure access to the conditions for living a minimally good life and the things that make lives minimally good. It does so, in part, because policymakers must understand the conditions for securing minimally good lives (and not just the things that let people live minimally well) to protect everyone's ability to live well enough. Moreover, policymakers must help people secure an adequate range of these conditions even though some of them are only instrumentally important for securing the things that make lives minimally good.

Put simply, this chapter proposes that free, reasonable, and caring agents should put themselves in others' shoes in considering what each person needs to live at least minimally well—even if that person wrongly believes they need more or less than they possess.[5] They should ask themselves whether they would now be content to live others' lives as those persons. The next subsection explains what it means to say that people need an adequate range of the fundamental conditions for securing meaningful pursuits, relationships, pleasures, knowledge, appreciation, worthwhile activities, and other life-improving goods. Subsequent sub-sections explain the (reasonable, free, care) mechanism for filling in details in this account more precisely (what constitutes, reasonable free care, appropriate empathy, contentment, and why we should employ the test). Although subsequent sections explain what this requires at some length, consider briefly here what makes people *reasonable*, *caring*, and *free*. *Reasonable* people see other people as moral equals and are appropriately impartial. *Caring people* attend, and respond, to others' interests appropriately. People have the relevant *freedom* when their judgments about life quality do not result from adaptive preferences, coercion, nor constraint.[6] Subsequent sub-sections also explain how this mechanism—buttressed by deliberation and debate—can help us decide what basic minimum people need in the real world. I do not propose an ideal observer theory about what a basic minimum requires in every possible world. Hence, reasonable, free,

---

[5] As subsequent chapters explain, I focus here on what basic minimum is necessary to respect our common humanity (whether the scope of basic justice is properly national or global). Subsequent chapters also argue that the way we understand what constitutes a basic minimum may affect how we must treat people in our private lives as well as in our roles as citizens and members of the global community. Finally, I intend this account to be sensitive to empirical evidence and useful in the actual world. For other reflection on welfare in this vein, see Tiberius (2008) and Haybron (2013).

[6] People can have this freedom under coercive laws—though these laws cannot undermine their access to a wide enough range of basic liberties.

caring people considering what others require to live minimally well need not act flawlessly nor have full information. They must only have the relevant information to arrive at an informed judgment about what others need to live well enough. Still, this chapter suggests that neither the first- nor third-person perspective alone will let us arrive at an adequate account. Rather, it employs the second-person perspective of free, reasonable, care.[7]

The Adequate Range of Fundamental Conditions for Securing the Things That Make Lives Minimally Good Lives

What does it mean to say that people need an adequate range of the fundamental conditions for securing meaningful pursuits, relationships, pleasures, knowledge, appreciation, worthwhile activities, and other life-improving goods? This sub-section explains each part of this claim in turn.

Consider, first, what it means to say that people only need an *adequate range* of conditions for living minimally good lives; their lives should contain enough things of value, pleasure, and significance even if they remain imperfect and far from excellent. Human lives completely devoid of significance and value, full of pain and suffering, do not qualify as minimally good. On the other hand, even lives that do not qualify as minimally good often have some significant, pleasurable, and valuable things in them. Minimally good lives are well worth living, not just endurable. Minimally good lives at least reach the lowest levels of flourishing.[8]

The fundamental conditions (resources, capabilities, and institutions) for living a minimally good life include the conditions *necessary and jointly sufficient for* securing enough of the things that make lives minimally good (relationships, pleasures, knowledge, appreciation, worthwhile activities, etc.).[9] Things are *necessary for* living a minimally good life when one cannot live such a life without them. When one has all the conditions one needs to secure

---

[7] Ultimately this chapter provides a coherentist argument for its account of the minimally good life. That is, I argue that each substantive condition in its account of the minimally good life is plausible though, ultimately, we should see if free, reasonable, and caring people can vindicate these conditions. Similarly, if a free, reasonable, and caring person would not agree with what I say about the substantive conditions, I take that as a mark against accepting the idea that as free, reasonable, caring people we should put ourselves in others' shoes in deciding what they need to live minimally well.

[8] The flourishing at issue here goes beyond what is *good for* a person and what someone who cares about another would choose for them. People can live flourishing lives and sacrifice some interests even though those who care about them would not choose this for them. See discussion below and in the subsequent chapter.

[9] Empirical evidence supports many of my claims about what people need to live minimally good lives (Waterman, 1993; Keyes, 2002; Lelkes, 2005).

the things that make one's life minimally good, the conditions together are *jointly sufficient* for such a life. However, one also needs some conditions that are merely *important* for living minimally well (and not strictly necessary on their own for doing so); one cannot have only a single, difficult path to securing the things that make one's life minimally good (Raz, 1986).[10] Conditions are *important for* living a minimally good life when they make a central, or characteristic, contribution to an individuals' ability to live such a life (Nussbaum, 2011). At least for secure access to the things one needs to live minimally well, one requires an adequate range of decent agency-supporting options (Wolff and de-Shalit, 2007). Moreover, many different sets of fundamental conditions can make lives minimally good, though everyone needs some of the same things (e.g. clean water).

Many *fundamental conditions* for minimally good lives exist. People require resources, capacities, and institutional structures among other things (Liao, 2015). Everyone needs adequate food and water. Most require some amount of education, shelter, and other resources. Furthermore, people must secure basic capacities, liberty, and autonomy (Griffin, 1986; Nussbaum, 2011). Everyone should have the ability to think and connect with other people, understand and embrace things of value, and develop skills (Nussbaum, 2011). People also require social and institutional structures to develop their capacities and secure the things that make lives minimally good. In short, everyone requires the internal and external, natural and social, conditions for securing these things.[11]

One has *secure* access to the things that make one's life minimally good when one can attain them easily enough and one is not at high risk of losing this access.[12] One must have good prospects of securing, and maintaining, these things if one tries. Some determinants of one's prospects include: one's

---

[10] Although these are also technically necessary conditions for living minimally well, on my account they merit mention separately for this reason.

[11] Although these are normative claims, good social and institutional structures are important for almost all of the fundamental conditions for such a life (Gupta, Davoodi, and Alonso-Terme, 1998; Yontcheva and Masud, 2005; Santos-Paulino, 2012; Helliwell et al., 2018).

[12] More precisely, one has sufficient security when there is no serious reason to doubt that one will continue to have the things that make her life minimally good. That is, one can maintain enough of the things that contribute to one's ability to live minimally well in a wide enough range of possible futures. Of course, it is hard to judge when this is the case as many different things can contribute to one's ability to live minimally well. A reasonable, caring, free person must consider "the degree to which each of these goods must be enjoyed securely, and . . . the relative importance of the secure enjoyment of each good" to each person's overall security (Herrington, 2015, 35). Still, when the person has sufficient security, and there is no serious reason to doubt that she will continue to have the things that make her life minimally good, a reasonable, caring, free person should be content to live her life as that person. I discuss further below what makes someone reasonable, caring, and free and how such people might arrive at such a judgment.

chance of success, and what one has "to sacrifice to achieve that probability of success" (Wolff and de Shalit, 2007, 72). One's attainment of some of the things necessary for living a minimally good life cannot come at the cost of attaining other things on the list. Moreover, one should not have to accept large risks of failing to secure things one needs to live well enough to secure other things one needs (Wolff and de Shalit, 2007).

Secure access to the things that make lives minimally good helps people live well enough at all times and overall. Those who lack sufficient security often suffer from fear, anxiety, stress, poor health, and other direct, and indirect, negative consequences of this insecurity (Daemen, 2022a; Daemen, 2022b). Most people need more than reasonable hope to sustain aspirations and agency—they require confidence in a good enough future. The insecure often have difficulty planning well for the future or carrying out their plans (Oberdiek, 2012). Sometimes insecurity forces people to engage in activities that put them at high risk of harm (Wolff and de Shalit, 2007). People may live well enough for some time without secure access to some of the important conditions for living minimally well. However, losing secure access to enough of these things typically undermines individuals' ability to live minimally well. Insecure access to some of the things people need to live well enough can also undermine their secure access to others (especially as most people rightly prefer not to be exposed to significant risk to their lives and livelihoods) (Finkelstein, 2003). We are harmed when our interests in being free from some kinds of risk are set back and some risks undermine our dignity or status as moral agents (Placani, 2016).

Moreover, security partly constitutes a minimally good life. Those living close to the poverty line without adequate health insurance or welfare provisions often fail to live well enough precisely because their situations remain so precarious. The insecure can easily lose other things they need to live minimally well. Furthermore, insecurity itself often undermines individuals' ability to live well enough. One has serious reason to doubt that those who are extremely insecure can live their lives well even if they luckily remain otherwise above the threshold for a good enough life, free from fear and anxiety about their situation, and with sufficient autonomy and other things that they value. Sufficient security is important for a minimally good life, in part, because it helps people relate to the world in important ways—it "reflects and shapes one's attitudes ... to threats" (Wonderly, 2019). It is the objective basis for believing that things are sufficiently likely to go well enough. Insecurity often undermines individuals' confidence in themselves, others, and their circumstances, making it difficult for them to reason well, engage in plans, and act to achieve their ends (Bowlby, 1969; Perry, 1997; Mikulincer and Shaver, 2015). Although some insecurity is ineliminable—and may even be desirable because it can, for instance, motivate us to act and strive for things we are not sure of attaining—sufficient security is a precondition, and component, of a good enough life. Those who lack sufficient security often do not feel at home in the world, safe, calm, strong, or courageous enough to trust in themselves, others, and their circumstances, and those who do not do not fare well enough (Maslow, 1942; Blatz, 1966; Bowlby, 1969; Rivera, 1977; Ainsworth, 1988; Jones, 2004; Ainsworth, 2010; Mikulincer and Shaver, 2015; Jones, 2019; Wonderly, 2019; Hassoun, 2024).[13]

It is not enough for a child living or working in hazardous conditions to fortuitously maintain relationships, knowledge, health, etc. The child must not suffer exposure to such risk.[14] We consider whether individuals' lives qualify as minimally good from an ex-ante perspective. So, the child's life does not qualify as minimally good in the sense at issue here because her prospects are precarious. The child has a justified aspiration to a secure future. A good enough life requires significant freedom from high risk of potentially debilitating vulnerability. It requires decent options that support agency. (Those who deny this can still accept my account as a view of what the basic minimum requires to make sure people have a good enough *chance* of a decent life.)[15]

Finally, many things contribute to minimally good lives including *relationships, pleasures, knowledge, appreciation,* and *worthwhile activities* (Griffin, 1986; Arneson, 1999; Tiberius, 2008). Exactly what things a person needs to live a minimally good life will depend on the person's character and circumstance (Kraut, 1994). That said, what someone requires does not

---

[13] Again, the claim here is not that these people have a right to the kinds of attachments that will help them live well enough, nor that others must provide them. I just claim that people need sufficient trust in themselves, others, and their circumstances to make and carry out the kinds of plans that will let them live well enough. Moreover, people plausibly require not just subjective security but the objective basis for this security (contra: Herington (2015)). People must have sufficiently good options from which to choose (Raz, 1986). However, care and concern for others typically enhance individuals' quality of life.

[14] Note that it is not enough to have a range of options nor even a decent chance of maintaining what one needs to live minimally well. The child might survive in other ways (e.g. by working in the local market); perhaps she even has a lottery ticket that gives her a good chance of faring much better in the future. Still, there is serious reason to doubt that the child can live well enough. Security requires good options and limits the risk of failing to secure, or maintain, the other things one needs to live well enough.

[15] The account provides a basis for a plausible basic minimum. I do not think it is a problem if it diverges slightly from intuitive conceptions of what people need to live minimally well in this respect.

completely depend on what that individual happens to desire, their psychology, and socialization (Arneson, 1999).[16]

I cannot hope to give a full account of each of the things that contribute to minimally good lives here, but consider briefly why people often need relationships, pleasures, knowledge, appreciation, and worthwhile activities to live minimally well. Worthwhile activities often give people a sense of the meaning essential for a minimally good human existence. Usually, people must have the freedom to choose from more than one thing worth doing to exercise sufficient autonomy to live well enough. Most people need not realize everything they set out to accomplish, many need not achieve much at all. Still, most find making some small contributions important for living a good enough life. Similarly, both small and great pleasures contribute to our ability to live minimally well. They give our lives variety and interest. Most of those with lives devoid of pleasure have severe depression. They may lack the desires necessary to engage fruitfully with others and the external world. Aesthetic appreciation and deep knowledge and understanding typically contribute to individuals' ability to live well enough too. But even if people can live minimally well without either, they need some kinds of knowledge and appreciation. To live well enough in our times, most people need at least an elementary education (and usually much more than that). People also need the ability to appreciate the things that help them survive and flourish. Moreover, most people find close personal relationships add great value to their lives. Those without friends or family may find it hard to live minimally well (especially if they lose these relationships early). That said, not every relationship adds value to our lives—those who simply leech off others may not fare better for their relationships, for instance. Though most of us might fare better by doing more to foster and sustain relationships, good relationships cannot normally require too much of those who care for others (Collins, 2013). (Subsequent chapters will argue that good societies have to aid those who cannot otherwise attain the care they need by, for instance, providing care homes for the elderly and mentally ill.)[17] This list may contain other

---

[16] The evaluative standpoint relevant for determining what a particular individual needs is not the standpoint of that individual. Rather, as I explain below, it is the perspective of a reasonable, caring, free person who puts themselves in that individual's shoes. The evaluator must have all the relevant information in considering what is necessary to live well as that individual.

[17] Even the most introverted hermits need some care in infancy to survive to adolescence. People might often do well to open themselves up to opportunities to connect with others—whether by talking more with neighbors or taking in a lonely soul for Christmas. In fact, most of us might fare better ourselves if we took proactive steps to not only care for the sick and elderly but also connect with others in our communities where, with the rise of new technologies, a pandemic of loneliness threatens mental and physical health. And, while we cannot help some people secure the relationships

things. Severe forms of discrimination and inequality can also undermine individuals' ability to live minimally good lives, for instance (Sen, 1999).[18] Protecting individuals' ability to live minimally well safeguards their basic moral status or dignity (Tasioulas, 2013; Killmister, 2016). Together, however, these things protect and help constitute our common humanity. They allow us to live a distinctively human, and valuable, form of life.[19]

To some extent, historical circumstances, geography, culture, and even individual differences determine what people need to live minimally good lives (Gallup and Sachs, 2001). As Adam Smith pointed out—in some societies, people need a linen shirt to take part in public life (Smith, 1904; Chase and Bantebya-Kyomuhendo, 2014). Some people will not even secure adequate nourishment if they lack access to culturally appropriate food (Sen, 1999). Some commit so strongly to particular (valuable) cultural practices, ways of life, or societies that they can only flourish within them.[20] Other people require opportunities or resources they cannot secure when, or where, they live but that they might foreseeably secure in the future. Yet others may need things that they cannot ever secure (e.g. drugs to treat their terrible health conditions that will not exist for hundreds of years). Sometimes we just have to say that someone cannot live a minimally good life in her world (though she should get as close as possible to living such a life). We can also recognize that we do not live as long as we might, but we often live minimally good lives for some time. So, even if most people require things they cannot secure to live well enough at some times, a basic minimum can still require helping people get as close as they can to flourishing in their times.[21]

People often fail to understand what they need for a minimally good life (Sen, 1980; Sen, 1999; Haybron, 2007; Haybron, 2008). While it matters that we all fulfill some important desires, some things contribute to our flourishing for other reasons. Matters of pure preference and true urgency differ.[22]

---

they need to flourish, good social institutions and societies might do much more to provide people with opportunities to connect with others and essential support for those unable to care for themselves.

[18] Although slaves might fight valiantly against their oppression, they do not have everything to which they have a justified aspiration as a matter of basic right as long as they are enslaved.

[19] If our relationships, worthwhile activities, and so forth contribute to good human functioning (as a system), we might come up with a fairly comprehensive list by employing a perfectionist methodology. Good relationships, for instance, may sustain the kinds of human development that allows for participation in worthwhile activities etc. I do not attempt to make this case here, however.

[20] Perhaps some can only flourish in cruel, or otherwise depraved, societies. However, if these cases exist, I believe they are extremely rare. In any case, they present the apparent tragic dilemmas that the final chapter discusses at some length.

[21] See discussion in notes below.

[22] See Scanlon (1975). Though I do not think consensus in a society determines the latter.

Things that make our lives go better often surprise us (Haybron, 2007; Haybron, 2008). However, it will not matter too much for the arguments that follow whether one accepts all these claims. At this point, it is only important to understand what it means to say that people need an adequate range of the fundamental conditions for securing meaningful pursuits, relationships, pleasures, knowledge, appreciation, worthwhile activities, and other life-improving goods.

The Justifiable Aspiration/Basic Right Standard

How can we figure out, more precisely, what things people need to live well enough? Consider the last component of this book's account of the minimally good life that provides an overarching mechanism for doing so: *People must secure those goods a reasonable, free, caring person would (in conversation with others) set as a minimal standard of justifiable aspiration/basic right*. To explain this idea, this section first distinguishes the justifiable aspiration standard I endorse from a lower reasonable affirmation standard that I do not rely upon here. Second, I give a quick, non-technical, overview of the core idea. Third, I explain what it means to say that people are *reasonable, caring*, and *free* more precisely. Fourth, I explain the test's nature and with what reasonable, caring, free people would rest *content*. Finally, I consider the kind of *empathy* involved in "putting oneself in others' shoes" or thinking about others' lives "as those people."[23] Subsequent sections explain why the proposed mechanism for figuring out what people need to live minimally good lives will likely yield good results, why people should employ the mechanism, and how to apply it.

First, consider how what people need to live the kind of minimally good lives at issue here differs from the much lower standard applicable for reasonably affirming that even some of the most severely disadvantaged live minimally good lives. This book focuses on what will enable people to live minimally good lives in what we might call the "justified aspiration as a matter of basic right" sense; it argues that everyone should get as close as possible

---

[23] Like Crisp (2006), I offer a virtuous observer theory, though I am not concerned with the level at which compassion gives out and I try to fill in the details of the kind of empathy at issue (also see Crisp (2008)). My account provides a mechanism that can let us make progress is identifying minimally good lives that might serve as a plausible basic minimum. Moreover, it relies on a different kind of empathy than Darwall (2002) advances in providing an account of how we can determine what benefits people. See discussion below, and for more on empathy and moral reasoning see Kauppinen (2013).

to securing this standard (Haybron, 2013, ch. 8).[24] Note that I use the phrase *justifiable aspiration/basic right* in a purely technical sense—we would normally say people can justifiably aspire to secure significantly more than a basic minimum. It seems fine for people to aim much higher (and perhaps also lower) than the threshold for a minimally good life. Here we consider just what standard everyone should plausibly get as close as possible to securing. When someone does not reach this standard, moreover, we can sometimes still "reasonably affirm" that the person lives a minimally good life in a different sense—they may attain a good enough life *given the constraints of possibility* (Haybron, 2013, ch. 8). Even some of the most severely mentally and physically disabled people live minimally good lives in this "reasonable affirmation" sense (Kittay, 2005). Those with significant physical and mental illnesses may have great material wealth and enjoy close human relationships among other things.[25] The first sense of the minimally good life—relevant for specifying what people can justifiably aspire to attain as a matter of basic right—plausibly demands much more than the second—what we need to reasonably affirm that someone has had a minimally good life, given the constraints of possibility. But this book focuses on the former. What kind of lives people can justifiably aspire to attain as a matter of basic right depends only partly upon the limits of what people can secure. Sometimes we just have to say that people cannot secure everything they have a justifiable aspiration to attain. We must do so when reasonable, free, caring people cannot rest content with securing what these people can attain because these people need more to avoid a serious risk of being unable to live their lives well. That said, even the most disadvantaged should still get as close as they can to the *justifiable aspiration/basic right* threshold. Or, at least, this book argues that a plausible basic minimum requires that much.[26]

---

[24] This book does not claim that people have rights to what it is impossible to provide. Moral requirements may compete. I believe, however, that people can have claims to things they cannot secure and that some rights will just tragically go unfulfilled (Hassoun, 2020a). See subsequent chapters' discussion.

[25] It is possible to use different labels for the two concepts at issue here if one prefers. Some will object to using the term "minimally good life" in two different senses even if we are clear about what sense is at issue in any case. Others might object that it is stigmatizing, or constitutes a failure to respect common humanity, to say those who live lives we should affirm do not live "minimally good" (or good enough) lives in any sense. However, we could not then, legitimately, say people have a right to live a minimally good life in the justified aspiration/basic right sense. Still, those who prefer to use the reasonable affirmation conception of the minimally good life can refer to the conception of the basic minimum at issue here *as a life reasonable, caring, free people would contently live*. I will, however, continue to use the shorter locution "minimally good life" here. Those who prefer different terminology can substitute another term as they see fit.

[26] Further work is necessary to specify what qualifies as getting closer to the threshold for living a minimally good life in the relevant sense. Still, it is this minimal standard that lets us explain why there is often something tragic even about some lives we can reasonably affirm—those who live them

Second, consider the core idea behind the mechanism I propose for how—as reasonable, free, caring people—we can figure out what someone needs to live a minimally good life in the "justified aspiration/basic right" sense: We should ask whether we would be content to live another person's life as that person. That is, we consider how we would fare *if we were that person* in making this determination and whether we would now be content to live their lives. Suppose we consider what someone about whom we know little will need for a life at the lowest level of flourishing.[27] It seems reasonable to maintain that the person's pleasures, relationships, and worthwhile activities (etc.) must sufficiently compensate for their difficulties, pains, losses, and frustrations so that one would not seriously doubt their ability to satisfactorily live it. Though determining when their life's downsides outweigh the upsides requires understanding what is significant to a person and how to balance the importance of many different things—from resources to autonomy—in their life. It may be reasonable, for instance, to sacrifice a great deal of pleasure for one's children or for a worthwhile achievement or cause (and doing so can—but will not always—help one live well enough). So, we must consider the individual's psychology, history, and circumstances and must put ourselves into the other's shoes in asking whether we would now be content to live their life as that person.[28] Some people may sacrifice a lot for others and still live excellent, never mind minimally good lives. On the other hand, some people admirably sacrifice their own life quality for others. The question here is not whether any given reasonable, caring, free person would trade her current life for a minimally good one—many fortunate individuals would not. Rather, we must ask whether there are any serious reasons to doubt that the person we consider can live their life well enough.

We can employ this test to ask whether individuals are faring well enough at a time, but usually we are concerned with their ability to live well enough over

---

have a justified aspiration as a matter of basic right to secure much more. The fact that we can reasonably affirm the lives of some of the most severely disabled does not show that they have enough for a basic minimum. Finally, in specifying a basic minimum I do not intend to deny that other things may matter more than providing that minimum for all. We must also be sensitive to the costs to others in setting the basic minimum. That said, I believe it is incredibly important to help people live well enough and there is a discontinuity in the reasons we have to help people flourish at this threshold (also see subsequent chapters' discussion).

[27] We might also get a sense for what makes lives minimally good by considering what makes our lives distinctively human. Though the things that make our lives distinctively human must also be valuable enough to make lives minimally good (Dorsey, 2010). It is hard to see how a life qualifies as minimally good if it does not guarantee for people the things necessary for a distinctly human (and valuable) existence.

[28] Again, when I say a reasonable, caring, free person should consider whether they would contentedly live another's life as that person, I mean that they should consider how they would fare if they were that person.

time. So, we normally ask ourselves if we would be content to live another person's life simpliciter when we reflect on what people need to secure and maintain a basic minimum. That said, we sometimes have reason to focus on smaller time periods. A policymaker in a ministry of health might consider, for instance, whether people need pain medication when undergoing particular medical procedures to fare well enough at that time. There are hard questions here about what constitutes the relevant contexts for judging whether someone lives well enough overall. They might be relative to existing resources or understood timelessly. I suppose, however, that we should judge quality of life in the real world and that resource constraints limit, but do not fully determine, what qualifies as a good enough life even in our current context. Sometimes we must say people just lack the resources they need to live well enough.

Third, to see how we can figure out what people can justifiably aspire to secure as a matter of basic right, I must explain, or stipulate, the choice situation from which judgments of life quality must be made more precisely.[29] Consider what it means for people to be reasonable, caring, and free. As I use the term, *reasonable* people see other people as moral equals and want to live with them on fair, mutually agreeable terms (Rawls, 1971; Rawls, 1980). Reasonable people want to cooperate with others and "share in common burdens" appropriately (Rawls, 1980, 529).[30] They can revise their ends on rational grounds but also understand that everyone has the standing to make claims to protections of their fundamental interests (Rawls, 1980). Moreover, reasonable people are appropriately impartial—they do not privilege the greater interests of some over others.

Other people's legitimate interests move those who care about them (Nussbaum, 2006).[31] *Caring people* attend, and respond, to others' interests appropriately. That is, they notice, aim to understand, and try to address others' needs (Steyl, 2020). More precisely, I suppose caring people want, and act, to promote others' interests when appropriate. This requires giving others' interests due weight. Sometimes caring for others requires flexibility or restraint. Other times it requires helping people to help themselves. Sometimes,

---

[29] I would like to thank the reviewers for pushing me to clarify the arguments in this section. The next section defends the claim that we should employ this standard out of concern or respect for common humanity.

[30] They may disagree about what is appropriate and need not think this can be determined by bargaining even in an appropriately specified original position. I also note some differences from John Rawls' conception of free, equal, moral persons. I do not suppose all people are free or equal in Rawls' sense because I do not exclude those who lack basic capacities from my conception of basic justice. Nor am I concerned only with what legitimate or just institutions might require, so my account of the *reasonable* also differs in important ways from Rawls'.

[31] Although people can also care for themselves, I focus here on what we need to care for others.

caring people must nurture or provide for others' basic interest (Noddings, 2002; O'Dowd, 2016). Yet other times, caring people will help develop or protect these interests as well as sustain them. Often caring people must ask people what they need in order to figure out the best ways of helping them (and even whether people require assistance in the first place). Caring people are "attentive, responsive, and respectful" (Engster, 2005, 55). When people care for others appropriately, they often (at least implicitly) communicate their concern for others and develop important relationships with them.

People *have the relevant freedom* when they have sufficient internal and external liberty. People have internal liberty when they can recognize and respond to value as they see it. External liberty is, roughly, freedom from interference. People have sufficient internal and external liberty for our purposes when they do not form, nor endorse, adaptive preferences that undermine their evaluations of life quality. People have sufficient external liberty when they have the decent options and bargaining power they need to arrive at such judgments (Raz, 1986; Hassoun, 2012).

Fourth, consider how reasonable, caring, free people would think about the standard necessary for living a minimally good life and in what contentment consists. They would not set a standard for other people under which reasonable, caring, free people themselves would not contently live (Rawls, 1971; Rawls, 1980). Reasonable, caring, free people should be content to live the "merely" minimally good lives the least fortunate will live when setting this standard.[32] The question is not whether the person one is deciding for will be content, as that person's preferences may be adaptive. Rather, the question is whether a reasonable, free, caring person would now (reflecting on, and considering but not occupying, another person's life) contently live that life as that person.[33] *Contentment* constitutes a judgment—that there are no serious reasons to doubt others' lives can be well lived—informed by feeling or affect.[34] The discontented reject, and often feel strongly averse, to living a life precisely because they believe there are serious reasons to doubt the life can be well lived and, hence, that the non-comparative costs of living the life

---

[32] Again, the question is not whether any given individual would trade her current life for a minimally good one—many fortunate individuals would not—but whether the life is good enough on its own terms for the person who must live it.

[33] And recall that, when one is free, one will not form, nor endorse, adaptive preferences that undermine one's judgment even though one understands them.

[34] Here I draw on Harry Frankfurt's account of contentment, though he was primarily concerned with what constitutes sufficient economic resources (Frankfurt, 1988, 95–116).

are too great.[35] The reasonable, free, caring person must fully understand the other person's circumstances, psychology, and history in deciding whether they would contently live as the other person (Frankfurt, 1988, 95–116).[36]

The idea that a reasonable, caring, free person must be content to live the lives she would say other people need may seem to guarantee too much or too little. It does not. In deciding whether a life qualifies as minimally good, the free, reasonable, and caring person will not only consider the person's circumstances, psychology, and history. She will recognize the normal limits of the human situation. She will give due weight to others' rights and the cost to other people of helping the person reach the threshold.[37] At the same time, the reasonable, free, caring person does not issue a comparative judgment, nor one determined by available, nor potential, options. People may need things to live well enough they simply cannot access in their societies.[38]

Finally, consider what kind of *empathy* people need to put themselves in others' shoes or think about whether they would be content to live others' lives as those people. We can contrast the relevant kind of "projective empathy" with the proto-sympathetic empathy, or sympathetic concern, Stephen Darwall argues we must employ in thinking about our moral obligations to others (Darwall, 2002, 62; Coplan and Goldie, 2011).[39,40] To have projective

---

[35] Although one must consider the balance of good and bad things within life, the balance with which a reasonable, free, caring person should rest content is absolute and not relative to opportunity costs. It should not depend on available, nor potential, options for that person (nor the judge's own level of resources, opportunities, welfare, and so forth). Still, contentment has to do with whether we feel the need to sacrifice significantly not to have to live the life we consider. Reasonable, free, caring people would not contently live lives that are just full of pain and suffering. Nor would they contently live lives that are just barely worth living as (presumably) there are serious reasons to doubt one can live such lives well enough (or the lives would be well worth living).

[36] Again, this way of thinking about contentment draws on the Frankfurtian view extended by Huseby (2020). It provides a tool that can help us think about where to draw a sufficiency threshold.

[37] Reasonable, caring, free people committed to respecting individuals' common humanity must heed the costs other people must bear of providing the standard they set. One cannot ask some to sacrifice too significantly for others' less significant interests. So, reasonable, caring, free people will rest content with a minimally good (as opposed to extremely good or excellent) life.

[38] This may even be the case for most people if we cannot access healthcare or other goods that will let us live well enough in our current conditions—and, if that is so, we may only have to help people get as close as possible to living minimally good lives.

[39] Reasonable people must view other people as free and equal and consider what they would need to possess Rawls' two moral powers, but caring people also understand that not everyone can or should try to secure these powers (Rawls, 1971; Kittay, 2005). Some people are not even capable of forming conceptions of the good and acting on them and reasonable caring people cannot ignore their existence (Rawls, 1971; Rawls, 1980). Rawls is probably right, however, to say reasonable people should not allow envy to affect their judgment but should tolerate diverse viewpoints and abide by the principles of justice they endorse. Moreover, they should be realistic and unbiased. The mechanism I propose for arriving at a judgment about others' quality of life also gives one some critical distance from previous experiences and socialization. Discussion and deliberation can help ensure the judgment is relatively free from framing effects.

[40] Different sufficientarian accounts endorse different ways of thinking about the threshold for a good enough life—e.g. see Frankfurt (1988, 95–116) and Crisp (2006)—but the arguments that follow also aim to establish that different accounts will yield different results.

empathy reasonable, free, caring people must try to fully understand emotionally, and otherwise, how other people live. They must appreciate other people's history as well as their current states. When we empathize in this way, we share other people's feelings as their perspectives warrant (Darwall, 2002, 62; Coplan and Goldie, 2011).[41] As Adam Smith put it: "in order to enter into your grief, I do not consider what I, a person of such a character and profession, should suffer, if I had a son, and if that son were unfortunately to die; but I consider what I would suffer if I were you, and I not only change circumstances with you, but I change persons and characters" (Smith and Haakonssen, 2002, §371; Coplan and Goldie, 2011). Projective empathy differs from proto-sympathetic empathy (a version of the sympathetic concern Darwall endorses).[42] Proto-sympathetic empathy requires self-consciously reflecting on the state of the person with whom one empathizes (Darwall, 2002, 67; Coplan and Goldie, 2011). Reasonable, caring, free people will projectively empathize with other people but then consider what they would need to contently live other people's lives as those people in their current states. This second-person perspective gives them sufficient space from others' desires, beliefs, and perspectives to avoid forming or endorsing adaptive preferences in making this judgment. They will not just consider how other people do, or might, feel about their states.[43]

Moreover, sympathy—"a feeling or emotion that responds to some apparent obstacle to an individual's good and involves concern for him, and thus

---

[41] This is not to say that we can access the others' states directly. Our simulation of others' states often misfires, in which case, we do not actually empathize with them correctly. But, on my view, empathy is also different from Amy Coplan's and Peter Goldie's characterization in "Understanding Empathy" on which: "empathy is a complex imaginative process in which an observer simulates another person's situated psychological states while maintaining clear self-other differentiation. To say that empathy is 'complex' is to say that it is simultaneously a cognitive and affective process. To say that empathy is 'imaginative' is to say that it involves the ... representation of a target's states that are activated by, but not directly accessible through, the observer's perception. And to say that empathy is a 'simulation' is to say that the observer replicates or reconstructs the target's experiences, while maintaining a clear sense of self–other differentiation" (Coplan and Goldie, 2011, 5–6). On my account, empathy is more akin to what they call "other-oriented perspective-taking" on which, "a person represents the other's situation from the other person's point of view and thus attempts to simulate the target's individual's experiences as though she were the target individual" (Coplan and Goldie, 2011, 10). Moreover, I agree that it "requires greater mental flexibility and emotional regulation and often has different effects than self-oriented perspective-taking" and their understanding of empathy (Coplan and Goldie, 2011, 10). Some people cannot projectively empathize with others, but I believe that people need this form of empathy to arrive at a well-informed judgment about the overall quality of others' lives. We probably have to employ different forms of empathy and concern for different purposes and situations.

[42] Darwall says sympathy "is a feeling or emotion that responds to some apparent obstacle to an individual's good and involves concern for him, and thus for his welfare, for his sake" (Darwall, 2002, 67).

[43] For more on why we must also care for other people to figure out what they need, see Nussbaum (2006).

for his welfare, for his sake"—will not suffice for two reasons (Darwall, 2002, 67; Coplan and Goldie, 2011). First, one needs to do more than care only about how a person's life goes for her sake to determine whether she can reach a basic minimum; one must understand her life. One must properly focus on the loss of the child, not on just how bad the person who has lost the child feels to understand that loss in that life. Second, one should care about *more* than how a person's life goes *for her sake* (or even whether she has *choiceworthy* options) when reflecting on what she needs to live a minimally good life; one should care about a person simpliciter.[44]

To see both points, consider a slightly different case where the child suffers from a serious illness. If one focuses on how the parent feels, one may try to help her in a variety of ways. The parent may benefit from letting someone else care for her child. But if one focuses on the ill child, and knows what it means to be the parent, one may know that for that person to live even a minimally good life, she cannot give her child up.[45] Doing so would blight her life even though it may benefit her, and no one would blame her for choosing to give the child up.[46] To get as close as possible to living a minimally good life, if the child cannot recover, she may need a lot of assistance in caring for her child.[47] If we focus on what that person experiences, we can give her experiences due weight. Still, we should care about

---

[44] Individuals' projects and perspectives inform the quality of their lives but do not completely determine this quality as people often make mistakes about what they need. Moreover, some things contribute to a person's quality of life even when they do not benefit that person. Consider again those who sacrifice greatly for a great cause.

[45] One may need to experience some states—like parenthood—to fully understand them, but even those who have not had relevant experiences might learn enough about what they are like by talking to people who have had the experience. They can then exercise the significant imagination required for appropriate care. As I explain below, discussion can help us improve our judgments. Still, it is important to recognize that our own knowledge has limits and not all reasonable, caring, free people can make the requisite determinations about the quality of different people's lives because they lack essential information.

[46] Here I am supposing we know enough about the parent's history, psychology, and circumstances to make this judgment. There may be some parents who could freely give up a child and still live good enough lives and others who can recover from such a loss. It is also clear that many of those who simply lose children, or other loved ones, can live good lives despite their grief even if it undermines their ability to live well enough for some time.

[47] Kagan draws the boundaries between what is good for me and my life in this way: The experience machine affects my life but not what is good for me. How a stranger fares affects neither what is good for me nor my life unless I invest time etc. in the stranger's success, in which case her welfare may affect the quality of my life (Kagan, 1994). We might call the boundaries Kagan draws on a life—*life internalism* and call those I propose *life externalism*. For, on my account, even the stranger's success might help make my life good. Though I do not think the stranger's success is likely to greatly affect my ability to reach a basic minimum. Nevertheless, saying that others' wellbeing affects the quality of my life makes it reasonable to think that we owe people a functioning economic system (many others' success) as a basic minimum.

more than what is *good for* someone when considering what makes her life minimally good.[48]

So far, this chapter has set out the minimally good life account of the basic minimum. The preceding sub-sections explained what people need to live minimally well and this book's mechanism for filling in details in the account. The next section will explain why the proposed mechanism yields plausible results, why people should employ it, and how it works in practice.

3. Arguing for Justifiable Care in Practice

Consider why the proposed mechanism for figuring out what people need to live a minimally good life yields plausible results. I must empathize with other people appropriately when considering what they need to live minimally well. If I do so, and possess sufficient freedom, I will set a standard for other people under which I would contently live as they do. To see why, consider why I might set a different standard for other people from the one I would demand for myself. I might do so because I privilege my own less important interests over others' greater interests (I am not reasonable). I might also fail to set a sufficient standard because, although I am impartial, I fail to care appropriately for both other people and myself (I am not caring). Finally, I may simply lack decent options or suffer from autonomy-undermining coercion or constraint myself (I am not free).[49] Put another way: If I am reasonable (appropriately impartial), I will only set for other people a standard under which I am content to live as they will. If I am caring, I will set a standard that I believe suffices for others. If I am free, and appropriately empathetic, *and have all the relevant information*, I am unlikely to make a mistake about whether the standard is sufficient.[50] Deliberation with other reasonable, free,

---

[48] Even if this suggestion fails, however, and we should employ Darwell's sympathetic concern instead, the other components of the account can remain intact. See preceding note for some discussion of the distinction between life quality or flourishing (at issue here) and wellbeing (typically understood as concerned with what is good *for* a person). On my account, we can improve individuals' wellbeing by doing things that are good for her without doing enough to make her life minimally good. Most, but not all, accounts of *welfare* in the literature focus on wellbeing, but I try to use the term *welfare* ecumenically throughout.

[49] There is some tension between the kind of appropriate impartiality required for reasonableness and caring sufficiently for others. The reasonable, free, care standard requires dealing appropriately with this tension by requiring us to put ourselves in others' shoes before arriving at an appropriately impartial judgment about their life quality (giving others' interests due weight as well).

[50] Of course, even a reasonable, free, caring person may make a mistake and set the standards too high or low. But if her standards are initially too low, really understanding the history, circumstances, and experience of a person in the proposed circumstances should encourage her to revise her standards upwards. Similarly, if the impartial decider has unreasonably high standards, considering how

caring people can help resolve remaining disagreements about what a minimally good life requires and ensure appropriate standards.[51]

This method for figuring out what people need to live a minimally good life will not resolve all disagreements; it is not an ideal observer theory of the minimally good life, but a way of making moral progress in the actual world as long as we buttress it with discussion and deliberation (Sobel, 1999). People can fail to freely occupy an appropriately impartial deliberative stance in a way that provides some space for reflection relatively free from framing effects.[52] No one is fully reasonable, caring, or free. We all lack relevant information about other people's lives. Still, we should empathetically put ourselves in others' shoes and think hard about whether we would contently live their lives in trying to arrive at plausible judgments about their lives' quality. Deliberation may help people guard against unintentional biases. It can help us figure out what reasonableness and caring require in many particular cases.[53] By correctly employing this method, we demonstrate respect for others' common humanity.

We must employ the reasonable, free, care standard to respect each person's common humanity.[54] Where, as subsequent chapters explain, *respect for our common humanity* resides in safeguarding these kinds of important (caring, reasonable, free) relationships with other vulnerable members of our moral community. It requires equal and due consideration of interests as well

---

someone who has much lower standards feels (where these standards are themselves reasonable) may encourage her to revise her standards downwards.

[51] Consider how a hedonist might insist that she would contently live the life of a happy slave even if the slave only values things on some objective list that she cannot secure while enslaved (Feldman, 2004). One might object to the hedonist's conclusion in two ways on this account. First, one can say that the hedonist is unreasonable or insufficiently free in accepting adaptive preferences from an external perspective. Second, one can argue that they do not care enough about what is good for the person, which requires thinking about their values in deciding for them. Finally, note that the fact that the mechanism is intended to work in the real world (where people are not very good at giving others' interests equal consideration) also explains why people will have to care for others and take their interests very seriously.

[52] People's judgments are influenced by their current standing and values and there is no fully impartial perspective, but I believe we can often think well about whether we would now contently live someone else's life (with their values, history, etc.) and that this is how we should decide whether someone can secure a basic minimum. Consider the case of the Amish girl discussed below. The fact that, in many ways, our lives might be better and worse than those of the typical Amish person does not make such judgments impossible.

[53] Here I suppose that discussion and deliberation among wise, informed, consistent, unbiased, caring people can help us make moral progress. Of course, in situations where unjust norms are widespread, and people fail to care enough for others, they will often make mistakes about what a minimally good life requires.

[54] It is not a heuristic device for figuring out what a minimally good life requires that we can use once and discard but a perspective we have reason to take up in caring for, and respecting, others.

as freedom.[55] We are embodied creatures and require many different kinds of care and concern to fulfill our needs over the course of our lives.[56] To provide equal, and due, consideration of individuals' interests in figuring out what they need to live well enough, we must be reasonable—demonstrating appropriate impartiality (Hassoun, 2017; Hassoun, 2020a; Hassoun, 2021a). Similarly, if we care for people in the way I have outlined, we give their interests due weight in considering what they need to live well enough. Our common humanity does not merely require formal, but substantial, recognition. Respect for common humanity's ground lies, in part, in the fact that we are all needy, vulnerable creatures who stand in important relationships of care and concern to others.[57] We are free, equal individuals whom no one can unjustifiably coerce or constrain (Locke, 1689; Hassoun, 2020a). So, coercion and constraint should not determine what qualifies as a good enough life for free (equal) individuals: We must not suffer from autonomy-undermining coercion and constraint in reasoning about what a minimally good life requires for others.[58]

Adopting the reasonable care standard to think about what people need to live well enough, we have reason to endorse many of the things on the common lists of what makes lives minimally good so it provides a plausible basis for an account of the basic minimum. Not everyone needs everything on any given list. Some need things that do not appear on common lists. Still, as Richard Kraut suggests, most people need "cognitive, affective, sensory, and social powers (no less than physical powers)" to live minimally good lives (Kraut, 2007, 137). Most also need some amount of autonomy, capacity for action, liberty, and understanding (Griffin, 1986). Moreover, deep personal relationships, accomplishments, and aesthetic experiences often contribute to minimally good lives (Kauppinen, 2013). Other plausible characterizations of what minimally good lives require exist too (Nussbaum, 2011). Not everyone will agree, but wise, informed, unbiased, consistent, caring people should.[59]

---

[55] We are all vulnerable in the sense that we can easily lose access to what we need to live well enough. Of course, people often fail to respect others' common humanity precisely because they fail to consider others' interests or give them due weight.

[56] It is possible, of course, that we owe other creatures similar care and concern for similar reasons, though I set these issues aside in this book.

[57] Each person's ability to live at least a minimally good life matters to the relationships they might, and will, stand in to others too, though for simplicity of expression I often focus on those relationships in which people currently stand.

[58] In very unjust societies people may have trouble occupying this perspective. Although they need to do so to properly evaluate life quality, cross-cultural discussion and deliberation may help them get closer to this ideal.

[59] Reasonable, caring, and free people should, more generally, converge on a small plurality of plausible characterizations of conditions for minimally good lives. See discussion below.

30   A MINIMALLY GOOD LIFE

To see more clearly how the account works in practice, consider how reasonable, caring, free people might reason about a few concrete cases. Suppose that policymakers must decide what someone in South Africa's Limpopo province needs to live minimally well. They consider the life of a typical child who sometimes lacks adequate food, water, and sanitation and who will probably not attain more than an elementary education (De Cock et al., 2013; OECD, 2019; South African Government, 2020). Though the child may be healthy, she almost certainly lacks secure access to the institutions, resources, and the capabilities she needs to live a minimally good life. Reflecting on what she needs to maintain decent relationships, pleasures, knowledge, appreciation, worthwhile activities, etc. can guide policymakers in trying to improve her life prospects (and help many of her contemporaries as well). Policymakers may disagree about some things—does the child need access to higher education to live well in her circumstances? The answer may depend on the opportunities available in her community to those without this education. Raising the general level of education may provide more opportunities as well as increase competition for available jobs. Still, the data show that youth who do not get a high school education in South Africa often fail to secure jobs (OECD, 2019).[60]

Consider, next, how a reasonable, caring, free person would evaluate the life of a 14-year-old Amish girl. Suppose the girl loves her family and community and was baptized into the Amish church. Then she decides she wants to go to college. The girl must determine whether to leave her community or stay. There likely exist serious reasons to doubt whether she can live her life well enough at least in the short term. Even if the girl eventually flourishes in the outside world, she may lose her family and community which she values greatly. Moreover, since she will lack her family's support and information about the outside world (never mind financial and other resources), she will likely have trouble leaving. Perhaps she can live successfully within the Amish community. Fully understanding and empathizing with her, however, one could also see how she might not. How can policymakers help the girl secure the autonomy-promoting options and other things she needs to live minimally well? Perhaps they cannot do much besides finding ways to make the transition to the outside world easier for the girl, if she decides she wants to leave the community. On the other hand, they might partner with the Amish

---

[60] Other accounts of the minimally good life (and of the basic minimum more broadly) may agree on the results in many cases, but they will disagree in others.

community to try to come up with better solutions for similar children in the future.

Finally, consider a single parent of three kids who lives in Colorado, has minimal savings, and who lost his job during the COVID-19 pandemic when he got hit by a car, developed a serious heart condition, and could no longer work. Can that parent continue to live minimally well? Can his children? The parent may well lose access to the relationships, pleasures, knowledge, appreciation, worthwhile activities, and other things that make his life minimally good. His disease, and its treatment, may cause significant pain and kill him young (threatening all these things). Moreover, the US social safety net often fails miserably. Suppose the parent does not have a strong social support network. He might not have the resources he needs to get to the food bank, never mind pay rent, once his normal unemployment benefits run out. Medicaid and the Affordable Care Act may provide some relief from medical costs. However, the future of the Affordable Care Act is anything but certain and the parent may have difficulty enrolling in Medicare.[61] Moreover, he may be unable to afford the premiums for other insurance options. So, he lacks secure access to the healthcare he needs to live minimally well. The parent may also have a hard time getting access to housing and other benefits and the family may not qualify. Furthermore, if he has some college education, even Meals on Wheels and similar organizations may not help.[62] Finally, if the parent cannot provide for his children, they may have to go into foster care—notorious in the United States for providing inconsistent support and supervision that can also threaten children's ability to live minimally well (Finkelstein et al., 2002; Wertheimer, 2002; US Department of Health and Human Services, 2019). At least, without a better social support system in place, both the parent and his children are at high risk of being unable to live good enough lives.[63]

One can debate my judgment about each of these cases, but I hope they demonstrate how reasonable, caring, free people can think clearly about what they would need to fare well enough as those people. At least, the mechanism I have provided can help us make progress in thinking about what people need for minimally good lives when we understand how children in a South

---

[61] Recall that security is important for a minimally good life. Perhaps one could argue for a constitutional right to healthcare on this basis, though I leave this possibility for future inquiry.
[62] I have tried to secure this kind of aid for a friend who was in this situation but does not have a family and failed, though perhaps things have changed in the past year or two and they differ for a family.
[63] I suppose here that he has excellent parenting skills and I acknowledge that foster care may benefit both children and their parents in some situations.

African township, a young woman in the Amish community, and a parent in Colorado are likely to fare.[64]

4. Conclusion

This chapter set out a new minimally good life account of the basic minimum.[65] The next chapter explains some advantages of this account of the basic minimum over the most plausible alternatives. Subsequent chapters argue that we must ensure everyone can live well enough when we need not sacrifice so much to help them and propose a particular way of helping people do so (Hassoun, 2009; Hassoun, 2016).[66]

That said, this chapter's account of the basic minimum is compatible with many different theories of what justice and morality require more generally. One can accept this chapter's account of what people need to live minimally good lives and a very different account of the conditions under which we must help people live such lives.[67] One might argue, for instance, that it is only when people act responsibly and we can help them at low cost that we should ensure they secure the basic minimum.[68] One can also endorse the account and claim that we owe people much more than the ability to live minimally good lives. One might argue, for instance, that justice or morality requires a much more substantive commitment to equality.

Moreover, the minimally good life account's advocates can endorse different ways of helping people secure a basic minimum. On some sufficiency

---

[64] Once one understands what people need to live minimally well, one can also better help meet those needs.

[65] Please see Hassoun (2017) and Hassoun (2020a) for some preliminary work on this topic and Hassoun (2021a) and Hassoun (2021b) for further discussion of these ideas.

[66] My account of how we should help people below the threshold is silent regarding whether we have any obligations to aid those above the threshold and we can combine it with different views.

[67] Just because someone needs something to live even minimally well does not mean that they have a claim to it. For the account to provide a basis for political and human rights obligations, it cannot require the (nomologically, if not politically) impossible (Gilabert and Lawford-Smith, 2012; Brennan, 2013). Moreover, helping people live minimally well will not always take lexical priority over fulfilling other rights and obligations. Though I will argue that doing so has significant weight insofar as it protects our common humanity. Individuals can plausibly claim the proposed basic minimum at least when others can help them live minimally good lives without sacrificing too much (Arneson, 2004; Segall, 2014; Nielsen, 2016; Herlitz, 2018). Presumably, we do not have to help people secure what they need to live even minimally good lives when we must sacrifice things of greater value to do so (Fried, 1976). If, for instance, helping a few people live minimally well tragically prevented us from saving many others' lives, we might have to focus on saving as many lives as possible (Arneson, 2004).

[68] To arbitrate between competing obligations, one must consider their ground. For more on how I believe we should think about potential conflicts between rights, see Hassoun (2020a).

theories, we must prioritize helping people rise above the threshold (Dorsey, 2010). On others, we can help many far below the threshold get closer to it before helping fewer people close to the threshold rise above it (Widerquist, 2010). On yet other theories, we can help many people above the threshold rather than help one person below it (Shields, 2018). Subsequent chapters defend a roughly prioritarian account of how we should help people below the threshold in present generations that also attempts to respect the separateness of persons (also see Hassoun, 2009; Hassoun, 2016).[69] Still, one can accept the account of the sufficiency threshold I have defended here and a very different account of how we should help people reach it. One only needs to agree that the reasons we have for helping people shift once they reach the threshold: We have especially weighty reasons to respect, protect, and help everyone live at least minimally well out of concern for their common humanity (Shields, 2012; Shields, 2018; Shields, 2020).[70]

---

[69] My account of how we should help people below the threshold is silent regarding whether we have any obligations to aid those above the threshold and we can combine it with different views.

[70] Again, subsequent chapters defend this conclusion, and the minimally good life account lets us bracket many important disagreements about what social justice requires in providing a standard on which we can secure broad agreement. For instance, it does not require people to have everything from which they might benefit or that they might choose. On the account, people only need an adequate range of the things that let them live minimally good lives. People only require all the things that are necessary and jointly sufficient, and some that are simply important, for living a minimally good life. People need not even secure everything that might contribute to their ability to live a minimally good life. They only need a sufficient range of the things they require (and that are important) for living such a life.

A Minimally Good Life: What We Owe to Others and What We Can Justifiably Demand. Nicole Hassoun, Oxford University Press. © Nicole Hassoun 2024. DOI: 10.1093/9780191946455.003.0002

2

Good Enough?

Other Accounts of the Minimally Good Life

1. Introduction

What basic minimum, if any, do we owe to co-citizens or members of the larger global community? Does it suffice if a young mother can find shelter from an abusive partner or must society also help her secure food, job training, or even a job? Should we have public works programs to help people in times of emergency? Must rich states, or their citizens, assist people in poorer countries and, if so, to what extent? Must even the most neglected and impoverished access essential vaccines and other medicines? How can we determine how much an adequate social welfare system requires? What minimal standard of provision can people plausibly claim? To answer any of these questions, we must first know what constitutes a basic minimum.[*] The previous chapter defended a new mechanism, or procedure, for arriving at an account of the basic minimum. It also outlined an account of what we owe to others simply in virtue of our common humanity.[1] Subsequent chapters argue that legitimacy, global justice, respect for human rights, and beneficence at least require helping people live minimally good lives. This chapter argues that the *minimally good life account*, unlike the main alternatives, provides a necessary and sufficient standard of minimum provision (one that gives each person a basic minimum they plausibly require).[2]

---

[*] This chapter draws on: Hassoun, Nicole. 2021a. "Good Enough? The Minimally Good Life Account of the Basic Minimum." *Australasian Journal of Philosophy* 100 (2): 330–34. It also draws on: Hassoun, N. 2021. "Sufficiency and the Minimally Good Life." *Utilitas* 33 (3): 321–336.

[1] Recall that, respect for our common humanity requires equal consideration of interests, as well as freedom. Moreover, this respect's ground lies, in part, in the fact that we are needy, vulnerable creatures standing in important relationships of care and concern to others.

[2] Different possible bases for a basic minimum exist. On a capability view, for instance, we must provide people with whatever they need to secure the requisite sets of valuable functionings (activities and states) (Sen, 1980; Nussbaum, 2000b). Alternately, on a resource view, we must only provide everyone with sufficient goods. Moreover, different accounts set the threshold for a basic minimum at different levels (they include different capabilities or resources etc.). Although this chapter cannot

More precisely, this chapter considers accounts of the sufficiency threshold that draw on competing currencies of (basic) justice. Those offering these accounts do so in the context of larger arguments about why we should help people secure a basic minimum and what exactly this requires. Different accounts serve different purposes. Some focus on political—e.g. justice or human rights-based—obligations. Others defend individual moral obligations to help people secure a basic minimum. Still, their arguments' success hinges on whether they provide a plausible account of the basic minimum. That is, arguments about the basic minimum—and the role it should play in moral and political theories—depend on its nature. So, I consider here whether the alternatives provide plausible accounts of a basic minimum that might play a role in larger arguments about what we owe to one another out of concern for our common humanity.

Although one might suppose that each author can define a basic minimum as they like and then argue that we owe people this minimum, their arguments cannot succeed if they do not offer a plausible account of what it is we owe people in the first place. Moreover, we can reasonably consider what qualifies as a plausible basic minimum before considering whether we owe people any such minimum. Consider an example from a slightly different domain. Suppose one thinks that we owe people equal welfare and that this requires helping the less well-off no matter the consequences for the better-off. Those who object to this view may reject either the claim that we must strive for equality or the claim that we should care about welfare per se (or both) (Arneson, 2005). It makes sense to consider whether welfare is the right currency of justice in evaluating the theory before turning to the claim that we should strive for equality. (Though one could also proceed in the other direction and consider whether we should care about equality before considering whether we should strive for equality of welfare, in particular.)

In any case, I will just consider whether the best alternatives provide a plausible basic minimum here. Proponents of the main competing accounts of the basic minimum I will consider intend them to support obligations to help people reach a threshold like the one this book defends. That is, they defend moral or political obligations to help people secure a basic minimum. So, considering their accounts in the current context seems reasonable. At least, I think this is legitimate given that subsequent chapters engage with competitors' larger arguments about the conditions under which we must

---

canvas every possible combination of bases and thresholds, it argues that its account has some advantages over the main competitors.

help people secure a basic minimum. Subsequent chapters argue that this threshold should play a role in our moral as well as political theories about what we owe to others.

What follows starts by reminding readers of the minimally good life account's most important features, before considering the main alternatives in turn. It suggests that most competitors either focus too narrowly on what people *think* they need or focus too widely on what people *generally* require for a basic minimum. So, they fail to capture everything people can plausibly claim as a basic minimum and/or suggest that people require some things that they cannot plausibly claim. An adequate account should attend to differences between individuals but cannot rely entirely on what people think they require even after significant reflection. That is, I suppose we want an account of what each person needs for a basic minimum but that we cannot neglect differences between individuals that can ground their claims.[3]

2. How We Should Understand the Minimally Good Life

Recall that, on my minimally good life account, people need an adequate range of the fundamental conditions for securing meaningful pursuits, relationships, pleasures, knowledge, appreciation, worthwhile activities, and other life-improving goods. Specifically, people must secure those goods a reasonable, free, caring person would (in conversation with others) set as a minimal standard of justifiable aspiration/basic right.[4]

Recall each component of this account briefly. First, the adequacy threshold for securing the fundamental conditions for a minimally good life must ensure that the life is at least well-worth living, though it need not qualify as an excellent, nor even a very good, life.[5] Lives at the lowest levels of flourishing qualify as minimally good.[6] People require all the necessary, and jointly sufficient, conditions for securing the things that make their lives good enough. Moreover, people need some conditions that just help them secure these things—those that make a central, or significant, contribution to their

---

[3] This seems particularly important for grounding human rights that protect individuals.
[4] The previous chapter defended the claim that we should take this perspective in thinking about what people need to flourish and explained why it should help us understand what people need as a basic minimum.
[5] Recall that lives must be more than just barely worth living to qualify as even minimally good.
[6] Recall that the flourishing at issue here goes beyond what is good for a person and what someone who cares about another would choose for them. People can live flourishing lives and sacrifice some interests despite the fact that those who care about them would not choose this for them.

ability to do so. Second, I call the internal and external, natural and social, conditions for securing the things that make life minimally good *fundamental*. Besides satisfying material needs, people require resources, capacities, and social and institutional structures to secure the things that make lives minimally good. Third, one has *secure* access to the things that make lives minimally good when one is not at significant risk of losing access (for further discussion, see Chapter 1). Fourth, many things make lives minimally good including *relationships*, *pleasures*, *knowledge*, *appreciation*, and *worthwhile activities*.[7] *Recognition* and *respect* that safeguard dignity, or common humanity, also affect individuals' ability to live minimally good lives.

Finally, we can determine what minimally good lives require by considering how reasonable, caring, free people would set a minimum for justifiable aspiration as a matter of basic right. *Reasonable* people want to cooperate and live with other people on fair terms (Rawls, 1971). They can revise their ends on rational grounds. They also understand that everyone has the standing to make claims to protections of their fundamental interests. Moreover, reasonable people are appropriately impartial. Setting aside special ties to others, they do not privilege equally important interests of various people differently. *Caring* people empathize with others to understand their circumstances, psychology, and history and give their interests due weight (Nussbaum, 2006).[8] They are motivated to help others. Finally, *free* people have sufficient internal and external liberty. They neither form nor endorse adaptive preferences that undermine their evaluations of life quality. Moreover, they have the decent options and bargaining power they need to judge whether lives qualify as minimally good (Raz, 1986; Hassoun, 2011b; Hassoun, 2012).[9] Reasonable, free, caring people would set a *minimal standard for justifiable aspiration/ basic right* under which they would contentedly live as others do, fully understanding others' circumstances, psychology, and history. When people secure the justifiable aspiration/basic right standard, there is no serious reason to doubt that they can live their lives well. We should not ask people whether they want different conditions as they may have unrealistic aims, adaptive

---

[7] The previous chapter discussed the things people need for a minimally good enough life at a greater length and subsequent chapters consider what we must do to support individuals in securing these things.

[8] Reasonable, caring, free people must fully understand emotionally, and otherwise, what it is like to live as others do by putting themselves in the others' shoes (appreciating their history as well as their current state). Again, Darwall calls this "projective empathy" (Darwall, 2002, 61–62). When we empathize in this way, we share other people's feelings as their perspective warrants (Darwall, 2002, 62).

[9] Living in a rule-governed society does not necessarily undermine freedom.

preferences, or poor bargaining positions. Rather we ask whether reasonable, free, caring people would contentedly live as others do.

The previous chapter explained how the account lets us arrive at concrete answers to questions about what people need to live minimally well, but it is important to see how the account can work in practice, so consider one more case. To live minimally well, does a young immigrant to the US who has trachoma need access to treatment that can protect her sight? I believe that if we put ourselves in her shoes, we will conclude that she does. Although we can reasonably affirm lives without sight, trachoma threatens individuals' ability to live well in the justified aspiration/basic right sense. It often prevents poor people from providing for their families and reduces their life expectancy significantly (Etya'ale, 2001). Even in rich countries, like the US, blindness often undermines individuals' ability to live well enough at least for some time (Dowling, 2020). Those who lose their sight may lose access to the resources they need to reach, and stay, above the justifiable aspiration/basic right standard over the course of their lives in US society. People fear going blind more than any other disability as vision loss often negatively affects subjective quality of life, independence, mental health, cognition, social function, employment, and educational attainment and can contribute to falls and other injuries (National Academy of Sciences, 2016). Immigrants to the US often have little social support. They may have trouble navigating new surroundings, especially if they do not already speak English. They may also lack jobs and adequate social services if blindness impairs their ability to support themselves. If we organized US society differently, and people did not place such a social premium on sight, the blind might fare well enough. Still, given that low-cost antibiotics and surgery can treat the young woman's condition, and absent the deeper structural changes to address the challenges blind people face, no one can reasonably assert that providing treatment costs others too much (Baltussen et al., 2005).[10] In any case, whether she will live well enough while blind depends on her history, psychology, and so forth.

3. Alternative Bases for the Basic Minimum

With the broad outline of the minimally good life account and how we should think about others' ability to reach this threshold in mind, this section

---

[10] Structural change may do even more to help individuals to live well enough—no one should get trachoma in the first place.

considers some of the account's advantages over the main competing welfare and capability accounts of the basic minimum.[11] Again, I will argue that the main competitors fail to capture all the things that people can plausibly claim as a basic minimum without suggesting that people require some things that they cannot plausibly claim. I consider, first, some accounts that focus too narrowly on what people *think* they must secure for a basic minimum before turning to others that focus too widely on what people *generally* require for this minimum. Making this case will support the conclusion that we should, instead, put ourselves into others' shoes and think about what each particular individual needs from the second-person perspective.

Consider, first, the most developed narrow account of the minimally good life in the literature. In *The Basic Minimum*, Dale Dorsey endorses a theory much like Joseph Raz defends in *The Morality of Freedom* (Raz, 1986, 308–309). On this account, to fare minimally well, people need success in valued projects. These "global" projects provide long-term goals that help unify people's lives (Dorsey, 2012, 39–41).[12] Dorsey says we should make sure individuals would still endorse their projects with coherent and complete preferences (Dorsey, 2012, 89).

There is a lot to admire in Dorsey's account. His view highlights the importance of helping individuals carry out their life plans and the centrality of those plans for good lives. Moreover, Dorsey attends to differences between individuals in a way that several of the other views this chapter will consider do not (Dorsey, 2012, 10). Different people have different values and can succeed in different projects. Dorsey also connects his account of what we owe people as a basic minimum to the nature of the good life as he sees it, and

---

[11] The account also has some advantages over some of the most sophisticated arguments for providing people with equal resources (Dworkin, 2000). First, people need many things besides resources such as liberties and the background conditions that support choice. People need the natural and social conditions for securing things that make lives minimally good. They need the conditions for autonomy, basic capabilities, and decent institutions. Even a robust basic income simply will not suffice. Some require education, social and emotional support, and other things besides resources to live well enough. People cannot purchase some of these things. Providing them does not impose excessive costs, or unreasonable obligations, on others. As capability theorists point out, we should care about what people can be and do as well as what resources they have (Sen, 1999; Nussbaum, 2011). Second, in practice, resource theories fail to provide a necessary and sufficient standard of minimum provision, because such theories fail to attune sufficiently to differences between individuals. Any particular basket of resources (or resource-based insurance scheme) is likely to leave some without enough and may give others too much (Sen, 1980; Arneson, 2013; Begley and Durgin, 2015).

[12] Several other authors endorse something like Dorsey's view and these views often have similar problems. See e.g. Sher (2014). Many views in the literature on sufficiency theory also face similar problems to those facing the other accounts this chapter considers. See e.g. Huseby (2010) and Shields (2018).

helping people carry out their life plans arguably deserves a great deal of weight in deliberations about how to help people.

Unfortunately, Dorsey's view does not guarantee enough for some and may provide other people with too much for any plausible basic minimum. Individuals' values and life projects matter, but other things do too.[13] We cannot just help people satisfy complete coherent preferences that constitute unifying life projects if, for instance, they completely and coherently adapt to a bad situation.[14] A horribly abused woman whose unifying life plan involves continuing to live with her abuser does not plausibly live a minimally good life, even if she has completely and coherently adapted to her situation. She may prefer, all things considered, to suffer her abuse in silence because she loves her partner and consistently maintain this distorted preference even if she knows what it is like to live free from abuse. Moreover, even if people prefer to remain in dire poverty after experiencing many alternative possible lives in which they are not impoverished, they do not live minimally good lives. (Reasonable people might maintain their preferences even after experiencing alternative possible lives where they are not impoverished because they will lose their particular attachments in these alternatives.)

Dorsey would respond that his view does not fall prey to most versions of the problem of adaptive preferences and that his account of the basic minimum is not too low.[15] Dorsey distinguishes shallow from deep adaptive

---

[13] I believe we sometimes have "moral reason to force people to live lives they do not value" (Dorsey, 2012, 78). Consider someone who will become a mass murder and coherently and completely value killing other people if she never attends anything beyond primary school. Should education through age 16 prevent her from forming these preferences, we should require her to complete this education. However, I consider paternalism further below.

[14] For the same reason, it may not do to ground sufficiency in agency or autonomy alone, although agency and autonomy plausibly provide part of its ground (Nielsen, 2016). Consider, for instance, some of the account's advantages over James Griffin's ground for human rights in normative agency understood as a more general account of the basic minimum. Griffin maintains that people should have the things necessary for normative agency (Griffin, 2008). This agency requires autonomy or the ability to form a conception of the good life, liberty, or freedom from interference and constraint in pursing this life, and some minimum provision of things like education. I believe some things people need for a basic minimum they do not need for normative agency (Tasioulas, 2013). Most people require some decent relationships and worthwhile activities for a basic minimum even if lacking them will not undermine agency (Liao, 2015). Moreover, all people should have some things as part of the basic minimum, even if they lack liberty and autonomy or agency. This includes infants, very young children, and the severely mentally disabled (Hassoun, 2013).

[15] Dorsey does admit that some deep adaptive preferences pose a problem for his theory but insists that his account of the basic minimum is high enough. He acknowledges that some preferences would not be revised even with full knowledge of what the experience of living the relevant alternative lives is like because they are central parts of a person's conception of the good. But he claims that adaptive preferences are only a problem if they are preferences for the worse and notes that preferences for the worse need not be adaptive (Dorsey, 2012, 101). Dorsey draws many helpful distinctions in pinning down the exact nature of adaptive preferences. He points out that even people with decent options who do not prefer the worse option and who have autonomy can have adaptive preferences. He notes that often, at some level, people do not judge that they will fare best by fulfilling adaptive preferences

preferences. Shallow preferences would be revised if one's conception of the good were complete and coherent and rendered a consistent ranking of preferences across all possible changes in capabilities, circumstances, and environments. Furthermore, in rendering this ranking Dorsey specifies that one must test one's preferences against one's value judgments about the quality of other (metaphysically) possible lives (with full knowledge of what the experience of living those lives is like) (Dorsey, 2012, 93–94). Deep adaptive preferences would not be revised even after this experience because they are central parts of a person's conception of the good (Dorsey, 2012, 101). Dorsey contends that if we have coherent consistent preferences, lives will not be preferred simply because one is unable to live them or because one has been indoctrinated into having them because one will experience alternative lives. Moreover, Dorsey would insist that even deeply adaptive preferences of those who prefer the worst do not entail that his account of the basic minimum is too low.[16] After all, achieving a valued project has significant value on its own—even if it is not otherwise valuable. On his account, "a valued global project... requires that one live a life that is narratively unified, the activities of which maintain a shared meaning, such that this particular explanation of the meaning is part of an explanation of one's own assessment of that life as worth living" (Dorsey, 2012, 66–67). Dorsey says most such lives require agency and that requires food, water, shelter, etc. Although Dorsey admits that even a life of a destitute sex worker subject to coercion and violence might count as minimally good on his account, he says, "virtually no one will *value* the achievement of a global project *under such conditions*" (Dorsey, 2012, 67). So, although one could value some achievable life projects like being a destitute sex worker under terrible conditions, very few people would do so.[17] Moreover, he says that if someone values a love relationship enough

---

and, if they had better options, they would prefer other things. He also points out that capability theories (and many other welfare theories) can suffer from adaptive preferences. People can have adaptive preferences even if they have basic capabilities (and just fail to exercise them), for instance.

[16] This is more plausible if one accepts Dorsey's claim that committing to a basic minimum only entails that helping people reach the threshold should take absolute priority to helping others below it and weighted priority to those above it. In Chapter 5, I argue for a different way of helping people below the threshold that is not compatible with this way of understanding the basic minimum. In any case, as I suggest below, those who have a valued project may be so much worse-off (enslaved, abused, etc.) than those who lack one that I do not think it is reasonable to accept his view.

[17] For Dorsey, the basic minimum consists in engaging in a valued project—so, to the objection that valueless projects, or projects of distinctively negative value, seem to deprive one of a dignified life, he says this: "the relationships between the achievement of basic human dignity and the achievement of the basic minimum ... appears to be fully dependent on people's conceptions of the good" (Dorsey, 2012, 57). "Whether the basic minimum ... requires a given person to maintain a life of human dignity depends on whether this person values dignified vs undignified lives" (Dorsey, 2012, 57). Moreover, Dorsey contends, one needs to provide an account of dignity that is not grounded in

to consider her life worth living despite being an enslaved, destitute sex worker, that is enough for a basic minimum because it would be better to help someone else who was equally poorly-off but who lacked any valuable project. Dorsey then appeals to other values besides the basic minimum to reject slavery, destitution, etc. (Dorsey, 2012, 69–72).

However, this argument fails for three reasons. (1) Dorsey's basic minimum is too low. People who live in terrible conditions do often value their lives for their own sake, in part, because of their important projects—like raising children, helping their friends, and generally being a good community member. And it is not clear that, even after experiencing other lives, they would prefer a different life that is not attainable by them.[18] However, whether or not they continue to prefer their own lives upon appropriate reflection, enslaved, destitute, sex workers lack a basic minimum.[19] That is, even if people *do* value their lives in such terrible conditions after reflecting on them appropriately, they do not qualify as minimally good. Even if they have deeply adapted to their situations, the most impoverished, oppressed, etc. do not live minimally good lives.[20] Enslaved, destitute sex workers do not secure a basic minimum even if they reflect appropriately on and continue to value carrying out their life plan of having a child, for instance. This is so even if they value continuing to live their lives over any other possible alternative life they cannot actually live, and no further reflection or experience will change their mind. They may have secured a valuable life plan, but that is not enough for a basic minimum precisely because they remain enslaved, destitute sex workers. (2) Even if we should prioritize helping someone without a valued life project over an equally poorly-off person who lacks one, that does nothing to establish that one is above and the other below the threshold. In subsequent chapters, I argue against Dorsey's claim that we should always prioritize

---

some other value to explain why it is required for a basic minimum. But, note that the minimally good life view provides just such an account of what dignity requires.

[18] Why should we think that when someone has been indoctrinated into believing something is best for them (maybe via horrible abuse), experiencing alternative lives in which they are not abused will change their mind?

[19] I use these examples because I think it is even less plausible that people can secure a basic minimum if they have deeply adapted to situations in which they only have self-regarding projects—like achieving inner peace.

[20] If Dorsey includes a content constraint on acceptable preferences so that they require everything in the minimally good life view, I have no objection to his account. But since he wants to stay neutral between what he calls "weak strong" and "weak subjectivism"—and what he calls "weak strong" subjectivism says that preferences for the worse contribute to the value of one's life—, Dorsey must reject a content constraint. Both kinds of subjectivism reject a purely preferentist view—as the life at issue must contain some objective value. But, on "weak subjectivism" mere preference satisfaction does not contribute to a good life if it is preference for the worse (whereas on "weak strong" subjectivism it does).

helping people reach the threshold over helping those who are further below it. But even if we must prioritize enslaved, destitute sex workers who lack valuable life projects over enslaved, destitute sex workers who have such projects, none of these people reach the threshold for any plausible basic minimum when they remain enslaved, destitute sex workers. (3) The fact that other things besides the basic minimum matter does not establish that enslaved, destitute sex workers fare well enough either. I agree that there are many reasons to reject poverty and compulsory sex work independently from our concern for a basic minimum. Sexual slavery and destitution arguably violate other *Basic Rights* beyond one's right to a basic minimum. But Dorsey cannot establish that enslaved, destitute sex workers fare well enough by pointing that out. These people still lack a basic minimum because their slavery and destitution undermine their ability to live minimally well.

On my account, the impoverished much more plausibly need the health care, education, food, water, shelter, capabilities, and institutions that reasonable, caring, free people would require to contentedly live life in their shoes. To live minimally good lives, people need sufficient subjective welfare and valuable life projects can enhance individuals' life quality significantly, but people also need many other things to secure a plausible basic minimum. We must understand, for instance, that women need good options—often including significant financial, as well as social and emotional, support—to leave abusive partners. Often, they cannot secure a basic minimum without such support. At the same time, people might secure a basic minimum without everything they need to have the kind of unifying project upon which Dorsey focuses. Suppose someone with very expensive tastes would require nearly the whole of their country's gross domestic product to achieve their life's goals. Alternately, suppose that they only truly identify with a life project of causing massive harm to others. Why think these people require so much? At least, they do not need extreme wealth for any plausible basic minimum and harming others plausibly undermines, rather than promotes, their life quality.[21] Dorsey does not think people will opt for, and only rest content with, expensive or harmful life projects when they reflect appropriately upon their experience of many other possible lives. He points out that when people have

---

[21] If we stretch our imaginations and suppose some people really could require so much and could never adjust their aspirations downward without sacrificing their ability to fare even minimally well, perhaps they simply cannot live well enough. Although they have some claim to move up towards the threshold, as Chapter 1 explained, the costs to others limit what a minimally good life can require. Moreover, subsequent chapters discuss additional limits to justifiable costs in making the case that we must sometimes provide a basic minimum for others.

a severe disability and have no choice about whether to pursue their projects, we must sometimes help them. Moreover, we must do so even when it is very costly or they need much more than most people suppose a basic minimum can require. Furthermore, if people with expensive or offensive tastes do maintain them after appropriate reflection, Dorsey says these preferences are akin to disabilities and they may really constitute a basic minimum for those people. However, he seems to grant that this is sometimes extremely unintuitive. For, he says that we may want to make an exception to the general rule that the basic minimum requires giving priority to helping people carry out their life projects when these projects are too expensive or offensive and other things (of impersonal value) may matter much more than fulfilling some such preferences (Dorsey, 2012, 177–185).

More generally, the minimally good life account has some advantages over a range of alternative welfare accounts that might play a similar role in explaining what we, at a minimum, owe to people. Note, first, however, that the book's account is compatible with many of these theories. A reasonable and caring person may specify what someone needs to live a minimally good life in the way I have suggested because doing so will best promote welfare on a variety of subjective, hybrid, or objective list theories. So, even those who reject the arguments that follow may still endorse the broad outlines of my account.

That said, consider why we should reject many alternative subjective and hybrid theories as accounts of what people need for a minimally good life (Heathwood, 2005; Haybron, 2008; Tiberius, 2008; Dorsey, 2012).[22] On many subjective and hybrid theories, people must be able to endorse their lives, so we must take very seriously the first-person perspective. I believe some endorsement constraint is plausible if we are concerned with what is good *for* people, but we should reject it when we are considering what people need to reach a basic minimum.[23] Helping people secure what they value matters, but other things also matter for a basic minimum. I have just argued, for instance, that we cannot only help people satisfy complete coherent preferences that constitute unifying, or even valuable, life goals if they completely

---

[22] I will adopt Christopher Heathwood's categorization here and say subjective theories implies that something contributes to one's life's value "just in case either (i) she has a certain pro-attitude toward it, or (ii) it itself involves a certain pro-attitude of hers toward something" but refer to these pro-attitudes as values (Heathwood, 2014). I consider only hybrid theories that endorses these propositions and add the further constraint that at least some of the things that help people live minimally good lives must themselves be valuable.

[23] Recall that the minimally good life account is concerned with life quality not wellbeing. See Chapter 1 for some relevant discussion.

and coherently adapt to a bad situation.[24] The most abused, neglected, poor, and disadvantaged among us can often satisfy some preferences and may endorse their lives even on some of the most sophisticated accounts of what this requires (Dorsey, 2012). Rather, I maintain that what people need for a basic minimum should be sensitive to, but cannot be completely constrained, by their values. Often, we should respond to adaptive preferences by helping to improve the conditions under which people form and maintain, or change, their preferences.[25] A basic minimum must ensure for people sufficient subjective wellbeing. But, depending on what policymakers (or others) provide, people's points of view, and so their values, can change in better (or worse) ways.[26] Even individuals' most central values, never mind mere preferences, do not fully constrain what they need as a basic minimum.[27]

Consider a concrete example to see why what individuals value cannot constrain what they need for a basic minimum.[28] In *Valuing Freedom*, Sabina Alkire describes an aid project to help poor villagers improve their livelihood. The aid agency presented two options. The women might grow vegetables for export or roses to sell for decorating shrines. The women chose the roses

---

[24] For people to secure a basic minimum, they may require opportunities to improve their life prospects while maintaining their particular attachments, but sometimes people also need help letting go.

[25] Abused women may for instance require not just shelter but the possibility of leaving their partners without sacrificing their, or their children's, basic life prospects.

[26] This point will not necessarily count against idealized or informed desire views, but these have their own drawbacks. See Rosati (1995).

[27] Partly this is also because the quality of one's values have far ranging consequences for other people. Even if I am wrong about this, recall that some subjectivists may accept this paper's account for their own reasons.

[28] One might try to motivate a subjective or hybrid account of the basic minimum by appeal to the idea that, at least insofar as we want an account of what we might want political institutions to provide, we must stay neutral between conceptions of the good (Nagel, 1995; Rawls, 1999). Different people have different values and there are a wide range of reasonable and conscientious lives. Proponents of neutrality believe that political institutions should not privilege helping people live some of these lives over others. Doing so would fail to treat everyone equally. Moreover, some argue that perfectionist institutions that reject political neutrality would fail to respect those whose versions of the good life they do not privilege. Individuals' views of the good help determine their identities and give their lives meaning. Institutions that privilege some conceptions of what people need for minimally good lives over others will not secure their subject's allegiance or cooperation. So, perhaps the neutrality essential for stability can only support conceptions of the (minimally) good life with a strong endorsement constraint. Although I ultimately reject political neutrality, and this book aims primarily to engage with those who also endorse some kind of perfectionism, we can set this objection aside here. Subjective and hybrid accounts of the basic minimum do not leave greater space for disagreement about the good than more objective views. Subjective and hybrid accounts *are* accounts of what the minimally good life—or the basic minimum more broadly—requires that some conscientious and reasonable people reject. In accepting an endorsement constraint, political institutions privilege subjective and hybrid accounts of the good and neglect to advance more objective conceptions of the good life. See also the discussion below on the importance of understanding what a plausible basic minimum requires even if we sometimes cannot or should not help people secure this minimum.

because they found the work more meaningful; it supported one of their valued life projects—it helped them honor their gods (Alkire, 2002). Alkire rightly believes that we should help people live lives they value.[29] At the same time, this project's value went beyond giving the women meaningful work. It also helped them feed their families, send their children to school, secure basic health care, and so forth. Sometimes helping people honor their gods helps them secure a basic minimum.[30] We may even have to help them honor their gods to ensure they secure such a minimum. Suppose, however, that planting roses did not help the women improve their livelihoods after all. The women must still have adequate food, water, shelter, and so forth to secure a basic minimum. Moreover, this claim does not depend on their valuing doing so as much as honoring their gods (or at all). They might prefer we aid them in building additional temples when the roses do not grow. To secure a basic minimum, people must live minimally good lives even if that does not help them secure (other) things they value. What people need for a basic minimum should respond to their preferences in some ways, but preferences cannot fully constrain the minimum.[31]

Consider next some wider and more objective accounts of the basic minimum. Matthew Liao provides the main objective welfare account of the

---

[29] More precisely, I do not think endorsement is strictly required for a minimally good life but can agree that endorsement at least improves many individuals' life quality.

[30] I believe this is often the case even where people have mistaken beliefs. They can realize other values such as an opportunity for introspection or connection with other members of their communities. Moreover, people often secure a sense of meaning from religious activity. At least, fulfilling religious values may contribute as much to flourishing as fulfilling other preferences not grounded in fact.

[31] Alternately, consider this case as a challenge to subjective views: Suppose your child wholeheartedly endorses being a lazy drunk and hurts people in predictable ways. She often lies, cheats, and harms other people to get what she wants. Such a life is pitiful, rather than minimally good. I imagine here a slightly altered version of the main character in the TV program *Shameless* who does not ever feel remorse for her actions. You should not say that insofar as this character acts as she wants, she fares well enough. Rather, she needs psychological and addiction counseling to reach the threshold for a basic minimum. Even if your child never changes her mind, or you can no longer help her because doing so would imperil your own ability to live well enough, her life may be far from minimally good. So, although the arguments I have offered may not convince every committed subjective/hybrid welfare theorist of this point, I believe that an adequate account of the basic minimum must extend beyond such subjective and hybrid accounts of welfare traditionally construed. Perhaps we can decide what people need for a basic minimum by appeal to appropriately laundered (or idealized) preferences, values, or what not, and this paper's proposal may provide one way of thinking about that. But idealization is not likely to fulfill a strong endorsement constraint (people do not always care about their idealized desires) and there are some serious questions about the confidence we can have in our idealized judgments. Moreover, subjective accounts also face a different puzzle. It is possible that people might make it the case that their lives can only be minimally good if they have things that are not valuable (if we do not also add the implausible constraint that securing things one values can only increase life's value when these things are actually valuable). That is, they may decide to value only valueless things, which might make it the case that they can only be brought up towards the threshold by getting the (non-valuable) things they value. I set this point aside here, however.

(minimally) good life in the literature. As Rowan Cruft helpfully summarizes Liao's compelling view, it focuses on what "*human beings qua human beings need in order to . . . pursue . . . basic activities*" (Cruft, 2015, 103). These activities affect people's lives as a whole. They improve the quality of our lives qua human beings rather than qua individuals (Liao, 2015, 81). Some examples include "deep personal relationships with, e.g., one's partner, friends, parents, children; knowledge of, e.g., the workings of the world, of oneself, of others; active pleasures such as creative work and play; and passive pleasures such as appreciating beauty" (Liao, 2015, 81). One does not need virtue or excellence to live a (minimally) good life on Liao's account. Rather, one requires "various goods, capacities, and options that human beings qua human beings need" (Liao, 2015, 82). People may require some of these fundamental conditions only to secure some of the basic activities, but Liao specifies that everyone has a right to all of them. Moreover, he says people should have "an *adequate range* of fundamental goods, capacities, and options so that they can pursue those basic activities that are characteristic of a minimally decent human life" (Liao, 2015, 82).

Because Liao's account is broad and pluralistic it captures many of the things people need to secure a plausible basic minimum, but I also have a few worries about his account. My main concern is that people may not secure the basic minimum when they have what people qua human require for a good life. Some people require much more than others to pursue basic activities and secure the things that make their lives minimally good. Individuals may have idiosyncratic needs for health care or social conditions that most people do not require for a basic minimum. A pregnant woman requires pre-natal care to live minimally well although most people do not require this care. Similarly, someone with a rare disease might need a treatment no one else needs to live minimally well. So, to decide what people can claim, Liao must provide an account of what it means to require something *qua human*.

Liao says some things about what people require *qua human*, but he must say more. He says that what he needs as a philosopher, he does not require *qua human*. Similarly, he says what someone needs to live a life devoted to helping others that person does not require *qua human*. However, it is not clear why the pregnant person requires treatment qua human rather than qua pregnant woman. Nor is it clear why a person with a rare disease requires treatment qua human rather than qua that individual with that rare disease. At least, most people do not need pre-natal treatment never mind treatment for an extremely rare disease. So, what people *typically* need cannot explain what these people require *qua human*. Perhaps the *severity* of the need—its effect on fundamental human interests—can explain when people require something *qua human*.[32] But, then we need to know what effects are severe enough and what fundamental interests count. Moreover, even the most idiosyncratic needs can affect fundamental interests—a pianist needs fully functional fingers qua pianist but, if she loses her ability to manipulate them, that might prevent her from feeding her family and remaining well nourished herself.[33] Perhaps the idea is that the basic minimum is *universal*; it is concerned with what anyone (in similar locations, circumstances, and times) would require. Everyone should be able to flourish. So, anyone who was a pregnant woman would require pre-natal care, anyone afflicted with a rare disease would need treatment for their particular disease, and anyone who was a pianist would require fully functional fingers. But, then all needs may ground rights on Liao's account. Some philosophers arguably require books to live minimally well, especially if they cannot otherwise take care of themselves and their families. On the other hand, those who require things not everyone in their situation would need would still not secure what they require for a basic minimum on this interpretation of the view. In any case, to

---

[32] One might also consider basic needs views as potential accounts of the basic minimum because they focus on deprivation and play a large role in the literature on sufficiency theory as well as in accounts of global poverty and human development (Axelson and Nielsen, 2016; Brock and Miller, 2019; Huseby, 2020; Timmer, 2021b). Harry Frankfurt has one of the best-developed and most influential accounts of needs, so consider his view briefly here. Frankfurt says people need whatever will let them avoid harm (Frankfurt, 1988, 104–116). More precisely, on Frankfurt's account, we need the inescapably necessary conditions for avoiding harm. Frankfurt says people need everything 'necessarily necessary for avoiding harm' (Frankfurt, 1988, 112). Although he does not provide an account of *harm*, Frankfurt says harm makes people worse-off than before. He also says that one's situation must improve to avoid harm if otherwise one's situation will become worse. Moreover, he says remaining in a bad condition harms people because then they have more bad things in their life (Frankfurt, 1988, 110). Unfortunately, Frankfurt's account does not provide adequate independent grounds for deciding what qualifies as a basic minimum. Partly for this reason, it suggests that people need things that they do not require for any plausible minimum. People do not need everything that lets them avoid all (e.g. very minor) harms as a basic minimum. Sometimes, we must even help people secure things that harm them in some ways for the sake of their greater good. Some people need chemotherapy (even though it harms them in many ways) to avoid greater harm. Finally, we must sometimes give people things that do not let them avoid harm but help them flourish (e.g. some kinds of education). The root of the problem for harm theories stems from harm's ambiguous nature—there exist different baselines for harm. On some accounts, harms make people worse-off (Kagan, 1998). However, on these accounts, fair economic competition may harm a millionaire even if it costs them very little (e.g. a dollar). Moreover, if people only experience harm when made worse-off, we do not harm children by failing to provide them with an education when they would not otherwise secure it (though, intuitively, they do need education). On other accounts, harms violate rights or basic obligations. But then, we need an independent account of these rights or obligations to make use of this conception of needs. Here I think needs theorists might do well to appeal to the minimally good life account (Hassoun, 2013). They can say people need whatever lets them live at least a minimally good life.

[33] I focus here on what I suppose is a more realistic case than one in which the pianist can only fare well enough with functioning fingers because she needs to make music to flourish though if nothing could make such a pianist's life even minimally good if she loses her ability to play, it seems plausible that she needs music to reach the basic minimum.

justify his view, Liao must provide an account of what it means to say someone requires something *qua human*. Moreover, insofar as he aims to capture only what people characteristically require for a minimally good life, his view will fail to capture what every person needs for any plausibly basic minimum.

I expect that a commitment to feasibility—or providing a theory that might respect the limits of what we can achieve through political institutions—lies behind Liao's focus on what people characteristically require for a basic minimum (Gilabert and Lawford-Smith, 2012). After all, he intends his account to provide a basis for human rights and not just our moral obligations. Perhaps we must focus on what people characteristically need for the purposes of creating public policy.[34] Policymakers typically have limited resources. Perhaps we simply cannot meet everyone's needs given that some require extensive resources.[35] So, Liao might insist that we specify the minimally good life in a way that focuses on what people characteristically require as a basic minimum within feasibility constraints.

There is something to this reply, but I believe that we need a deeper account of the basic minimum that can explain what every person needs even when political institutions cannot help everyone. After all, Liao focuses on what human rights *each person* can claim, and institutions that only provide

---

[34] Note, also, that David Braybrooke also has a well-developed account of basic minimum that focuses on what people need to carry out some key social roles, though his account was developed for a very different purpose (Braybrooke, 1987). On Braybrook's account, policymakers determine what people need via a consultative process. First, they specify a list of necessary goods that enable people to fulfill four social roles: parent, worker, citizen, and housekeeper. Then, policymakers specify minimum standards of provisions so each member of the population can carry out each role. Braybrook says that the list may never be fully complete and is sensitive to changing social conditions but insists that even many young people who reject the above roles, and elderly people who no longer fulfill them, need the things that his account provides. However, the fact that some people need things that they do not need for the four social roles Braybrooke endorses (parent, worker, citizen, and housekeeper) means his account cannot provide a plausible basic minimum for *all*. Even some of the poorest and most oppressed can often raise children, maintain their houses, work, and function as citizens (Hassoun, 2013). Still, many lack secure access to the things they need to keep doing so and some can do little more than this. Moreover, people do not always need to function in the ways Braybrooke suggests if they do not, and will never, want to do so to secure a plausible basic minimum. Consider a monk who does not, and never will, want children. It seems, Braybrook's account cannot provide a plausible threshold for a basic minimum for each person (though it may fulfill his aim of providing an account of what people *generally* need that may be useful for some policy purposes). I have argued for this conclusion at length elsewhere (Hassoun, 2013). Both Braybrooke's and Frankfurt's accounts may, however, suffice for policymakers interested only in arriving at a rough characterization of what people generally need. Moreover, there are other alternative accounts of needs, though many focus on what people need for autonomy and I reject the idea that people only need what will help them secure autonomy as a basic minimum below (see, for instance, Copp (1998, p. 125) cited in Page (2007, 17)). Finally, note that people politically contest needs (Fraser, 1989). I hope that considering what people need to live well enough may help resolve some political disputes in a way that acknowledges the importance of our common humanity and protects the most vulnerable among us (Fraser, 1989; Hassoun and Brock, 2012; Hassoun, 2020b).

[35] In which case, Liao might argue that they should focus on standard threats to individuals' ability to live minimally good lives.

what people characteristically require for a basic minimum cannot plausibly protect the human rights of all precisely because some have uncharacteristic needs. A good account of the basic minimum should attend closely to differences between individuals and what they require even if policymakers cannot help everyone. We need a standard that is universal in the sense that it does not neglect the needs of some nor let anyone fall through the cracks. So, a good account of the basic minimum should explain what every person needs. Though it may be impossible to help everyone secure a basic minimum in some situations, we must acknowledge that some will not reach the minimum precisely because we cannot help them. That is what allows us to recognize tragedy and respond to it appropriately. We can often improve our institutions and come up with better public policies that meet these needs but, to do, so we must know that they exist. Subsequent chapters argue that we must often help people secure a basic minimum. Here, however, I only consider the basic minimum's nature and practical limits that determine what we should do cannot determine what people require so directly.[36] We should recognize what everyone needs for a plausible basic minimum even when we cannot help everyone. (I consider how we should respond to apparent tragedy in later chapters.)

I also have another reason for rejecting Liao's account of the basic minimum: People must have more than just the ability to *pursue* the things that make their lives minimally good (as Liao does not take pursuit to require success) (Liao, 2015). People must actually attain these things to reach any plausible basic minimum. Liao might say that we can never guarantee that people live minimally good lives.[37] Rather, we can only help ensure that they have the fundamental conditions for living such a life. It is true that we cannot guarantee that people live minimally well because (say) they might get an incurable illness. Still, they do not live well enough (at least at the time) when they get sick. People must have sufficient health to live minimally well even though we cannot always ensure that they live well enough. So, a minimally good life requires securing, and not just pursuing, some things.

More generally, we should not just focus on capabilities in setting the basic minimum, though capability theorists correctly point out that people require

---

[36] Subsequent chapters also argue that individuals must sometimes act outside of institutional constraints to help people secure a basic minimum.

[37] I also think some things contribute to individuals' ability to secure a basic minimum that cannot, on their own, impact individuals' lives as wholes. Much of our lives' value comes from things that individually do not amount to much but, collectively, constitute a great portion of our happiness (Duflo and Banerjee, 2022). Moreover, we need some things (like pain medicine) to live minimally well at particular times even if they do not impact the quality of our lives on the whole.

much more than basic activities for this minimum (Pogge and Pogge, 2002).[38] The problem with capability theories is that they just ensure people *can* secure a basic minimum and fail to ensure people *actually attain* one even when we can easily help them do so. So, although one can convert this chapter's account of the basic minimum into a capability theory *if* one believes that people must only be *able* to live minimally good lives, I do not believe we should do so.[39] Some capability theorists argue that we never have to ensure people live minimally good lives because that requires paternalism—we must only make sure people can live such lives.[40] But even ensuring that people can secure and maintain basic capabilities may require paternalism.[41] We may have to tax those who cannot otherwise secure these capabilities to pay for what they require (Dorsey, 2012; Wolff and de-Shalit, 2007; Pedersen and Midtgaard, 2018). So rather than saying people must just be capable of living minimally good lives, I believe we should say everyone has a justified aspiration to live minimally well (Arneson, 2005).[42] If a reasonable, free, caring person put herself into the shoes of someone capable of living minimally well but who made bad choices, she should not say the person has the basic minimum. If the person needs inexpensive mental health (or other) care to avoid severe pain and suffering (though they can purchase expensive care themselves, they just will not do it), the person needs inexpensive care to attain a plausible basic minimum.[43] It matters that people actually secure whatever they need to live minimally good lives and capability accounts fail to ensure people *actually attain* any plausible minimum even when we can easily help them do so.[44]

Some capability theorists might argue that their accounts better respect the limits on obligations to help people secure a basic minimum (Enoch, 2016).

---

[38] Though Liao says basic activities can include passive as well as active pleasures, good relationships, and knowledge, it matters what individuals can be as well as what they can do (Liao, 2015). Many kinds of people can live minimally well, but people must live decent lives to reach the threshold for any plausible basic minimum. So, some people fail to live minimally good lives even though they have liberty, autonomy, "the option to have social interaction, to acquire further knowledge, to evaluate and appreciate things, and to determine ... [their life's] ... direction" (Liao, 2015, 82). They simply fail to exercise their capacities and avail themselves of good options.

[39] Some capability theories say that children must secure functionings, but I know of none that ensure adults flourish.

[40] On paternalism also see (Hanna, 2018).

[41] See Claassen (2014) for discussion of some of the ways in which capability theories arguably require paternalism.

[42] Of course, every account must answer hard questions about what to do if it is impossible to help everyone secure a basic minimum. I consider these questions in the final chapters.

[43] I discuss limits to our obligations to provide a basic minimum for others in subsequent chapters.

[44] So, although I will sometimes focus on what people need to live minimally good lives in what follows, I believe people need more than the ability to live minimally good lives.

They might argue that we should not specify the basic minimum in a way that neglects these limits. Perhaps helping people secure more than central capabilities keeps them from taking responsibility for their lives, undermines the social bases of self-respect, diminishes individuals' moral status, or treats people as if they lack the capacity to form, revise, and pursue their own conceptions of the good (enough) life. Doing so might also undermine autonomy, disrespectfully suggest that individuals lack the ability to shape their own lives, or even undermine their ability to live well enough overall. People need to take responsibility for their own lives and require self-respect to flourish, and good institutions will respect individuals' moral equality. Moreover, much of our lives' value comes from exercising our capacity to form, revise, and pursue our own conceptions of the good (enough) life (for critical discussion, see Dworkin (2000); Shiffrin (2000); Nussbaum (2006); Quong (2010); Birks (2014); Carter (2014); Robeyns (2016)).

Subsequent chapters engage with different ways of understanding the limits on obligations to help people secure a basic minimum,[45] but limits on what we owe people cannot determine what they need to reach a plausible threshold any more than our inability to help them. Sometimes we just should not help people reach the threshold, even when they will not reach the threshold without our help. Sometimes helping people secure anything more than capabilities may keep them from taking responsibility for their lives, undermine the social bases of self-respect, diminish individuals' moral status, or treat people as if they lack the capacity to form, revise, and pursue their own conceptions of the good (enough) life. Even when that is so, knowing that people cannot reach a plausible threshold without greater assistance allows us to recognize that something is not as it should be. This recognition gives us a reason to search for alternative options. Perhaps there is a respectful way of encouraging responsible behavior that will help people live minimally well. Or perhaps we can change the situation so that we can permissibly help people live such lives or they will help themselves. So, it seems worth inquiring into what qualifies as a plausible basic minimum even when we do not have to help people secure so much.[46]

---

[45] Though I do not endorse the limits suggested above, I agree that much of our lives' value comes from exercising our capacity to form, revise, and pursue our own conceptions of the good (enough) life. Moreover, I believe that good institutions should respect individuals' moral equality, provide the social bases for self-respect, and encourage individuals to take responsibility for their own lives.

[46] This is even the case if we should never help anyone reach the threshold and, again, this book's concluding chapters consider how we should respond to apparent tragedies.

Even if capability theorists disagree and maintain that people must only be capable of living minimally good lives, the minimally good life account has another advantage over at least the best-known capability theories because it attends more closely to individual differences and has a more expansive ground (Nussbaum, 2007; Ruger, 2010; Venkatapuram, 2011). Nussbaum says, for instance, that a "fully human" life includes threshold levels of capabilities for life, health, bodily integrity, sensation, imagination, thought, emotions, practical reason, affiliation, connection with other species, play, and control over one's environment (Nussbaum, 2011). Not everyone needs everything on this list as a basic minimum. Some committed city dwellers do not value, and may not benefit from, connecting with other species (though everyone's survival and flourishing depends on some other species). Many of these people can secure a basic minimum even if they cannot connect with other species and even if they lack effective access to nature conceived more broadly. Why must these people even be able to access nature if they do not value doing so and will never come to value connecting with other species? I agree that people need some good options from which to choose even though they will not choose all of them. Still, not everyone needs this particular option. On the other hand, particular people may need capabilities Nussbaum has not listed—e.g. the capability to participate in their particular religious community—to live even minimally well.

David Axelsen and Lasse Nielsen's "Sufficiency as Freedom from Duress" provides the best developed capability account of the basic minimum in the literature on sufficientarianism. Axelsen and Nielsen value individuals' capability to succeed but only in central areas of human life; free from "pressure that would impede any normal human being's ability to succeed in a similar situation" (Axelsen and Nielsen, 2015, 416). They specify that central areas of human life include one's ability to meet needs for "basic health, decent housing, adequate education, and so on," but also capabilities for "rational development and critical thought, respectful social relations, and political freedoms" (Axelsen and Nielsen, 2015, 409). Elsewhere Axelsen and Nielsen claim that people should have three broad types of capabilities: "1) capabilities related to biological and physical human needs; 2) capabilities related to fundamental interests of a human agent; and 3) capabilities related to fundamental interests of a social being" (Axelsen and Nielsen, 2016, 4).[47] They deny

---

[47] Axelsen and Nielsen could offer a similar theory that stresses the separate spheres of justice, but we need an overall evaluation to decide whether people are all things considered above the threshold for a basic minimum. This is because improvement in different spheres will not always compensate

that preferences, welfare, or wealth matter and say (basic) justice only concerns what has value "from any perspective" (Axelsen and Nielsen, 2015, 412).[48] Moreover, Axelsen and Nielsen specify that individuals must have enough of all the things that help them succeed. Finally, they reject tradeoffs between an individual's ability to secure some of these things and others. On their view, several different sufficiency thresholds exist, but I am considering their account of the threshold explained above as an account of the basic minimum (Axelsen and Nielsen, 2016, 12).

Axelsen and Nielsen's account faces some challenges: It may fail to recognize people's claims when they require more (or different things) to live a minimally good life than most require (central capabilities). Imagine someone who can only flourish with access to nature (and suppose I am right that this is not a central human capability). This person may need access to nature to flourish, but Axelsen and Nielsen's account may not provide it. The person may have all the requisite biological/physical, agential, and social capabilities they specify. If so, their account is not appropriately sensitive to differences between individuals.

Axelsen and Nielsen say that people only need central human capabilities for a basic minimum because they think that justice only concerns what has value "from any perspective" (Axelsen and Nielsen, 2015, 412). To motivate their claim that justice only concerns what has value "from any perspective," Axelsen and Nielsen argue that we should reject preference-based theories of welfare (Axelsen and Nielsen, 2015, 412). They explain how their account avoids the "problems of adaptive preferences, false consciousness, and expensive tastes" (Axelsen and Nielsen, 2015, 410).[49]

As we have seen, however, it is possible to reject preference-based theories of welfare in many ways. We need not focus only on what is valuable from any perspective to explain why we do not generally have to help people fulfill preferences for things that do not help them live minimally well over central human capabilities (and whatever else they need to live well enough). The minimally good life account does so by adopting the second-person perspective of reasonable, free care.

---

for decrements in others, while different improvements and decrements in others can balance each other out (Arneson, 2005).

[48] Although they focus on full (not basic) justice, I consider here whether their theory provides a plausible account of basic justice—or what we owe people simply out of concern for our common humanity.

[49] Also note that Amartya Sen's purely procedural proposal for determining capabilities using public input, though useful for many policy purposes, is not likely to provide a plausible account of what different people need to attain a basic minimum unless the choice situation is defined along the lines I have suggested.

Moreover, people must sometimes fulfill idiosyncratic needs (that are not sub-species of generic needs, e.g. for freedom or social recognition) to secure a basic minimum. The minimally good life account's advocates acknowledge this, but Axelson and Nielsen must deny it. Again, a great pianist might need reconstructive hand surgery that others do not require to continue to provide for herself and her family (and, hence, reach any plausible basic minimum). So Axelson and Nielsen's argument does not establish that justice only concerns what has value "from any perspective" in the sense at issue (Axelsen and Nielsen, 2015, 412). People cannot just secure central human capabilities when they require something more than, or different from, what most people need to secure a plausible basic minimum.[50]

More generally, this book's view has some advantages over many objective theories that focus too widely on what *most* people require for a basic minimum. This book's account of the basic minimum acknowledges that people often need different things to live minimally well (see e.g. Griffin, 1986; Kraut, 2007, 137). Some people need particular relationships, communities, or resources to flourish that most others do not. At the same time, the minimally good life account can explain why the things on the common objective lists often contribute to flourishing. Everyone arguably requires some "cognitive, affective, sensory, and social powers (no less than physical powers)" to live well enough (Kraut, 2007, 137). People also need some liberty, autonomy, capacity for action, and understanding to live minimally well, while accomplishment, aesthetic experience, and deep personal relationships can help them do so (Griffin, 1986). Similarly, life, health, bodily integrity, sensation, imagination, thought, emotions, practical reason, affiliation, connection with other species, play, and control over one's environment often give lives significant value—though not everyone needs all of these things to flourish (Nussbaum, 2000a, 71).

---

[50] Not "everyone needs to be equally well-off in regards to housing, health, security, and nutrition to lead successful lives" (Axelsen and Nielsen, 2015, 421). Still, if liberal neutrality does not protect everyone's ability to live well enough, we must reject it. The next chapter argues that Axelsen and Nielsen wrongly suggest that claims to assistance only exist if "everyone can reasonably accept the relevance of the reasons given for [these] claims" (Axelsen and Nielsen, 2015, 411). In some historical periods, the majority of people have failed to understand, or care about, others' needs simply because those people had disabilities or belonged to minority groups and I do not think all of these people were unreasonable (they were just wrong). Even cross-cultural agreement arrived at via deliberation and discussion may be a far cry from truth. We should care about others who need things to live well enough that most people do not need even if most reasonable people fail to recognize their claims. Of course, Axelsen and Nielsen may insist that most people historically (and perhaps the majority of people in many countries today) were (and are) unreasonable. However, they must then provide a substantive account of what reasonableness requires. To fully substantiate their account, they must also defend the claim that their particular account of what reasonableness requires is the correct one to apply for their purposes.

Finally, unlike many competing objective theories, this book's account provides a unifying mechanism for determining what people need to reach the minimally good life threshold. We consider what reasonable, caring, free people would set as a minimal standard of justifiable aspiration in deciding what each person needs to live well enough (Kraut, 2007; Fletcher, 2013).[51] Moreover, this mechanism garners some support from the fact that we should reflect with reasonable, free, care on what basic minimum is justifiable; we should care for, and respect, people as free and equal individuals whose choices about how to live should not result from coercion and constraint.[52] Concern, or respect, for our common humanity requires this reasonable, free, care in determining what others need to secure the basic minimum.

---

[51] Figuring out what constitutes a basic minimum is not the same as understanding why it matters that people have the things that they need to live minimally good lives, but all other (objective, hybrid, and subjective) theories need to explain this as well. We can always ask why pleasure, desire fulfillment, knowledge, appreciation, success in significant plans, etc. make one's life better. Given the diversity of things that can, and often do, contribute to individuals' quality of life, it may be an advantage of this chapter's account that it is compatible with different explanations of how, and why, these things contribute. We should not sacrifice wisdom or sensitivity to the reasons why our lives can be valuable at the altar of simplicity. There are many ways in which things can make different people's lives better in different circumstances. Theories that provide a unified account of why things contribute to the quality of people's lives can help us recognize important sources of value but are unlikely to exhaust them. Moreover, these theories may fail to attend carefully enough to differences between individuals.

[52] Furthermore, I believe the way this book proposes figuring out what a minimally good life requires is better than the main alternative objective accounts of how we should decide what people need for a basic minimum. Consider for instance a perfectionist and eudemonistic theory that is roughly Aristotelian (Sorabji, 1980). On this account, we have to live within the constraints of nature but also live well within those constraints. This is the life of reason and virtue. On such accounts, a minimally good life is "an active virtuous life which has available to and for it and adequate supply of external goods" (Annas, 1993, 368). Why think this is definitive of a minimally good life? Perhaps one will only think so if one approaches the question of what makes a life minimally good from the first-personal perspective asking: "What kind of life should I on the whole live?" What view is "capable of organizing and focusing all the concerns and aims of my life as a whole; [what view can] encompass everything worthwhile in my life"? (Annas, 1993, 85). But, even if reflection and cultivating the disposition to live virtuously are the only reasonable options to pursue (which I doubt), cannot one also be virtuous and miserable (Wolf, 1982; Tiberius, 2008; Haybron, 2017)? (A miserable life would fall below the basic minimum on any adequate account.) Moreover, this view has trouble explaining why many other things are necessary for a basic minimum besides virtue. If other things are necessary for happiness or the minimally good life (as Aristotle admits), why? There are two ways of thinking about the value of external goods: They can contribute to the minimally good life (1) independently or (2) only in virtue of advancing virtue. If one accepts the former view, the theory may lack a plausible unifying mechanism (at least virtue fails to unify the things on the list). If one accepts the latter view, there are many unintuitive consequences: We do not want children to have external goods only for virtue nor do we want many of the things that we want only for virtue. Moreover, many things contribute to the quality of our lives in ways that have nothing to do with virtue (Annas, 1993; Haybron, 2017). The minimally good life account avoids these problems as it focuses on what we need to live well enough together (and it may be Aristotelian if, as some argue, Aristotle's foundational question was more social in nature). Moreover, if it is plausible, it suggests a diagnosis for what has gone wrong here: the first-person perspective is not the right one for arriving at an account of the basic minimum any more than the third-person perspective. Rather, one needs to put oneself in others' shoes *before* adopting the first-person perspective.

4. Conclusion

This chapter defended the minimally good life account of the basic minimum. It argued that this account has some advantages over the main competitors. Unlike subjective and hybrid welfare accounts, the minimally good life does not focus too narrowly on what people *think* they must secure for a basic minimum. Unlike objective welfare and capability accounts, it does not focus too widely on what people *generally* require for a basic minimum. It also ensures that when people reach the threshold for a minimally good life, they *actually attain* a plausible minimum. Moreover, although the minimally good life account is broad and pluralistic, it offers a well-grounded unifying mechanism for determining what people require to live well enough. So, the chapter argued, it better protects *everyone's* ability to secure *everything* they need to reach a plausible basic minimum without suggesting people require things they do not. Understanding what kind of basic minimum people need can help us determine what types of social safety nets suffice in the face of pressing global threats—those that at least protect individuals' ability to live the minimally good lives to which they can justifiably aspire as a matter of basic right. The next chapter makes this case.

3
The Minimally Good Life and Basic Justice

1. Introduction

What do we owe to others as a matter of basic justice? What can we claim for ourselves? Many propose competing answers to these questions (Moellendorf, 2002; Caney, 2006; Brock, 2009; Gilabert, 2019).* This chapter argues that *the minimally good life account of what we owe and can demand as a basic minimum* provides a plausible new alternative. The account leaves room for pure charity or altruism while acknowledging the importance of freedom, rights, and responsibility for human lives. Much of our lives' value comes from the ways we can, and do, care for others but also from how we can freely care for ourselves. This account requires us to sacrifice anything others need to live a minimally good life that we do not similarly require. However, it does not say we owe others everything they desire or from which they might benefit. So, it generates significant demands, but it also limits these demands significantly. Moreover, the account treats people equally requiring that we help others live minimally good lives where this does not imperil our own ability to do so. At the same time, we can demand the assistance we need to live minimally good lives when that does not require others to sacrifice their ability to live such lives. So, the account reconciles the perspectives of those who must give with those who require aid (Mill, 1863, ch. 5; Hassoun, 2021a). Finally, I argue that: The account (1) carves out a path between socialism and social democracy on the left, and traditional forms of luck egalitarianism and libertarianism on the right, (2) can inform theories of what we owe to people in our personal as well as political lives, and (3) differs from many other major accounts of basic justice.

---

* This chapter draws on: Hassoun, Nicole. 2022. "The Minimally Good Life Account of What We Owe to Others and What We Can Justifiably Demand." Special Issue on Basic Needs: Normative Perspectives, *Lessico di Etica Pubblica* 1 (2022): 107–126. http://www.eticapubblica.it/

Let me start by explaining what I mean by *basic justice* in more detail. An account of *basic justice* explains what basic minimum we must provide for each other simply out of respect for our common humanity. Where, as I explain below, *respect*, or *appropriate concern, for our common humanity* requires equal consideration of interests as well as freedom. Common humanity's ground lies, in part, in the fact that we are needy, vulnerable creatures who will, and do, stand in important relationships of care and concern to others. We may need to limit what basic justice can demand in some circumstances (when acting on concern for common humanity requires sacrificing something of greater importance).[1] Moreover, sometimes we owe particular others care or concern that goes well beyond what respect for common humanity demands. Still, I believe this care should not normally come at the cost of doing what respect for common humanity (*basic justice*) requires. Full justice, never mind morality, plausibly demands much more than respect for common humanity—e.g. equal opportunity. Still, in my view, ensuring basic justice typically takes priority over other requirements of justice.[2] Making this case will explain what hangs on ensuring a basic minimum for all—the significance of failing to provide this much for others.

2. Desiderata for a Successful Theory

In Peter Singer's seminal article "Famine, Affluence, and Morality" he suggests two different principles governing the aid we owe to others that might inform an account of basic justice (Singer, 1972). On the weaker principle, we must only give up what is not morally significant to aid others. On the stronger principle, we can only retain things morally comparable to what others will lose without aid. Although Singer framed his argument around a single rescue case, it extends to all cases where we can aid someone who lacks adequate food, water, shelter, and so forth. Since many such people exist, and not enough others will provide aid, everyone has a great number of opportunities to aid (Arneson, 2012). So, to aid others, even Singer's weaker principle requires us to sacrifice everything that lacks moral significance. His stronger

---

[1] There are, of course, different ways of thinking about duties and their limits. See Hassoun (2020a) for some discussion.

[2] As I explain below, this concern should also take precedence over other plausible requirements of justice—including the fair equality of opportunities portion of Rawls' difference principle. Moreover, if the minimally good life account of what we owe, and can demand, as a basic minimum is correct, it supports a discontinuity in the importance of promoting individuals' ability to flourish at the threshold for such a life—reasonable, free, care helps justify this special concern.

principle requires sacrificing everything that we do not need to avoid what others will suffer without our aid. We must even give up parts of our bodies if others need them more.

Consider Singer's stronger, more demanding, principle first. I believe we should reject the idea that we must sacrifice organs without which we might live (e.g. one of our eyes) to aid others. We do not have to do so to save others' lives never mind help them live minimally well. At least, basic justice does not require so much. People may nobly donate an organ to a loved one, or even a stranger, but they do not have to give up so much. There should exist some realm—that includes significant bodily integrity—where we do not have to sacrifice for others even if that means they do not survive or flourish (though, arguably, states can require people to get vaccinated, and even give blood, to help others in some circumstances). Moreover, I believe this realm should extend well beyond our physical limits at least to the property we need for health and life (though people may have to give up all the property they do not need to live well enough).[3] Consider the following case. Suppose that a refugee camp lacks enough anti-malaria pills for everyone, and one refugee luckily secures a pill. Although it would be nice for the refugee to share the medicine, she does not have to share. At least, the requirement to share demands too much if the protection half a pill provides will not suffice to ensure her healthy survival given infection (even if half of a dose would provide some protection). In any case, I suppose here that an adequate account of basic justice cannot *demand too much* in the sense that it requires us to sacrifice life or limb (or our ability to otherwise live well enough) for others.

That said, not every kind of demandingness poses a problem for a principle intended to explain what we owe to others and can reasonably demand as a matter of basic justice; theories can fail to demand enough as well as demand too much.[4] I believe that, under its most plausible interpretation,

---

[3] I take this as a starting point for argument here but, as I hope will become clear below, I would ground a right to bodily integrity in concern or respect for our common humanity. We are embodied creatures not (just?) free souls and have basic interest in food, water, shelter, and the other things we need to survive and flourish. Though we may willingly sacrifice ourselves for others in some circumstances, we fail to respect our own common humanity if we do so in others. Similarly, no one can require some to sacrifice themselves for others because that fails to duly respect their common humanity. One might think of the right to be free from such an obligation as a personal prerogative, but it is grounded in impartial concern for our common humanity that recognizes others' similar rights. Respect for common humanity supports a unified threshold for both what we can demand from and what we must provide to others. See John (2011) for further defense and recall previous chapters' arguments concerning security in good enough lives. There exist serious reason to doubt those whose bodily integrity remains insecure have good enough lives, see also the discussion below.

[4] There are many accounts of demandingness (Goodin, 1995; Arneson, 2004; Philips, 2008; Gilabert and Lawford-Smith, 2012; Gheaus, 2013; Brennan, 2013; Gilabert, 2017). Some object to principles that require people to do what produces the best results, run contrary to agents'

Singer's weaker principle fails to demand enough. He does not explain what counts as *morally significant*. But, if people need not sacrifice anything that affects the quality of their lives, this principle does not demand enough. We must often sacrifice morally significant things—e.g. time with our children—to help others. (On the other hand, if this principle requires us to sacrifice whatever we do not need to live well even when others can live well enough without our help, it demands too much. I consider below, and in the next chapter, several theories that make the principle precise enough to evaluate.)

Besides what people must sacrifice for others as a matter of basic justice, whether people will have enough under any proposed principle matters; ceteris paribus, an adequate standard must *demand enough* so that no one can reasonably doubt that anyone who attains it can flourish. That is, I will suppose that people need to live choice-worthy lives and have enough of the things that make their lives good for them. Even if people have everything they would choose, however, that may not suffice. Some will reject this desideratum, but I believe we should endorse it. The monk who only wants solitude and those who commit suicide for a great cause may live choice-worthy lives (Arneson, 1999). Still, we cannot just provide people with these opportunities. No one should have to sacrifice that much. Serious reasons exist to doubt that people who only have these options can flourish. Similarly, people who value little (e.g. the severely depressed) do not, thereby, sacrifice their rights to more. We may just have reason to make it possible for these people to fare better.

A theory that fulfills the above desiderata leaves significant room for pure charity or altruism but acknowledges the importance of basic rights, as well as freedom and responsibility, for human lives. While we must often help others secure a basic minimum, we do not have to give others everything from which they might benefit. Both benefactors and beneficiaries have basic freedom, rights, and responsibilities (Locke, 1689).[5]

Moreover, a theory that fulfills the desiderata above—that does not demand too much and yet demands enough—provides a unified threshold

---

inclinations and desires, conflict with self-interest, or leave little room for agents' personal concerns. So, we not only require an account of what makes a theory too demanding, we need to know why that kind of demandingness, or infeasibility, undercuts the theory. Here, however, I defend the proposed desiderata only by appeal to the coherentist justification one might endorse if they accept the proposed theory or the concrete judgments about the counterexamples I offer to alternative views. For I primarily aim to develop a view that satisfies these requirements.

[5] See discussion in notes above and recall that basic justice does not exhaust our moral claims. We may, for instance, have obligations to loved ones that allow us to prioritize saving them over strangers. Though special obligations do not generally trump the claims of common humanity.

for what we owe and can demand from others. In doing so, it reconciles the two perspectives on what we owe and can reasonably demand (that of those who might give and those who might receive) so they do not remain, as Mill suggests, each from their "own point of view... unanswerable" (Mill, 1863, ch. 5). If an account sets different standards for what we owe and can reasonably demand as a basic minimum, some might have to sacrifice things for others that they could not reasonably demand. At the same time, others might not have to sacrifice things that they could reasonably demand. Barring relevant differences between individuals, such accounts lack appropriate impartiality.

3. The Minimally Good Life View

Recall my proposed *minimally good life account of the basic minimum*. On this account, people need an adequate range of fundamental conditions for securing meaningful pursuits, relationships, pleasures, knowledge, appreciation, worthwhile activities, and other life-improving goods. Specifically, they need those goods a reasonable, free, caring person would (in conversation with others) set as a minimal standard of justifiable aspiration/basic right.

Lives qualify as minimally good in the "justified aspiration/basic right" sense when they satisfy *reasonable, caring, free people*. Reasonable people are appropriately impartial—they see other people as moral equals and want to live with them on fair, mutually agreeable terms (Rawls, 1971). They understand that everyone has the standing to make claims to protections of their fundamental interests (Rawls, 1980). Caring people empathize with others and try to promote their interests at least in proportion to their weight (Nussbaum, 2006). They will sacrifice some of their own interests to do so.[6] Free people have sufficient internal and external liberty; adaptive preferences, poor options, and limited bargaining power do not undermine their judgments of life quality (Raz, 1986; Hassoun, 2011b; Hassoun, 2012).[7]

The basic idea behind the account is simple: People should be content to bear the costs of living the "merely" minimally good lives the least fortunate will live when setting the standard fully understanding their circumstances,

---

[6] Again, the kind of empathy at issue is "projective empathy" (Darwall, 2002, 61–62). When we empathize in this way, we share others' feelings as their perspective warrants and put ourselves in others' shoes understanding their circumstances, history, and perspectives (and this is distinct from the sympathy Darwall (2002, 62) endorses).

[7] As previous chapters explained, free people can still live under coercive laws.

psychology, and history.[8] We do not ask whether the least fortunate rest content with their conditions. They may have adaptive preferences or poor bargaining positions. Rather we ask whether a reasonable, free, caring person would now, considering how they would fare if they were those people, contently live those lives. In making this determination, people must fully understand others' circumstances, psychology, and history (Frankfurt, 1987). Wise, informed, unbiased, consistent, caring people reflect on what they would need to be content to live others' lives in others' actual conditions where many lack wisdom, information, impartiality, consistency, and due concern for others (Hassoun, 2021a).

The proposed method for figuring out what people need to live minimally well will not resolve all disagreements, but it can help us make moral progress in the actual world if we buttress it with discussion and deliberation. I just hope that we empathetically put ourselves in others' shoes and think hard about whether we would be content to live their lives as those people in trying to arrive at plausible judgments about whether others live well enough. So, the proposed method for figuring out what people need to live minimally well, if not contractualist, is at least discursive. By employing this method, we demonstrate respect (or appropriate concern) for others' common humanity.[9]

Reasonable, caring, free people should agree that to live a minimally good life, a person's *relationships, pleasures, knowledge, appreciation, worthwhile activities, and other life-improving goods* must outweigh their difficulties, losses, pains, and frustrations. They should not reasonably doubt the person's ability to live their life satisfactorily (Hassoun, 2021a). Though some may have idiosyncratic needs and might only rest content with a lot of resources or with valueless pleasures, people can make mistakes about what they need. Moreover, everyone must secure all the necessary conditions for living minimally good lives and an *adequate range* of the things that are merely important for living such lives. Furthermore, they must have *secure* access to these things so that they can attain, and maintain, them without too much

---

[8] There is room for reasonable disagreement about what a minimally good life requires, but reasonable, free, caring people should understand that different people need different things when they empathize with them appropriately and have the relevant information. Moreover, recall that they are appropriately impartial and will promote others' interests at least in proportion to their weight.

[9] The fact that the mechanism is intended to work in the real world (where people often fail to give others' interests equal consideration) also explains why people will have to take others' interests very seriously. Although my case does not hang on this claim (and those with different perspectives on it may accept my argument), I believe that reasonable, free, caring people with full information will rarely make a mistake about what people need to live minimally good lives. That said, it is very difficult to explain what full information requires and to make this case. However, see Railton (1986) and previous chapters' discussion.

difficulty. Securing some of the things people need to live a minimally good life cannot come at the cost of securing other things. The *fundamental conditions* necessary and important for people to secure the things that make their lives minimally good differ, but they include capacities, resources, and institutions among other things (Liao, 2015).

Moreover, as previous chapters explained, violating bodily integrity, basic capacities, or autonomy threatens everyone's ability to live minimally good lives (Hassoun, 2021a; Hassoun, 2013). Recall the previous chapters' argument that people even need medicines that help them get eye exams to protect them against serious risks to their ability to live minimally well (because an adequate basic minimum requires *secure* access to what people need to live well enough): Vision loss often negatively affects subjective quality of life, independence, mental health, cognition, social function, employment, and educational attainment and blindness can contribute to falls and other injuries (National Academy of Sciences, 2016).

Consider the worry that, since the account attends closely to individual differences, it cannot protect everyone's bodily integrity. Some may worry that there exist cases where some (very fortunate) individuals can suffer a natural loss of a body part (e.g. a finger) without any risk to their ability to live minimally well even for a time. If so, perhaps those individuals can live well enough even without bodily integrity. Moreover, such people may have to sacrifice their bodily integrity to help others live minimally well. So, some may claim that the minimally good life account cannot demand enough and demands too much.

I reject this worry. On my account, basic justice requires that people have *secure* access to an *adequate range* of the things necessary and *important* for living minimally good lives.[10] Importantly, bodily integrity protects secure access to this range of things. Consider societies that do not protect individuals' bodily integrity or, worse, require some to sacrifice their bodily integrity for others. One has serious reason to doubt people can live well in such societies—hence they do not reach the justifiable aspiration/basic right threshold for a minimally good life on this book's account.[11] As previous chapters explained, on some accounts of what people need to live minimally well, people do not require so much. This account focuses, however, on the

---

[10] Again, what range suffices for each person may differ but reasonable, free, caring people must also empathize appropriately with others and possess the relevant information to determine, via discussion and deliberation, what range suffices for most.

[11] Even coercive institutions that only threaten to remove fingers for crimes, fail to guarantee subjects the security they need to flourish at all times.

kind of lives reasonable, free, caring people would be content to live and I believe they would demand bodily integrity.[12] It sets a minimal standard for justified aspiration everyone can plausibly claim as a basic minimum.

Consider, then, one reason why people must at least help each other live minimally good lives when that does not require sacrificing their own ability to do likewise. They must help others live such lives to respect each person's common humanity. Since we are all human, everyone has an equal claim to freedom, but also to reasonable care and concern. Some other basic rights views might justify similar conclusions. I believe, for instance, that concern for freedom, rationality, fair cooperation, needs, and interdependence may well ground similar claims. Here, however, I provide a new account of the basis for such rights as well as a new account of what we owe to others and can reasonably demand as a basic minimum (Hassoun, 2013).[13]

One might try to ground the claim to respect for common humanity and explain its nature in different ways, but I believe that its ground lies, in part, in the fact that important relationships of care and concern to others participating in our uniquely human moral community support, and partly constitute, our distinctively human forms of existence.[14] Our relationships

---

[12] Even if I am wrong about this, the account's main advantage is the flip side of this limitation: Unlike the main alternatives, the account rightly justifies differential protections for different people. At the same time, the account can explain why people often require equal treatment: equal opportunity for participation in public life is plausibly important, for instance, for protecting our common humanity (in our political relationships). It is possible to add an additional requirement of respect for bodily integrity to the account if necessary. Moreover, other requirements of, or reasons besides, basic justice may require protecting bodily integrity. People may, for instance, merit protection against standard threats to their ability to live well enough. And, if some very fortunate individual can suffer a natural loss of a body part (e.g. a finger) without any risk to their ability to live minimally well even for a time, perhaps policymakers should say that they should not require priority treatment when they can direct scarce medical to others who need them to live well enough. (Though hopefully we will have enough to help all live much more than minimally good lives.) Perhaps such people will even have to sacrifice their bodily integrity for others in some (very tragic) circumstances. Suppose, for instance, that even though legal changes ensure that everyone becomes an organ donor when they die, there still are not enough kidneys to save the life of one child. Suppose, moreover, I am a perfect match and medical tests reveal that I will continue to live a good life with only one kidney for my remaining years and that my family members could do so as well. Do I do nothing wrong if I just walk away? This is not entirely clear to me. That said, I will continue to suppose the account can protect bodily integrity here. Moreover, I believe that reasonable care often requires providing much *greater* protection for bodily integrity to those who need it than many alternative accounts. It can explain, for instance, why a pianist may require even very expensive reconstructive hand surgery to continue to provide for her family without undue hardship, though surgery that restores basic function might suffice for most.

[13] See the previous chapter's discussion of Liao (2015) and Hassoun (2013) for further criticism of alternative human rights views.

[14] I do not have space here to defend this conception of our common humanity's ground against the main competitors, so I take it as a starting point for the argument. Some might equate common humanity with basic needs and agency, though not everyone can secure agency (Braybrooke, 1987; Brock, 2009; Risse, 2012, 74–82; Griffin, 2008). Moreover, as some of these authors acknowledge, it is not clear that people will have human rights to anything that does not fulfill these needs or advance

help constitute, and make possible, our distinctively valuable human form of life. As humans, we all need and benefit significantly from care and concern over the course of our lives.[15] Without this care and concern, we simply could not survive never mind develop or flourish.[16] We are all born equally free and everyone's ability to survive and flourish depends on many circumstances over which individuals exercise limited control. Those who fail to respect common humanity and, say, advance the claim that one sex or race should dominate another might reflect on this fact: People only have contingent freedom and we all share a distinctively human form of life participating, at different times and in different ways, in important relationships of care and concern.[17] Everyone equally has free will (or does not) and our basic freedom and constraint also help ground our claims to respect for our common humanity. No one deserves their fundamental freedom or constraint just by virtue of the contingent fact of their birth into these circumstances. Though,

---

their agency on such accounts (Griffin, 2008; Risse, 2012, 74–82). Similar points might apply to capability accounts of our common humanity (Nussbaum, 2007). Others suggest that our capacity to feel love, grief, guilt, hope, shame, and remorse can help ground our common humanity though it is not clear that these things can ground commitment to a robust basic minimum either (Gaita, 1999). Often global justice and human rights theorists appeal to common humanity without explaining its ground (Moellendorf, 2002; Caney, 2006; Gilabert, 2011). That said, some accounts of moral personhood or moral equality may play the requisite role. So, I discuss this account's advantages over George Sher's account of our moral equality in the next chapter (Sher, 2014). Sher's account fails because not everyone can cope with contingency on their own and some cannot respond at all to the misfortunes that befall them without assistance. Not everyone has beliefs, plans, or aims, for instance, and sometimes there is nothing we can do to ensure that people can live their own lives effectively. So, one of my account's advantages is that it does not exclude the severely mentally ill, incredibly disadvantaged, or other irremediably ineffective people. Another advantage is that my account does not clearly commit one to particular views on abortion, infanticide, or animal rights. What one will think about these topics depends on exactly how one thinks about personhood and our connections to those who are not obviously part of the human community. Animals and plants are, of course, subject to contingency and also participants in ecological forms of life that may have similarly great value. I discuss the grounds of moral personhood and my views on environmental ethics elsewhere: Hassoun (2008); Hassoun (2011a); Hassoun and Wong (2015); Kreuder and Hassoun (forthcoming).

[15] One can challenge the minimally good life account by pointing out that some people require loving relationships that they cannot easily secure, nor maintain, to fare well enough. If people cannot live minimally well without care and concern that we cannot rightly require others to provide, they do not have a right to this care or concern. That said, people can mistakenly believe they need particular relationships to flourish. Moreover, we can do a lot to provide good education systems that support social and emotional development and foster children's ability to form, and maintain, the kinds of deep attachments that generally contribute to good lives. Moreover, we should buttress our contributions to care work, and other forms of social support, to foster good relationships and help people who require significant forms of care and assistance live minimally well. Beyond respect for bodily integrity, we may also have significant obligations to engage more deeply with others in ways that enhance everyone's ability to live well enough.

[16] Again, I discuss the grounds of moral personhood elsewhere. See, for instance, Kreuder and Hassoun (forthcoming).

[17] Moreover, most people are subject to coercive rules over which they exercise limited control. So, the relationships at issue include (but are not limited to) political relations. These institutions are justified, in part, by the ways in which they help us live well enough together; they promote the common good and help us solve collective action problems.

we may deserve differential treatment for other reasons (e.g. based on how we respond under these constraints).[18] At different points in our lives, we all find ourselves needy and vulnerable. Moreover, even the most needy and vulnerable among us stand—and should stand—in important relationships of care and concern with others that help constitute, and make possible, our distinctively human form of life.

Consider, then, what respect for individuals' common humanity requires in more detail. As a human, everyone has an equal claim, or right, not only to freedom but also to reasonable care and concern. After all, important relationships of care and concern to others participating in our uniquely human moral community support, and partly constitute, our distinctively human forms of existence. So, we must help create the conditions under which people will lead morally (and otherwise) decent lives. We must respond to others' needs and claims to decent treatment. This arguably requires many things, but when people require assistance to live minimally good lives and no one else is providing this assistance, others who can assist without sacrificing so much must do so.[19] To respect individuals' common humanity, we must help one another live minimally good lives when that does not require sacrificing our own ability to do likewise.

In other words, I believe respect for common humanity generates significant obligations of global justice. Everyone—independent of citizenship or other affiliation—has an equal claim to freedom, but also to reasonable care and concern. We are equally free and deserving of our basic freedom and constraint and we are all needy, vulnerable, and interdependent. We stand—and should stand—in important relationships to one another that help protect, and constitute, our common humanity. So, we have reasons to respond to each other's needs and claims to decent treatment out of respect for our common humanity. We must respond to these needs and claims by helping each other live minimally well when doing so does not require sacrificing our

---

[18] Furthermore, we often survive these contingencies and can flourish under them, in part, because we all share a distinctively human form of life participating in different ways at different times in important relationships of care and concern. Each individual's participation in sustaining our valuable human forms of existence, moreover, helps explain the importance of protecting our common humanity. If this is right, our common humanity merits respect, in part, because of its nature: we are needy, vulnerable, interdependent creatures who stand in important relationships of care and concern to others participating in our uniquely human moral community (for further discussion see Chapter 4, §2).

[19] On my view, concern for common humanity cannot normally require some to sacrifice themselves for others but perhaps in emergencies, when there are a great many lives at stake, this concern could require such sacrifices. Alternatively, other principles of justice or morality might require such significant sacrifices.

ability to do the same.[20] Minimally good lives partly constitute, and help people secure, many valuable things: basic capacities, opportunities, resources, autonomy, and so forth. Moreover, we should provide this much for people because living such a life has such (intrinsic) importance for each person and their relationships to one another. And, I believe no one should have to sacrifice their ability to live such a life to help others for the same reasons; these claims are not limited by borders or politics.

Because protecting everyone's ability to live minimally well protects our common humanity and some of the key relationships we stand in to one another are political associations, these claims are plausibly political, or human rights, obligations.[21] We must treat all those to whom we stand—and should stand—in such relationships with the reasonable, free care we would only rest content to receive ourselves. There exist serious reasons to doubt that those who do not receive the aid they need to live minimally well will continue to do so. Other things beyond our common humanity may ground human rights, but respect for human rights requires us to at least protect others' ability to live minimally good lives when doing so does not require sacrificing anything as important (e.g. our own ability to live well enough) (Beitz and Goodin, 2009; Raz, 2015; Pogge, 2008).

On my view, states are the primary obligation bearers for fulfilling their subjects' rights because they are well placed to do so—even though states' specific obligations are derived from the more universal obligations outlined above (Hassoun, 2020a). Other states, and then the international community (individuals and other organizations who can assist), have secondary obligations to aid when states cannot, or do not, fulfill these obligations. Arguably, each person's common humanity gives them a justified claim, or human right, to others' aid, irrespective of country of origin or residence. So, where one's compatriots fail to provide the requisite assistance, the international

---

[20] Again, other reasons plausibly support these claims too. Although different people may require different things to live well enough, we show respect for common humanity when we give their lives due weight, and reasonable, free care requires helping people live well enough. I believe that no one really deserves the things they are born with—their talents, resources, institutions, and tools—and that people will try hard enough to live minimally well if they can. So, we should help everyone live well enough when they need assistance, though we do not have to give them exactly the same things and we do not have to sacrifice our own ability to live minimally well to help others. We can also recognize and reward effort and talent—especially when doing so helps people live (at least minimally) well.

[21] Although many gesture towards minimally good life accounts of human rights, I know of few human rights theorists who have even started to cash out accounts of what a minimally good life requires (Nickel, 2007; Brock, 2009; Tasioulas, 2015). For exceptions, see Hassoun (2013); Liao (2015); Hassoun (2021a). I criticize alternative accounts in Hassoun (2021a), (2021b) and Chapter 2 as I think most fail to attend carefully enough to differences between individuals and so fail to protect everyone's ability to live minimally well.

community must come to one's aid.[22] These rights do not preclude giving significant priority to compatriots' claims as long as doing so remains compatible with ensuring that everyone lives well enough (Brock and Hassoun, 2013; Brock, 2013). At the same time, we may have to improve international, if not global, governance significantly to ensure that everyone lives at least minimally good lives.[23]

Compare this with John Rawls' theory of international justice (Rawls, 1999). Although Rawls supports a basic list of human rights (life, liberty, property, and formal equality), on his account, deeply discriminatory societies may qualify as decent and the international community cannot intervene to change them (Rawls, 1999, 65). The minimally good life account would not support intervention that undermines individuals' ability to live good enough lives; it requires respecting the cultures and ways of life that support individuals' ability to live such lives. However, the minimally good life account requires international action (care and concern) to alleviate severe (e.g. autonomy-undermining) discrimination where this care and concern advance individuals' ability to live minimally good lives. The international community should, for instance, support education initiatives, and provide international aid, to advance gender equality.[24] At least, insofar as we must respect, protect, and fulfill a robust list of human rights to ensure that everyone can live minimally well, those who accept the minimally good life account cannot endorse Rawls' view.[25] Moreover, they cannot endorse strong forms of liberal neutrality that deny political institutions should help individuals live at least minimally good lives.[26]

---

[22] Though perhaps associative obligations can help us figure out which (equally needy) individuals have the strongest claims to our aid (Hassoun, 2021a).
[23] In fact, I would ground claims to states and, therefore, upon compatriots, in part, in respect or concern for common humanity.
[24] And, of course, other things matter besides what we owe to others and can reasonably demand as a basic minimum—intervention could be impermissible (or required) for other reasons.
[25] The final chapter explains further how we should respond to illegitimate rule that does not protect individuals' ability to live well enough.
[26] I endorse Steven Wall's (1998) arguments against these forms of liberal neutrality and, so, do not engage with these views at length here. However, I believe that political institutions can respect reasonable people with different views of the good (enough) life even in advancing some (sound) range of conceptions of such lives over others (Wall, 2017). There are many things of value besides neutrality (Raz, 1986, 162). Respect for common humanity and the relationships that make possible our valuable human forms of life require helping people live minimally good lives. Respect for common humanity may even do more to secure agreement and institutional stability than neutrality. That said, my view is compatible with a moderately strong commitment to neutrality as many lives will qualify as minimally good (Wall, 2017). Different people require different things to secure the basic minimum and individuals may have great discretion in forming and pursuing their view of the good life (Raz, 1986). Moreover, reasonable, caring, free people engage in discussion and deliberation about what different people require given their different circumstances, histories, and character. So, my view will respect the decisions about what lives qualify as minimally good upon which reasonable (free and caring) people can agree. For other compelling arguments against liberal neutrality also see Arneson (2005).

I believe, moreover, that because living minimally well matters so much to people and our relationships with them, we must help others in our personal, as well as political, lives. Our world seems terribly tragic—our national and international institutions continually fail to help millions of people around the world secure what they need for even minimally good lives (Hassoun, 2020a). Ideally, we should fix, or build, the necessary institutions to help everyone live at least minimally well, and individuals can often fulfill their obligations to help others flourish by doing so (Moellendorf, 2002; Brock, 2009). Still, where good institutions are missing and we cannot create them, individuals retain their claims to live at least minimally well. Those who can help them, without sacrificing their own ability to live well enough, should step up to bridge the gap. This is not merely supererogatory, but a requirement of reasonable, free care for others—a duty of basic justice.[27] In our tragic world, we must do more than assist in easy rescue cases, but we do not have to sacrifice our ability to live minimally good lives even to save others. Those who deny that individuals have significant obligations outside of their political lives to aid others might focus only on our obligations to help others by advocating for appropriate institutional change in what follows.

Subsequent sections (and chapters) explain why the minimally good life account's demands are appropriate but consider here the worry that individuals do not have to provide so much for others when their institutions fail. Some will maintain that the account will prevent people from spending time with their friends or family members when they could, instead, help others who are less well-off (Hampton, 1993). Perhaps the account is unreasonable or fails to consider limits to beneficence implicit in human nature. Perhaps basic justice cannot require helping others in our personal lives when that comes at any significant cost. Perhaps my account will only make people feel guilty for not doing more to help others (O'Neill, 2005).

The minimally good life account may not require as much as critics suggest but, even if it does require a lot in our tragic world, we should accept it. Ideally, individuals would only have to help set up and maintain good institutions and could then freely live their lives under those institutions' rules (Hassoun, 2020a). However, this may not suffice to ensure that everyone lives minimally good lives. If it does not, and an individual and their friends and family members have what they need to live well enough, I believe they should help others who lack what they need to live even minimally good

---

[27] The account does not have obvious implications for debates about abortion because it is not clear whether a fetus is a person. See Kreuder and Hassoun (2021) for discussion of moral personhood and the account's application to the case of abortion if a fetus is a person.

lives. That said, competing obligations to help friends and family flourish may outweigh, or trump, obligations of basic justice. That is, special obligations to those with whom we stand in intimate relationships may require us to prioritize helping our friends and family members live minimally well before helping others do so. So, the view might not be nearly as demanding as it seems. Moreover, the view is grounded in a conception of free, reasonable care and is appropriately impartial: We must help others only when we can reasonably demand help ourselves. So those who want to argue that it is unreasonable must provide a competing account of what free, reasonable care requires (or at least explain why they do not think we must care for others in this way). The account also demands less than straightforward maximizing consequentialist views like Singer's on which we must give up anything that can help another more (also see e.g. Unger (1996)). Finally, if most people simply cannot live up to this standard, even if we endorse these moral norms and make the requisite changes to institutional structures, that may just be the tragic state of our world too (Estlund, 2019). Again, the next chapter considers alternative accounts and explains why we must take up the slack when others do not do their part in helping people live at least minimally good lives.

Those who reject the idea that common humanity alone requires helping everyone live well enough should, however, still agree that we should help others live minimally good lives, irrespective of location, insofar as we subject them to coercive rules. I have argued at length elsewhere that there are many coercive international institutions (Hassoun, 2012). Property rights and rules of trade are often enforced with sanctions and bind people across borders. Borders, and even peacekeeping efforts constrain individuals' ability to do whatever they might like, and these constraints impact individuals' lives significantly (Hassoun, 2012). Legitimate rulers—who have a justification right to rule—cannot create rules for others under which they would not contently live as doing so is not reasonable (appropriately impartial) nor respectful of individual freedom. Legitimate rulers must ensure that their subjects can live well enough. So, at least as members of political societies subjecting each other to coercive rules (if not the global community), we should help each other live minimally good lives when that does not require sacrificing our own ability to do so (see Appendix I for further argument).

4. Locating the Account in the Literature

I realize, of course, that the preceding arguments will not convince everyone—even all of those who endorse the idea that we should respect individuals' common humanity. Some believe we do not owe people any basic minimum at all and might maintain that common humanity only demands respect for individual freedom. Most notably, libertarians, who reject positive obligations to aid others, do not think that we owe people any basic minimum (Nozick, 1974). Similarly, luck egalitarians and some deontologists think that desert, luck, responsibility, and so forth undermine individuals' claims to a basic minimum (Dworkin, 2000; Knight, 2015). But even some egalitarians and consequentialists may reject the minimally good life account of what we owe and can demand as a basic minimum, so I consider each of these views in turn.

I reject libertarianism—a family of political views giving near absolute priority to individual freedom from interference—because it has too impoverished a view of the basis for our common humanity.[28] We are not just free creatures but sensitive, insecure, related ones who require care and concern to survive, never mind flourish. We must have more than just the ability to choose our lives, we must have decent (choice-worthy) options. Libertarianism denies that an adequate account of (basic) justice requires reasonable care. But basic justice, not just charity, requires helping people live well enough. Respect for our common humanity—justice and respect for human rights as well as beneficence—demand this much. To see the problem with traditional (Nozickean) forms of libertarianism more concretely, recall that, on Nozickean varieties of libertarianism, everyone has rights to acquire and transfer their holdings. On Robert Nozick's view, justice in original acquisition requires respecting the Lockean proviso—that one leave enough and as good for others. However, on his view, property often merits respect even when respecting such property requires preventing people from securing what they need to survive (Nozick, 1974). Someone who develops a new medicine does not have to let other people access it (e.g.) even if no one can prohibit people from accessing a previously existing resource at a reasonable price. On this chapter's account, this view fails miserably (Hassoun, 2020a).[29] Of course, if libertarians endorse more plausible versions of the Lockean proviso that protect individuals' ability to live minimally well, they may endorse my account (Wendt, 2017).[30]

---

[28] That said, I believe libertarians should accept part of the argument I provide in Appendix I—that legitimate coercion requires ensuring autonomy—and I develop it at greater length elsewhere (Hassoun, 2012).

[29] If the minimally good life account is correct, legitimate rules must also require that the inventor let people access the drug to ensure that everyone can live minimally good lives (see Appendix I). At least this is so where they can do so while preserving incentives for innovation to protect individuals' ability to live minimally good lives in future generations. Rulers might do so by implementing alternative reward mechanisms for new innovations (Hassoun, 2020a).

[30] Some left-libertarians endorse a universal basic income and insist people only have rights to their fair share of natural resources, but also seem to believe this will suffice for people to attain a "*minimally adequate* or *sufficient* quality of life" (Steiner, 2009; Vallentyne and Steiner, 2009, 59).

Those in the roughly luck egalitarian camp might also accept the minimally good life view as a supplement to their own (Fleurbaey, 1995; Fleurbaey, 2008; Tan, 2012; Knight, 2013). On some traditional luck egalitarian (and related) views, people are responsible for their talents and preferences but not (e.g. brute bad) luck (Arneson, 2000; Vallentyne, 2002; Segall, 2010; Lippert-Rasmussen, 2011; Knight, 2013; Knight, 2021a). Ronald Dworkin believes, for instance, that we should distribute resources equally to satisfy individuals' preferences over goods in a way that respects the opportunity costs of our preferences for others.[31] He believes preferences and talents merit respect, but that we should limit the negative consequences of at least some kinds of brute bad luck (Dworkin, 1978).[32] So, if people do not choose to purchase adequate insurance for (expensive to treat) rare diseases that undermine their ability to live well enough, that is just too bad. Many luck egalitarians partition the factors that affect outcomes differently, however, and can accept the minimally good life account (Fleurbaey, 1995). Some suggest people are responsible for what they can control (the exercise of their will) and not for the resources or talents they possess where these things are not under their control. Others apply a different responsibility cut that sorts factors into things over which we can reasonably hold people responsible and things over which we cannot reasonably hold people responsible (presumably including some resources and talents) (Fleurbaey, 1995). If luck egalitarians accept that we cannot reasonably hold people responsible for living a minimally good life, they can endorse this book's argument. On such views, if people require more assistance to live a minimally good life than what they can attain given some responsibility cut, we should reject that cut. We must provide the requisite assistance.[33] Even when people have made mistakes that lead them to fare poorly, we should not

---

Although a universal basic income may help people live such lives, I have argued that people also require many other things to do so including basic capabilities, good institutions, and sufficient social support.

[31] Although Dworkin denies that he is a luck egalitarian, and one might give this class of theories a different label, I am interested here in theories that propose we hold people responsible for those things that are not a matter of (e.g. brute) luck.

[32] On some luck egalitarian views, we should only hold people responsible for the results of choices they are not morally obligated to make or refrain from making, as many situations present mixtures of brute/option luck (Lippert-Rasmussen, 2011). Some claim people are only responsible for decisions made with equal opportunity (Arneson, 2000; Vallentyne, 2002). Yet others maintain that we should not hold people responsible for bad outcomes they can reasonably avoid and, on some other views, differential option luck can be as bad as brute luck (Segall, 2010; Knight, 2013; Knight, 2021a). On many of these views, we are not obligated to assist those who cannot live well enough because they have, for instance, squandered their resource aimlessly drifting rather than working hard to provide for themselves. On the other hand, we must help people who are not responsible for their plights.

[33] Even careless motorcyclists or those who squander resources should receive emergency aid on this view, but that does not mean they do not have to pay back the costs of the care they receive. In tragic cases, where we cannot help all, perhaps we should prioritize those who we expect will not waste the aid they receive. Moreover, sometimes the best way of helping people is not to give them anything but to encourage them to help themselves.

let them languish below the threshold for a minimally good life. On the proposed responsibility cut, we should generally ensure everyone can, and does, live a minimally good life.[34] The cut makes explicit reference to what individuals need to live minimally good lives. This can help the luck egalitarian explain why we must provide the irresponsible with at least emergency care (Fleurbaey, 1995; Anderson, 1999; Albertsen and Lasse, 2020).[35] More generally, such versions of luck egalitarianism can support a social safety net to protect everyone's ability to live minimally well (Tan, 2012).[36]

Moreover, many who endorse traditional forms of relational egalitarianism might accept my account of basic justice (Vandamme, 2017).[37] Accepting my

---

[34] On this view, people cannot be responsible for falling below the minimally good life threshold. I take this to be a moral commitment—based on the view that people will try hard enough to live minimally well (much like the claim that all people are equal)—rather than an empirical claim. At least, one should grant that the claim that people will try hard enough if they can is only partly empirical. After all, we have to say what constitutes "hard enough" and consider what people "can" do. Given the difficulty of establishing the relevant empirical component of the claim, however, I believe it is reasonable to take the claim that people will try hard enough as a moral proposition—like the claim that all people are (morally) equal. After all, people rarely have a greater incentive to try to achieve something. So, if they fail to live minimally well, it does not seem reasonable to me to hold them morally responsible for trying harder. Of course, readers are welcome to disagree. Moreover, there are many other ways of responding to the harshness objection to luck egalitarianism (Barry, 2006) (for relevant discussion, also see Voigt (2007); Knight (2005)). Some luck egalitarians might stress the fact that most people who do things that seem irresponsible (e.g. who ride motorcycles without helmets) avoid injury, so many of those who end up getting into accidents that undermine their ability to live minimally well are not fully responsible for their poor luck. Some particular individuals may also lack agential control or have good excuses for what would otherwise constitute irresponsible behavior. Some may lack the mental capacity to make a responsible decision or inadvertently forget to wear a helmet. So, we may often have to provide emergency (or other kinds of) care to those who ride motorcycles without helmets (or make other seemingly poor decisions). Perhaps we can hold people responsible for their choice in ways that do not imperil their ability to live minimally well (Albertsen, 2020). Moreover, some argue that since people can change over time, or may lack free will, we should not let them bear the full costs of poor decisions (Knight, 2015). Alternately luck egalitarians could endorse 'responsibility-constrained sufficientarianism' or argue that there are other reasons to think the view will ensure everyone can live at least minimally well (Tan, 2012; Lippert-Rasmussen, 2015; Knight, 2022).

[35] A full account of what justice, never mind morality, requires of us can still consider responsibility, however. Moreover, if two people are unable to live minimally good lives and there is only enough to help one person do so (without asking anyone else to sacrifice their ability to live minimally well), perhaps we can consider the fact that only one has acted responsibly in deciding who to help.

[36] The next chapter discusses some other deontological theories that do not demand enough, and some that demand too much. On some accounts, people have a troubling amount of discretion and, on others, people do not even have to provide aid in easy rescue cases. Some hold rights-based views on which we have perfect discretion over how to use our bodies and property (though these views are much more plausible if they only govern the ways in which states can force people to help others) (Thomson, 1976; Lichtenberg, 2010). Others suggest that people have imperfect duties of beneficence that they can often fulfill as they like (Kant, 1785). Yet others maintain that morality cannot require we live altruistically focused, or even moral, lives (Wolf, 1982; Williams, 2006). Such views fail to demand enough when they say it is acceptable to leave people unable to live even minimally well despite the fact that it would cost others very little to help. Other views are too demanding if they require some to sacrifice their ability to live well enough for others (Kant, 1785).

[37] Of course, it will not suffice to eliminate status inequality if it does not ensure that everyone lives well enough. Relational egalitarians must hold that inequalities in resources, capabilities, or other goods apart from status matter because they undermine equal relations between individuals in a society (Anderson, 2010). But I believe they also matter for other reasons.

account does not require rejecting all relational inequalities, but those who think we should reject all relational inequalities should accept it. Proponents of relational egalitarianism care about how a distribution is determined and whether it undermines equal relations (Anderson, 2010). On their view, justice requires that people stand in appropriately virtuous relationships with others (Anderson, 2010; Scheffler, 2015). The relational egalitarian claim that justice depends on whether people who are mutually accountable, free, equal, "self-originating sources of claims" could reasonably agree to stand in their relationships to others inspires many contractualist theories (Rawls 1980, 546; Darwall, 2006, ch. 12; Anderson, 2010, 4).[38] Proponents of the minimally good life account believe that inequitable social relations—of status, standing, or authority—can undermine basic justice. These inequalities do so when they undermine individuals' ability to live well enough. Moreover, I have argued that inequality in the distribution of *other* goods undermines basic justice when these inequalities undermine individuals' ability to live minimally well because such inequalities are incompatible with respect (or proper concern) for our common humanity. Respect for our common humanity requires standing in good relationships with others.[39] Even if inequalities (or insufficiencies) that undermine individuals' ability to live well enough do not result from unjust relations between people, they result in unjust relations if left unaddressed. Moreover, virtue, and virtuous relations, are arguably part of a minimally good life at least for most people: We must help people live such lives when we can do so without sacrificing anything so significant. Otherwise we do not treat them well enough.

Many other (distributive) egalitarians and consequentialists can also accept the minimally good life view as long as they agree that we must adequately protect individuals' ability to live minimally well. We may best help people live well enough by promoting distributive equality or helping improve welfare, capabilities, resources, or other goods (Wilkinson and Pickett, 2011). Moreover, consequentialist and egalitarian considerations may guide how we

---

[38] Arguably, such people would not agree to coercive rules under which not everyone could live minimally well. If they did, that would not suffice for basic justice because it shows lack of due care and concern for others.

[39] Some people may require loving relationships to fare well enough that they cannot easily secure or maintain, but love is not something we can mandate. What we can do is support people in developing their ability to maintain decent relationships through education and, where necessary, counseling. Moreover, we often provide care and concern for those who cannot secure what they need on their own in residential facilities (e.g. group homes for the mentally ill). Though the account may provide reasons to buttress the kinds of support we provide significantly, it is often fair enough to insist that those who believe that they need particular relationships to live minimally well are simply mistaken. For relevant discussion, see Collins (2013) and Liao (2015).

help others as long as such theories include a (minimally good) life threshold below which none should fall and all should rise. Furthermore, adopting the minimally good life view helps address a basic problem for consequentialists and many egalitarians—individuals are separate human beings who merit respect as well as consideration (Persson, 2013; Hirose, 2015).[40] In most circumstances, we cannot simply aggregate their claims and sacrifice some for the sake of even a greater number of others. Only in truly tragic situations will we have to choose to help some live minimally well at such a high cost to others (or ourselves). (I discuss how we should respond when it seems we face such situations in the final chapter.) With the minimally good life threshold in place, no one will have to sacrifice parts of their bodies or the property they need to live well enough to help others, though people may merit significant praise for doing so when others are likewise imperiled (contra: Unger (1996); Singer (1972)). Moreover, we should normally give great priority to helping people live minimally well as opposed to, say, helping a much greater number of people who can already live excellent lives. If consequentialist and distributive egalitarian theories include the minimally good life threshold, they will maintain a substantive basic minimum above which all should rise and none should fall.[41] And, while a full theory of justice may require those with excellent lives to help the merely very well-off, such theories can recognize that basic justice does not require so much. (See Chapter 5 for further discussion of how we should help people below the sufficiency threshold as well.)

5. Appropriate Demands, Public Policy, and Obligations beyond Basic Justice

The minimally good life account can play an important role in many larger theories of justice, but it provides a distinctive explanation of what exactly we owe others as a basic minimum and why. It claims that we must, out of respect

---

[40] Some may also argue for sufficiency over more egalitarian views based on pragmatic considerations such as feasibility, though subsequent chapters argue that helping people reach the sufficiency threshold may demand a lot (Dumitru, 2017; Carey, 2020).

[41] Proponents of satisficing consequentialism—on which outcomes must just be good enough might specify that an outcome is good enough only if everyone lives a minimally good life (and explain that we must give enough priority to helping people below this threshold) (Slote and Pettit, 1984). Similarly, progressive consequentialism, on which we must only do something to improve the world, might plausibly specify that our "bit," or fair share, includes helping others live well enough (Jamieson and Elliot, 2009; Sinnott-Armstrong, 2015). It is not plausible that one has done enough to improve the world by, say, creating a beautiful work of art when one could instead save many lives without sacrificing anything significant at all. Proponents of this view should also specify that people must help others live minimally well when doing so does not require sacrificing their own ability to live well enough.

for our common humanity, help others live minimally well in the justified aspiration/basic right sense when we need not sacrifice our own ability to live this kind of life. Moreover, this book provided a mechanism for figuring out whether particular lives are good enough: As free, reasonable, caring people, we must consider whether we would now contently live others' lives in their shoes to respect everyone's common humanity.

The minimally good life account of what we owe, and can demand, as a basic minimum fulfills the desiderata with which we started—it does not demand too much, but it demands enough. It does not demand too much because it does not require some to sacrifice their bodily integrity, nor the property necessary and important for health and life to aid others, even if that means others do not survive or flourish.[42] It demands enough in that there exists no serious reason to doubt that an individual who reaches the justified aspiration/basic right threshold can live her life well. The minimally good life standard does not allow severe deprivations (or violations of bodily integrity), in part, because individuals require *secure* access to an *adequate range* of things necessary, and *important*, for living well.[43] On the minimally good life account, we must give some significant aid but do not have to provide others with everything from which they might benefit. The account demands enough, but it does not require too much.

Consider what accepting the minimally good life account of what we owe to others and can reasonably demand as a matter of basic justice implies for public policy. Though good reasons may exist to support social democracy or even socialism, the account requires neither; it only supports a minimal welfare state. It does not require social democracy because we do not plausibly have to ensure most people's access to higher education or the fine arts as a matter of basic justice; lacking these things does not threaten *most* people's ability to live minimally good lives.[44] I hope that helping everyone live minimally well

---

[42] My view is compatible with many ways of distributing the obligations to help people live minimally good lives. Still, I suppose that what each of us should do depends on what others actually do. In some circumstances, everyone has to provide all the assistance they can as long as that does not undermine their ability to live minimally good lives. That is, in a world where millions are suffering and dying young each year from easily preventable poverty-related causes, we must each do what we can to help before purchasing things we do not need to live minimally well ourselves.

[43] See discussion in notes above. Also note that coercive rules threaten individuals' ability to live minimally well if they cannot avoid such severe deprivations under these rules (Hassoun, 2013; Hassoun, 2021a; Hassoun, 2021b; Hassoun, 2021c). So, I do not think people can subject others to coercive rules under which they cannot access existing medical treatments if they suffer severe injury (e.g. if they lose an eye).

[44] What a particular individual needs depends on her psychology and history—so a great sculptor who has fully devoted her life to her art might not live minimally well without her art—but helping a few people access the arts is a far cry from social democracy for all.

does not require withholding funding for the fine arts (or higher education) but it might and, if so, that is the tragic state of our world. We should not build great monuments to any God before everyone can eat and secure the other things they need to live well enough. For similar reasons, the account does not require limiting rich people's ability to accumulate wealth (limitarianism) except where we must do so to ensure a basic minimum for all (Robeyns, 2019). Though, if we cannot otherwise help everyone live even minimally well, we may all have to cultivate less expensive tastes insofar as possible. The minimally good life account does not support socialism if most people can live minimally good lives even if they lack democratic control of the means of production, exchange, and distribution.[45] (Though, traditional forms of capitalism have yet to prove sufficient for people to live minimally good lives either.) Everyone may flourish best when people value helping others enough. The minimally good life account of the basic minimum comports with whatever social systems ensure people secure the things they need to live such lives.

The account supports a social and economic system that includes a robust social safety net. The system must help everyone live well enough whether we can best achieve this via basic income, negative tax, or alternative policies (Rappoport, 1924; Parekh, 1975; Van Parijs and Vanderborght, 2017).[46] I expect that, given the diversity of things people need to live minimally good lives, helping everyone live such lives will require many different institutional policies (Hassoun, 2012). We may have to promote individuals' ability to live well enough via conditional and unconditional cash benefits, capital grants, job subsidies, training programs, opportunities for labor market participation, and/or in other ways (Gough, 1994).

6. Conclusion

This chapter argued that we should help protect each other's ability to live minimally good lives as a matter of basic justice and the next chapter explains

---

[45] Workers in capitalist systems may be alienated from their humanity in the sense that they cannot express some fundamental aspects of their social personality through their labor. Still, it seems obvious that many workers in wealthy capitalist societies with robust social safety nets live minimally good lives. We fulfill many social needs in ways that do not involve our labor (e.g. through friendship) in these societies. Moreover, many other things that have nothing to do with the ways in which we labor contribute to our ability to live well enough. Though, of course, capitalism may ultimately prove unsustainable because it cannot support everyone's ability to live well enough.

[46] Given the extent of global poverty (and ecological limits we face), some argue that we must transform free market economic systems by limiting the wealth people can acquire significantly (Robeyns, 2017; Robeyns, 2019; Timmer, 2021b).

the advantages of this account of what we owe to others and can demand as a basic minimum over some more specific alternatives. More precisely, this chapter considered how this book's account of what basic justice requires carves out a path between libertarianism and luck egalitarianism on the right and socialism and social democracy on the left. It also explained how the minimally good life account fits into the broader literature on distributive and relational justice. These arguments may not convince those who embrace alternative perspectives, but they at least help locate this book's account in the literature on social justice and political obligations. The next chapter considers more specific alternatives to the minimally good life account. It argues that the main competitors are either too demanding, not demanding enough, or both.

On this book's account of basic justice, we must help others live minimally good lives when that does not require sacrificing our own ability to do so. The account can help ground a theory of global justice and human rights and guide individuals' action in their personal as well as political lives. The minimally good life account provides a unified standard for what we owe, and can rightfully demand, as a basic minimum. It treats both those who require aid and those who must provide it equally. The account requires us to give some significant aid. Yet, it does not demand that we provide others with everything from which they might benefit. The minimally good life account leaves room for pure altruism, or charity, and freedom, rights, and responsibility in human lives. It does not demand too much because it does not require people to sacrifice their own ability to live well enough for others. It demands enough because no one can reasonably doubt that those who secure the aid they need to flourish can live their lives well.

4

Advantages of the Minimally Good Life Account

1. Introduction

What do we owe to others and what can we justifiably demand as a matter of basic justice (that is, out of concern for our common humanity)? The previous chapter argued that people must help each other live minimally good lives when that does not require sacrificing their own ability to do likewise.* Our relationships of care and concern for others demand this respect because they help constitute our distinctively valuable human forms of life. We need these relationships to survive and flourish as free, but constrained, human agents vulnerable to the radical contingency that shapes our lives. Respect for our common humanity requires that we treat everyone with reasonable, free care and concern. We recognize others as free, equal individuals with the standing to claim decent treatment and this includes assistance in living at least minimally good lives when no one must sacrifice so much to help them. So, people have human rights that protect the flourishing relationships that bolster, and help constitute, our common humanity. Because some of the most important relationships we stand in to others are political, legitimate coercive states must fulfill their subjects' human rights to a basic minimum. But, even individuals, as part of the international community, must assist or rectify institutional failures to fulfill these rights and should hold each other to account. They must help others live minimally good lives when no one else is doing so—either by helping to build the requisite institutions where they are missing or by working to fill the gap. This chapter starts from the conclusion that, when we are considering cases where we do not stand in any special relationship to others whom we might aid beyond that of shared—or common—humanity, we cannot fail to do something to help a person live

---

* This chapter draws on: Hassoun, Nicole. 2022. "The Minimally Good Life Account of What We Owe to Others and What We Can Justifiably Demand." Special Issue on Basic Needs: Normative Perspectives, *Lessico di Etica Pubblica* 1 (2022): 107–126. http://www.eticapubblica.it/

minimally well at reasonable cost (Feinberg, 1984). It considers alternative views of what costs we must bear.[1]

Several competing answers to the question "How much must we be willing to sacrifice to help others live minimally well out of concern, or respect, for their common humanity?" seem plausible: (1) We must only do our fair share to help others (where this might be understood in different ways). (2) We must help people until they can help themselves live effectively, but we need not do more than that. (3) We need not sacrifice anything that can ground a requirement to help another, but we should be willing to sacrifice anything that does not ground such a requirement if our sacrifices are proportional to what others can gain with our aid. (4) We need not sacrifice anything that affects the quality of our own lives but should help improve others' lives whenever we need not sacrifice so much.

Recall that the previous chapter defended two desiderata for a successful account of basic justice. First, theories must generally *demand enough* so that no one can reasonably doubt that an individual who reaches the threshold for a basic minimum can live her life well unless doing so requires too much of those who must help. It claimed that people need more than choice-worthy lives—they must have enough of the things that make their lives good for them. There exist many views that satisfy this desideratum. It does not commit one to my minimally good life account of what we owe to others and can demand as a basic minimum. Since, however, I only aim here to address those who agree that people have some claim to assistance in living at least minimally good lives where the costs of aid are reasonable, I take this desideratum for granted.[2]

Because the question I aim to address is only "How much must we be willing to sacrifice to help others live minimally well out of concern or respect for their common humanity?", I can also grant that theories requiring us to sacrifice to help people secure more than a minimally good life *demand too much*. That is, although justice, or morality, may require much more, I will grant to those who prefer more minimal accounts, that theories requiring us to sacrifice to help people live very good or excellent lives demand too much.

---

[1] However, one can accept further constraints on this account of what we must give up for others if one does not find my arguments here compelling.

[2] Recall previous chapters' arguments against alternative capability and welfare accounts of the basic minimum. Similarly, accounts suggesting that people only need a short list of human rights—e.g. security, property, subsistence, formal legal equality, some freedom of conscience, and freedom from slavery and genocide—fail woefully because they do not ensure for people even choice-worthy lives (Miller, 1998; Rawls, 1999; Griffin, 2008; Blake, 2013). Those who have basic capabilities may fail to flourish and lack everything but the mere possibility of choice. Everyone needs some kinds of equal treatment and respect. No one should have to face pervasive discrimination in society that seriously threatens their ability to live a minimally good life.

That said, it may strike some readers as odd to set aside some competing accounts on the grounds that they require providing people with more than the basic minimum. After all, the theory I defend is much more demanding in some respects than many of those on which we must help people secure things they do not need to reach the threshold. On my view, we must sacrifice whatever we do not need to live well enough to help others. So, my view seems at least as open to the charge that it demands too much as the competitors'.

Note, first, that saying that competing accounts demand too much when they require us to sacrifice to help others secure more than a basic minimum, just amounts to the claim that no one should use them for this purpose. Many of these accounts were not intended as accounts of basic justice but of related phenomena—like beneficence or charity. I only consider here whether these views can provide plausible accounts of the costs we must bear to help people secure a basic minimum because they provide some of the most promising possibilities. So, in saying that they demand too much when they require more than this minimum, I do not deny that they can serve many other roles.

Moreover, the minimally good life view is not nearly as demanding as one might suppose on first sight. One reason for this is that the proposed threshold is quite high. Recall the previous chapter's claim that a good threshold for demandingness should be unified in the sense that we can only demand for ourselves what we must also provide for others. We must only give up what we do not need to live flourishing lives ourselves to help others who otherwise cannot live such lives. So, someone who is quite rich may not reach the threshold for a minimally good life if they suffer from severe, untreated depression. They may have to help others financially, but not at the cost of the social support and other things they need to achieve the psychological flourishing that lets them live a good enough life. People need not sacrifice the property or other things they need for life or health to aid others. Moreover, I do not provide a complete account of what justice and morality require. So, obligations to ourselves and our loved ones may limit the account's demands as well, though fulfilling these obligations should not generally come at the cost of failing to fulfill claims of common humanity.

Most importantly, however, my proposed threshold for what qualifies as too demanding and not demanding enough allows people to maintain the projects and commitments that give their lives meaning while at the same time recognizing that fulfilling the impartial claims of common humanity are also important for a life of integrity. There are limits to what justice, as a part of morality, can require of us (Wolff, 1982). We often identify deeply with the actions that flow from our important projects and neither can, nor should, step aside from them to consider their value from the impartial point of view (Williams, 1985). It is important that people can live with integrity and avoid alienation from their agency. Still, to live a life with integrity, we must sometimes *integrate* morality's impartial requirements with the other (partial) commitments that give our lives meaning so that we can respond appropriately to moral, as well as non-moral, values (Scheffler, 1994). Perhaps it is only at times of crisis, or pending tragedy, when we should question our commitments—never mind consider giving up our deepest projects or values. But, when others cannot live even minimally good lives without our assistance, and we face such a potentially tragic situation, we must sometimes adjust our aspirations, and even identities, in ways that allow us to act on the impartial requirement of respect for common humanity. One sacrifices one's integrity in giving undue weight to one's own interests over the interests of others in such circumstances.[3] In short, I propose that the appropriate balance between the requirements of impartiality and personal prerogatives supports both the requirements proposed here and the limits to the demands that follow.[4]

After all, my account also demands much less than some alternatives and not only because it does not require us to sacrifice anything at all to help those above the threshold for a basic minimum (it stays neutral on the question of whether we have any obligations to those above the threshold for a basic minimum). Recall that the previous chapter defended the desiderata that an adequate account of basic justice cannot require us to sacrifice the property or other things we need for health or life even to help others live minimally good lives. Some—like Peter Singer—advance incredibly demanding principles of basic justice requiring some to sacrifice their limbs, if not their lives, for others (see, also Unger (1996)). However, while it might be a noble act of self-sacrifice to give up one's health or life for another, I suppose here that requiring such sacrifices *demands too much*. After all, individuals cannot live their own lives if they lack the health and other things they need to do so, and we must only give to others what we can also claim for ourselves. At least, if any accounts of what we owe to others as a basic minimum in the literature demand too much, these do and the question at issue is really: "What else demands too much?".

---

[3] Sometimes we must give others' lives due weight to live good enough lives ourselves.
[4] This is a substantive view that I defend below and in the final chapter. However, metaethical considerations may support the claim that this is what integrity requires in our world where many people need assistance to live even minimally good lives (Scheffler, 1993, 125).

In any case, my aim here is primarily to address those who endorse the above desiderata. In what follows, I examine alternative views that are plausible on first blush, in part, because their demands seem more reasonable. I argue that the alternatives fail one or both desiderata above and sometimes that they have other problems (and I take this to provide a coherentist argument that helps justify the desiderata).

2. Alternative Accounts of What We Owe and Can Claim as a Basic Minimum

First, consider fair shares views of what we must sacrifice for others. Most of those who embrace fair shares views want to find something that "sets the case where one directly confronts a person in imminent danger of death or serious injury apart from the wider set of circumstances in which we have opportunities to prevent harm or alleviate deprivation" (Miller, 2019, 328). Proponents of fair shares views often hold that "agent-neutral principles should not under partial compliance require sacrifice of an agent where the total compliance effect on her, taking that sacrifice into account would be worse than it would be (all other aspects of her situation remaining the same) under full compliance from now on" (Murphy, 2000, 80). On these accounts, we ought to reject principles that require people to sacrifice more than they must if everyone did what they should. Rather, people should just bear their fair share of the costs of fulfilling our collective obligations to aid (Murphy, 2000, 74–101).

However, depending on what each person must do if everyone did their part, fair shares views may let people do almost nothing for others while leaving great needs unmet or require some to sacrifice everything for others.[5] Consider a case where an individual must only give a minuscule amount if others do their fair share: On this view, she might literally not have to lift a finger to help others in desperate need, so it would not even require easy rescue. At the same time, an individual's fair share may often implausibly require sacrificing the things one needs for life or health to aid others (recall that previous chapters defended the desiderata that an adequate account of basic justice cannot require us to sacrifice our health or life even to help others live

---

[5] See Appendix II for discussion of Liam Murphy's view.

minimally good lives—an adequate basic minimum should ensure that people have bodily security).[6]

One way of specifying fair shares is by reference to entitlements and what the ideal moral code requires (Arthur, 2002). This code contains the rules that, with full compliance, would produce the most good for society as a whole. So, proponents of fair shares views sometimes assert that, although the ideal moral code requires easy rescue, no one must sacrifice basic entitlements to help (at least distant) others (Arthur, 2002, 885–891). This is because the ideal moral code includes entitlements to one's person and property. Both security and property rights support the productivity that makes minimally good lives possible (Locke, 1689).[7] Proponents of fair shares views may, thus, conclude that requiring people to give up their security or property to help distant others live minimally well demands too much.

However, we must sometimes sacrifice some things to which people normally suppose they are entitled (e.g. property) to help others and not only in classic rescue cases. Often people can sacrifice a great deal of what they have without compromising their basic security or life quality and, thereby, save many lives or alleviate a great deal of suffering.[8] Moreover, helping others live minimally good lives when that does not require sacrificing our own ability to do so may well produce the most good for society (and the world) as a whole. If so, we should reject the entitlement/ideal moral code defense because it fails by its own criterion.[9]

---

[6] So, although it might be a noble act of self-sacrifice to give up one's health or life for another in the way that Singer or Unger require, I started from the desiderata that requiring such sacrifices also *demands too much*. After all, if any accounts of what we owe to others as a basic minimum in the literature demand too much, these do. In any case, I expect most people will endorse this desideratum and argue that my view demands too much as well. So, I primarily focus on theories that aim to limit the costs of aid in what follows.

[7] Some suggest that people will not be under any duty to help if we say others must pick up the slack since they can suppose others will fulfill their duty. So, first order morality should not require anyone to take up the slack (Cohen, 1989). However, whether this is so depends on individuals' psychological character, our understanding of these duties, mechanisms to enforce compliance, and many other things (Stemplowska, 2016). If there is greater need than those who pick up the slack might reasonably be expected to help alleviate, for instance, the argument does not work. Those who might free ride on others' efforts will still have to contribute (Stemplowska, 2016).

[8] Proponents of fair shares views cannot assert that my view cannot be part of the ideal moral code because it does not contain genuine entitlements as anything is potentially up for grabs. On my view, people remain entitled to whatever they need to live minimally well themselves and may also be entitled to things others do not need to live well enough.

[9] As the previous chapter noted, many other non-consequentialist theories are also troublingly minimal. Some hold rights-based views on which we have perfect discretion over how to use our bodies and property (Thomson, 1976; Lichtenberg, 2010). Others suggest that people have imperfect duties of beneficence that they can fulfill as they like (Kant, 1785). Yet others maintain that morality cannot require we live altruistically focused, or even moral, lives (Wolf, 1982; Williams, 2006). On many of these accounts, people have too much discretion in deciding whether to help others. Moreover, they are too minimal if they entail that people can neglect to help others even in easy

In any case, in our non-ideal world, many people fail to do what they should. So, we should not endorse the rules that would produce the most good for society as a whole if people did what they should. When some fail to do their part, others often must take up the slack to ensure everyone fares well enough.[10] Ideal theory, in our non-ideal circumstances, requires this much. An agent's fair share should depend upon how many people require assistance, how much assistance they need, and how many will help as well as what one can do for others without imperiling one's own ability to live well enough. It should not depend on just what people must do in ideal circumstances where everyone else is contributing.

Perhaps proponents of fair shares views might try to resist this conclusion by arguing that duties to rescue only arise when people are physically proximate and, when there are others who can assist, no individual has a duty to rescue until the duty is allocated via a fair procedure (Miller, 2019).[11] David Miller offers the most promising fair shares views of reasonable sacrifice along these lines in "The Nature and Limits of the Duty of Rescue" (Miller, 2019). He says that, normally, physical distance is relevant because it makes victims uniquely reliant on those who can provide aid and "if we claim . . . sovereignty over our personal space, we should also accept some responsibility to others for what goes on within it" (Miller, 2019, 331). Miller also says that our personal space can stretch much further than normal when needed for rescue, we cannot escape responsibility by moving out of a person's personal space once the duty has been triggered, but we can avoid moving into it. Moreover, when potential rescuers recognize "the victim as a person in need

---

rescue cases (because potential benefactors claim discretionary rights over their bodies or property, insist that they can just decide to help others later, or want to pursue personal projects or help those closer to them). Also see the previous chapter's discussion of many forms of consequentialism and egalitarianism.

[10] Recall that, our shared institutions plausibly have first-order responsibilities to help everyone live well enough on my account. Moreover, I argue at some length in Appendix I that, individuals as members of political societies subjecting each other to coercive rules we have primary obligations to establish the requisite institutions when the costs of doing so are reasonable. Finally, individuals, as part of the international community, have second-order obligations to rectify institutional failures or pick up the slack.

[11] Frequently arguments about aid devolve into consideration of highly idealized examples (cf. Unger (1996)), whereas I think it is often more pertinent to reflect on real world cases. Although in common law countries, good Samaritan laws have rarely been forthcoming, it seems clear that people ought to help others in many cases even when others are around who could also help but fail to do so. Consider what we think of those who witnessed Kitty Genovese's rape and murder in New York in 1964 but did not call the police just because others could. Few would deny that each person should have made the call even if others refused. It is, perhaps, less clear whether there is an enforceable duty to aid but, arguably, these duties are enforceable. Supposing someone without a phone could take one from an inactive neighbor to call the police and prevent the rape or murder, this seems permissible. Similarly, it seems there should be such a law requiring people to make the call if it works to help people to fulfill their moral duties in cases like this.

of help, and the victim likewise understands the rescuer as having the capacity to give it . . . [a] relationship is formed . . . the rescuer has directly confronted the victim as another human being in desperate straits" and must provide aid (Miller, 2019, 331). Finally, Miller maintains that the number of others who can help makes a difference to the nature of our obligations. When many people could rescue (and especially when the costs depend on the number of others who contribute), the duty is held by the group and consists in a duty to coordinate action. Once the group figures out how to aid, individuals must do their part (as long as the division of responsibility is fair considering individuals' capacities and so forth). If co-ordination fails, individuals have "a strong moral reason, but not a duty of justice, to rescue" (Miller, 2019, 335).

Miller says that when others who are equally well placed to help simply do not, that changes our moral obligations. For, justice provides "directives that apply to all moral agents in the same way, insofar as they are similarly situated. Its principles tell us how to act on the assumption that others, too, will follow them" (Miller, 2019, 337).[12] He considers a case where he and four other bystanders can rescue five victims. Once he rescues the first, no others will act. Miller says he has a strong reason to save the rest of the victims if the cost is reasonable, but no one can force him to do it and none of the victims are wronged if he chooses not to save them (Miller, 2019, 337). This lets us track the fact that the other bystanders are blameworthy for failing to act in a way that he is not. Otherwise, if the victims "wish to claim compensation for the injuries they have suffered as a result of not being rescued, they have as much reason to sue . . . [him] . . . as they have to sue the other four. But this is surely repugnant: saving them was the others' job," not his (Miller, 2019, 338).[13]

I believe Miller's account fails to recognize the importance of helping people who are not close by and when others could (but will not) assist.[14]

---

[12] Miller says "There may be other moral reasons that apply in circumstances where that assumption fails—supplementary directives that address that situation. But we misunderstand justice if we think that its purpose is to tell us how to act even when all around us are ignoring its injunctions" (Miller, 2019, 337). For relevant discussion, also see Lichtenberg (2013).

[13] Miller also seems to think that we should hold people responsible for doing their part and letting people off the hook by taking up the slack fails to treat them appropriately. I believe we can both maintain that there is an obligation to take up the slack and hold people responsible for failing to do their part. See Stemplowska (2016); Stemplowska (2019) for further discussion of issues with fair shares views.

[14] Miller also offers this argument, against consequentialists: Even if it is certain that someone can save a greater number of lives by helping those far away rather than someone right in front of her, she should nonetheless rescue the closest person. The other people she could help are not present at the time. Here I think Miller makes a mistake. After all, the far away others may also be uniquely vulnerable to the potential rescuer's decision about whether to aid. I suspect Miller is not considering this possibility. On the other hand, his argument against contractualists is compelling if not everyone is part of the relevant social contract: We have just as much of an obligation to save the life of a foreigner

Fairness should not take lexical priority over helping those in desperate straits (Stemplowska, 2016).[15] Duties to aid can be held by a group and we need to distribute them. Given the failure of coordination, and therefore potentially huge costs for the one person who must act (and who might be able to do very little alone), Miller provides a compelling argument for creating institutions, or agreements, to distribute the relevant responsibilities.[16] Moreover, I agree that vulnerability generates significant obligations and that one should aid when no others can, nor will, help. I also think that the kind of recognition Miller emphasizes—also evident in Jeremy Waldron's nice account of our Samaritan duties (Waldron, 1999)—explains why we should help others. But I think we *owe* others this kind of recognition. On my view, others' common humanity and our relationships require this recognition. Still, these obligations exist independently of the recognition. That is, we *should* empathize with others in the way respect for common humanity requires, though we often fail to do so (Atuire and Hassoun, 2023). As virtue ethicists might stress, we need moral education to enhance empathy and, thus, virtue. So, if someone fails to recognize others' needs, that does not alleviate their obligation. Finally, I believe our personal space should stretch as far as needed to enable rescue when we need not sacrifice anything more important to help others (like our own ability to live minimally well). Miller objects to this possibility by saying that although "the rescuer will always have a reason to help the victim, to turn this into an obligation would potentially diminish her freedom severely" (Miller, 2019, 333). But any time we must help others, that might diminish our freedom severely. If no others are around, one might have an onerous obligation to aid on fair shares views. Moreover, the fact that others are around, but do not help, should not affect the costs one must bear. Neither should the fact that someone is further away from a victim.[17]

---

as a co-national or co-citizen in desperate need. Ours is "a duty that one human being owes to another regardless of any pre-existing social or political relationship that may obtain between them" (Miller, 2020b, 326).

[15] Zofia Stemploska also points out that noncompliers often increase the burden of aid in other ways—e.g. we should help those in refugee camps because others have failed in their duties not to destroy their homes (Stemplowska, 2016). For a non-consequentialist argument for taking up the slack, also see Karnein (2014).

[16] See the previous chapter's discussion of how the obligations apply to legitimate institutions, and Appendix I. Ultimately, however, I think the buck stops with each one of us. That is, where the institutions to ensure individuals can live at least minimally good lives are absent, or broken, we must all help fill the breach.

[17] Miller is most concerned with wrongdoing and not costs, though we are considering whether one is obligated to bear the costs here. Moreover, I believe the kind of wrongdoing at issue for Miller is like the wrongdoing this book considers. After all, institutions must often require people to do their part to fulfill human rights though here I focus on making the case that (basic) justice at least requires individuals to help pick up the slack.

Finally, it is possible to recognize that our duties are importantly different in cases where everyone does their part to aid those in need and in cases in which many do not, and maintain that (basic) justice requires us to aid in both cases.[18] One can say: Ideally, everyone would only need to do their fair share and fulfill their primary duties—our primary obligations are limited to doing our part. Still, when others fail, we have back up duties to do more than our fair share and rescue those in desperate need. These secondary duties to help in non-ideal circumstances remain duties of justice owed to those in desperate need. If Miller denies this, he may also have to reject many social welfare programs that tax some of those who have already done their part to help the poor (Stemplowska, 2016). Nevertheless, one can maintain that we should not be sued for failing to fulfill our secondary duties when it is possible to hold others (with primary responsibility for aiding) to account.[19]

Second, consider the view that we must help others live effectively but need not help anyone achieve more than this. In *Equality for Inegalitarians*, George Sher argues that people should be free to set their own aims and pursue strategies to fulfill them (Sher, 2014). He believes our moral equality consists in the fact that we are all equally subjects of a life—agents with beliefs, plans, and aims who project ourselves:

> not merely as the locus of a kaleidoscopic sequence of unrelated feelings and experiences, nor yet as a rudimentary agent who at each moment will respond to...[our]...strongest urges, but rather as a continuing conscious subject whose earlier and later experience will be related by anticipation and memory, and whose earlier and later actions will be structured around plans that are aimed at implementing...stable though evolving reason-based aims. (Sher, 2014, 82)

Sher says this enables people to live a characteristically human life. He thinks institutions should protect each person's *fundamental* interest in living the

---

[18] On enforceability see Wellman (2001). But he says the fact that "the state does not need everyone's cooperation to supply its essential benefits" undermines individual obligations and I think it does not (Wellman, 2001, 748). Our obligations are conditional in this way: if states fail to help some people, individuals must pick up the slack. Some might object that individuals are not obligated to provide aid when their individual actions make no difference alone. For a response to this inefficacy objection see Hassoun (2020).

[19] Although I have argued that individuals fail to fulfill their human rights obligations when they do not pick up the slack, it takes further argument to establish what legal penalties they should bear for this failure in different circumstances. I am most concerned to establish that individuals are morally liable for picking up the slack when the costs are reasonable. Some of those who can assist at reasonable cost may not even be morally blameworthy for failing to do so given, e.g., the information available to them about their moral responsibilities.

life their "form of mental organization makes possible" (Sher, 2014, 94). People need the ability to live their lives *effectively*—successfully responding to the reasons their situations provide, forming intentions, and pursuing plans in light of those reasons (Sher, 2014, 96). People vary in ability to live their lives effectively. However, Sher maintains that once people have enough wealth, knowledge, skills, and opportunity, they can compensate for any remaining limitations in their ability to reason and pursue plans well. So, he says, further improving their access to wealth, knowledge, skills, and opportunities will not do more to help them live effectively. Sher believes people must just reach this threshold of effectiveness at which, he says, their fundamental interest become fully and equally protected. He endorses the significant inequalities in the wealth, knowledge, skills, and opportunities that remain. Moreover, his account of our fundamental interests purportedly grounds a requirement to let people suffer the consequences of their bad choices and, he thinks, poor decision-making capacity is often "innate and intractable" (Sher, 2014, 105).[20] Sher believes we owe people very little. We must only provide them with basic education and just enough resources and opportunities so that they can start to leverage them to increase their share without sacrificing their ability to live effectively.

I agree that people should be able to live their lives effectively when possible, but Sher's view implausibly allows one to refuse to help people in desperate need if they cannot live effectively. Sher thinks our moral equality lies in having a consciousness with structure "*that gives rise to a sense of time, reasons-responsiveness, and the interests that rational aims generate*" (Sher, 2014, 90). But some lack such consciousness and even those who have it may be unable to live their lives effectively even with significant aid.[21] Those who lack the kind of consciousness Sher values may be capable of gaining it. So, contra Sher, it is not enough to just help them secure the lives their current "form of mental organization makes possible" (Sher, 2014, 94). Moreover, even those who lack the kind of consciousness Sher values still have a variety of needs for food, water, shelter, and comfort (among other things). These needs

---

[20] Sher says "whatever else is true, a person is definitely not able to live his life effectively if his fortunes are systematically disconnected from his own decisions and actions. Someone whose deliberations never ended in decisions, whose decisions never issued in actions, or whose actions never affected his life in predictable ways would hardly be living his own life at all. He would be more a patient than an agent" (Sher, 2014, 104).

[21] In discussing animals' moral status, Sher expresses some ambivalence about whether our moral equality lies in simply having a consciousness or in having a consciousness "that gives rise to a sense of time, reasons-responsiveness, and the interests that rational aims generate" (Sher, 2014, 90). Ultimately, he endorses the later view.

persist whether or not people can reasonably respond to their rational aims, form intentions, and act on them. Those who must remain ineffective do not deserve less help when they cannot respond appropriately to contingency. More than how we respond to contingency, and our ability to respond, matters. So, it will not do to say that those who cannot live their lives effectively should just adjust their aspirations in light of what they can "realistically hope to accomplish" or alter them in light of unforeseen, changing circumstances (Sher, 2014, 126).[22] Even those who will never be able to respond well to contingency, and will remain unable to live their lives effectively no matter what aid they receive, should secure whatever contributes to their ability to live well enough. At least this chapter starts from the presupposition that this is so when the costs to others of providing the requisite aid are not too high.

Moreover, Sher neglects the fact that no one deserves their fundamental freedom or constraint, though they may deserve differential treatment for other reasons (e.g. based on how they respond to it). Everyone's freedom is contingent. Everyone equally has free will (or does not) and their basic freedom (and/or constraint) helps ground their common humanity (and claims under constraint). We often survive radical contingency and can flourish despite it, in part, because we share a distinctively human form of life. We participate in different ways, and at different times, in important relationships of care and concern. Often, we can only cope with contingency together—through these relationships. Moreover, I believe each individuals' participation in sustaining our valuable human forms of existence partly grounds a requirement to respect our common humanity.[23] That is, we can ground obligations of basic justice in appropriate concern, or respect, for our common humanity—the fact that everyone is equally subject to radical contingency and has to live with it as a member of our moral community standing in relationships of care and concern to others. On this view, we are not moral equals because we can cope with contingency alone. Rather, we merit respect for our

---

[22] It is one thing to say that we must learn to live within the ecological, and other, limits we face to help people live well enough. It is another altogether to say that the poor, oppressed, and otherwise deprived should just learn to be content with their lot. Moreover, no one is born with good reasoning ability, but most can improve their ability to reason with practice. Just like the other things people need to live well enough, we should help people make good decisions when we can without sacrificing our own ability to live minimally well.

[23] We often contribute to shared long-term projects or practices that depend on connections between individuals involved in a collective enterprise (e.g. advancing medical research). Moreover, we contribute to human cultures, practices, institutions, societies, and heritage. We care for the future of humanity through sustaining these ways of life as well as individual humans (Scheffler, 2016; Scheffler, 2018). Even those who seem to be fairly disconnected from many of these practices—the severely mentally ill, the homeless, etc.—contribute to important human forms of life and, importantly, opportunities for others to care for them.

common humanity because we have needs, vulnerabilities, and will and do stand in important relationships of care and concern to others participating in our uniquely human moral community. Some of those who lack hope, live in desperate poverty, or cannot secure adequate nourishment on their own cannot "think clearly," but many can (Sher, 2014, 130). Still, these people often remain at high risk of losing access to the things they need to live well enough, even when they can live their lives effectively.

Moreover, in our tragic world where so many cannot even live their lives effectively, Sher's view may require us to give up even what we need for life or health to help others. No single individual can help everyone attain basic education or reach the leverage threshold no matter what she gives up. Even collectively, we may be unable to provide enough assistance. Sher incorrectly supposes that the affluent need not sacrifice much to help those who cannot currently live their lives effectively, especially in the global context. The vast majority of the world's population still lives in desperate poverty and basic justice cannot require sacrificing the things one needs for life and health to help others (though those who do so may sometimes merit praise).

In short, Sher's view may require too much as well as too little—if helping others get to the effectiveness threshold requires sacrificing one's life or health, one need not do so. A plausible basic minimum must provide some people with much more than the ability to live effectively but cannot require anyone to sacrifice their life or limbs to aid others.[24] When misfortune strikes, we cannot just say that the poor, sick, and miserable should adapt to their circumstances. Nor should we say they have enough if they can still respond to reasons and pursue plans. We should help these people secure adequate food, water, shelter, health care, social and emotional support, and the other things that they need to live well enough, when doing so does not require us to sacrifice too much, precisely because their lives are so contingent.[25] It does not only matter that people can decide how to respond to contingency but that they fare well enough through its vicissitudes.

Third, consider a view on which we need not sacrifice anything that can ground a requirement to help another but on which we must sacrifice anything that does not ground this requirement to help people secure such life enhancing goods. Garrett Cullity, in *the Moral Demands of Affluence* (2004), argues that the affluent must sacrifice a significant amount to aid others.

---

[24] There are limits to the sacrifices people must make to help others even when they cannot secure a basic minimum. Also see Chapter 5 for discussion of how we should help people secure this minimum.

[25] Recall that everyone should get as close as possible to living a least a minimally good life.

Yet, he also claims that they need not sacrifice as much as theorists like Singer claim. Although Cullity intends to provide an account of beneficence, as he sets up the project, he engages with those who think basic justice requires we provide more aid. Moreover, Cullity provides one of the most promising accounts of what we must sacrifice for others. So, it seems apt to consider here whether his view provides a plausible account of what basic justice requires. Cullity argues that certain life-enhancing goods, like friendship, pursuing long-term projects, and living together in a community require partiality; friendship requires giving friends' interests special consideration that does not extend to everyone (Cullity, 2004, 129–130). Cullity then claims that we must help others pursue these life-enhancing goods. He calls these goods *requirement grounding* (Cullity, 2004, 143–145). By parity, Cullity suggests, agents can freely pursue these goods for themselves, even if it means not helping others. Furthermore, he thinks people can freely structure their lives around non-altruistic, requirement-grounding goods. This gives us permission to seek seemingly trivial goods that help us in a greater pursuit. For example, I need not volunteer for a lifesaving charity if volunteering prevents me from taking a friend to lunch. But, if I can choose a different life that is equally good (or not worse by a requirement-grounding margin), I should choose the one where I can best help others (Cullity, 2004, 147–150).

We should not use this view as an account of basic justice rather than beneficence, though it is more plausible than Arthur's, Miller's, Murphy's, and Sher's accounts. In some cases, it asks agents to sacrifice too little, and in other cases too much.

On the one hand, we might not have to help others secure everything that enhances their life quality by what Cullity thinks is a requirement-grounding margin even when we need not sacrifice anything that would affect the quality of our own lives by a similar margin. At least, we need not do so out of concern for common humanity. On Cullity's account, friendships and other non-altruistically focused pursuits always ground requirements to aid. But someone with a great number of friendships, and so forth, may be well above any plausible basic minimum. So, if losing a friendship does not pose a serious threat to that person's ability to live well, at least basic justice does not require us to help prevent that loss (though, as Cullity contends, it would be nice to do so!).

On the other hand, Cullity's view sometimes asks agents to sacrifice too little. Intuitively, we must sometimes give up things that Cullity believes ground requirements to aid those in desperate need. For example, it seems that an aspiring scientist ought to forego completing her biology homework one evening if it means saving a life (even at a great distance and as part of a collective endeavor).[26] One might even need to give up biology to pursue a different career as long as one could also do well enough given that career and even if it is worse for that person by what Cullity considers a requirement-grounding margin. This would not be the case when one's career is so tied up with one's identity that one could not live minimally well without it or when transitioning to another career would imperil one's ability to live minimally well. And, one might maintain that people need not give up anything as significant as their career to help people (and doing so may rarely help others).[27] Still, I think the burden of proof for making the case that people need not consider different careers when they can help more people live minimally well by doing so, lies squarely on those who would insist that they can do whatever they want. After all (by hypothesis), if we do not help others live even minimally good lives, they will lose something very significant. They will not live even minimally good lives. Moreover, by hypothesis, if someone who could aid others goes for her next best career option and helps those in need, she will still live a minimally good life herself. The cost on the other side of the equation equals the difference in satisfaction the person will secure in her favorite vs. second favorite career. This person may not lose much even if the difference qualifies as requirement grounding on Cullity's account. Cullity's account of what grounds requirements to aid does not plausibly account for what we owe to others simply out of respect for our common humanity.

Still, one might insist on a proportionality constraint on what we must give: Perhaps we need not aid others if we must give up more to do so than they will gain (Knight, 2021b). One could argue for a different conception of what makes an account of obligations stemming from concern for common humanity too demanding on this basis. Perhaps the aggregate welfare loss, if someone pursues her second-best career, will be greater than if she chooses her best option. Though she might aid someone just a bit who will otherwise not secure a basic minimum and perhaps even help them reach the threshold, some will insist that she need not do so unless the net gain is positive.

---

[26] Cullity wants to say people are less blameworthy, and may do less wrong, if they neglect to give to aid organizations than if they fail to help someone right in front of them for two reasons. First, if they give to an organization, their action alone will make little difference. Second, the need is more vivid when it is right in front of them. I am not convinced of either point, but we can focus on a case where the person is at some remove and one must coordinate one's actions with others.

[27] One might also worry about what would happen to funding for the arts or other social endeavors on this account, but the worry assumes that the arts do not help individuals flourish and not all art is expensive. Other things also matter besides helping people live minimally good lives. That said, respect for common humanity may require feeding people before building even the most beautiful monuments.

I believe that even if a large difference exists and there is an aggregate welfare loss if the person pursues her second-best career, someone cannot justify failing to aid another just by saying that she will benefit herself more if she secures her favorite job.[28] If one denies that people must sometimes sacrifice more for others than they will gain, one must let billionaires keep all of their wealth if they cannot bring billions of dollars' worth of benefit to those otherwise unable to live well enough. This is so even if the billionaires could help millions rise above the threshold while keeping millions for themselves.[29]

One might more plausibly add a different kind of proportionality principle as a limit to what we must sacrifice for others. That is, one might not think it reasonable to require someone to sacrifice a great deal and bring themselves down to the threshold to help another who is just below the threshold rise above it or even to help someone further below the threshold get closer to it. Perhaps there are even cases where it is better to help many people above the threshold than someone below it.[30] The next chapter considers how we should think about helping people below the threshold. It argues that it is normally best to help the least well-off, but we should also care about the number of people we can aid. Moreover, I have argued that the reasons we must help those below the threshold are very significant and they are exhausted once everyone can live at least a minimally good life. Competing obligations, never mind mere benefits to those who are already above the threshold, cannot normally trump obligations that stem from concern for our common humanity. Finally, for the sake of argument, this chapter grants that there may be no obligations to help people secure more than a minimally good life. Still, one might ground some limit to what people must give up for others when their aid can do a very limited amount of good in concern for common humanity. It also seems reasonable, however, to require such sacrifices. After all, the other person will not be able to live even a minimally good life without assistance. We should, in any case, reject the idea that we need not aid others if we must give up more to do so than they will gain.

---

[28] Although societies generally let people make career decisions for themselves, they constrain their options in other ways. Licensing and training programs, for instance, only allow the most competitive applicants to get positions in medical fields. Such constraints seem justified if they save lives and otherwise help more people live well enough.

[29] Although money has decreasing marginal utility, we may only be able to do a limited amount of good for some people with additional financial resources.

[30] Here I imagine it might take a lot of resources to bring marginal improvements in some individuals' life quality even below the threshold. We have no obligations to provide resources that make little difference to how individuals fare, and we should evaluate the impact of resources and other goods on individuals' life quality. Still, if someone is very poorly-off to start with even small differences in life quality may be quite significant for that person. But, even if everyone could live well enough and provide the requisite aid, one could argue that helping them would cost too much.

For similar reasons, we should reject the fourth view that we must sacrifice all, and only, what does not affect the quality of our own lives to improve others' lives as an account of basic justice.[31] In "The Ethics of Social Democracy" Richard Miller endorses the principle of *mutual concern* (Miller, 2010, 9–30). He says, "everyone's underlying concern for others ought to be sufficiently great that greater concern would impose a significant risk of worsening his or her life, if he or she fulfilled all further responsibilities; but apart from special relationships or interactions it does not have to be more demanding than this" (Miller, 2010, 15). "Underlying concern for others," requires that one help people meet their needs, which requires helping them avoid "a significant risk of worsening" their lives (Miller, 2001, 15). Besides self-reliance, Miller says people need:

> access to a variety of successes in living, for example, the enjoyment, development, and expression of personal affection and friendship; inquiry whose complexity, content, and demands suits their curiosity, interests, temperament, and capacity for learning; meaningful work and reciprocation for others; contributions in cooperation; the fulfillment of responsibilities that grow with growing capacities; the enjoyment of beauty; having fun. (Miller, 2015, 2–3)

He also specifies that mutual concern requires us to help people "to pursue enjoyably and well worthwhile goals with which ... [they] ... intelligently identif[y] and ... cannot readily detach" (Miller, 2015, 2–3). He asserts that these goals can include things like attending a play, purchasing designer clothing, or getting a Ph.D. If the fact that one cannot do these things makes one's life significantly worse, one can pursue them, and one should receive aid in doing so as long that does not require others to sacrifice anything that affects their life quality (Miller, 2010, 9–30).

Miller's account requires both too much and too little. Miller claims that whether or not an agent must sacrifice something depends on what effect this thing has on her quality of life. I believe we sometimes must sacrifice things that affect the quality of our lives, but we need not sacrifice everything that does not impinge on our quality of life. Intuitively, for instance, we may need

---

[31] Miller thinks these requirements only obtain within social democratic societies and we do not have to help others much at all until we fulfill these obligations to compatriots, but I take this to be incompatible with respect for common humanity. See Hassoun (2012); Brock and Hassoun (2013) for discussion of obligations of global justice for some defense of the global scope of claims of common humanity and the previous chapter for an extension of that view.

to sacrifice something as insignificant as our ability to (ever) buy fancy clothes or theater tickets to save someone's life, but basic justice does not require us to help people see Shakespeare or buy designer clothes, even if that will not impinge on the quality of our lives. Miller's account, however, makes the opposite claim.[32]

Those who disagree with my analysis can add a proportionality (or any other) constraint to the minimally good life view, but I believe that to respect everyone's common humanity, we should help everyone live at least minimally good lives if that does not interfere with our own ability to live well enough. Unless better alternatives exist, we can conclude that this book's minimally good life view provides the most plausible account of what we owe to others, and can demand, as a basic minimum in the literature.

3. Conclusion

Let me recap in setting the stage for subsequent chapters' discussion. The previous chapter argued that the minimally good life account provides a plausible standard for basic justice. The next chapter turns to questions about how we should try to help people live well enough. The final chapter considers what we should do when it does not seem we can help everyone or we will lose something at least as significant in the process. This chapter argued against alternative accounts of basic justice. One cannot say we must never sacrifice our entitlements nor that we must only provide life-saving aid in easy rescue cases. We must sometimes do more than our fair share when others fail to help. At the same time, if we are in very non-ideal circumstances, and doing our fair share requires sacrificing our ability to live minimally well, doing so may require too much. It does not matter how far away we are from those who require our aid nor how many others might help. We may also need to sacrifice significantly to help people who are already able to help

---

[32] The minimally good life account does not fall prey to this problem. People who think that they cannot live a minimally good life without ever seeing Shakespeare or purchasing designer clothes almost invariably make a mistake (even if they will have to learn to value differently if they cannot access these things and that will take some time). Of course, Miller focuses on mutual concern and not basic justice, though I focus on basic justice here. In the first part of this chapter, I considered the idea that individuals should not have to do more than their fair share. I do not believe this is the case in our non-ideal world. Still, some may fairly complain that those most able to adjust their aspirations will have to do more on the minimally good life account. Previous chapters suggested that states have primary obligations for providing the requisite assistance. Where primary obligations remain unfulfilled, however, and the more fortunate individuals must bridge the gap, presumably they should still receive compensation for doing more than their fair share.

themselves in some ways but who cannot otherwise live minimally well. Moreover, we must sacrifice some non-altruistically focused pursuits without which we can live minimally well to help others reach this threshold. That said, we need not help others secure all the friendships and other non-altruistically focused pursuits we might justifiably pursue ourselves. Or, at least, basic justice does not require so much. Moreover, we must sometimes help others live at least minimally well even at some net cost. We must sometimes sacrifice things that affect the quality of our lives even though we need not always sacrifice things that do not affect our life quality. Still, to secure basic justice for all, we must only help others live minimally good lives when doing so does not require sacrificing our own ability to live well enough.

5
Helping People Live Minimally Well in Present and Future Generations

1. Introduction

How should we help people live minimally good lives in present and future generations when doing so does not require sacrificing our own ability to live well enough? Answering this question could not be more important.* After all, almost any institutions or policies we might implement impact individuals' ability to live such lives in future, as well as present, generations (Caney, 2009; Gardiner, 2010; Moellendorf, 2014; Hassoun, 2015). Consider, for instance, a policy to reduce climate change. Even if the policy does nothing but prevent some of the deaths and migration that climate change will cause, the policy will likely impact how people in present and future generations fare and even how many people there will be in the future. If we do nothing, climate change will probably kill hundreds of thousands of people (Broome, 2005; IPPC, 2007). It will likely exacerbate extreme weather events like floods and droughts that kill people directly. Droughts and floods may lead to other problems like famine or disease. As sea levels rise, and many coastal areas are submerged, climate change will continue to increase migration (Mayell, 2002; IPPC, 2007). If people in present or future generations die as a result, that will change the size of the population in those generations as well as how people fare. If many of those who die would otherwise have reproduced, or climate change leads to migration that changes the number of children people have, that may also change the size of future generations. So, if a policy reduces climate change-related deaths or prevents mass migration, it will affect how people in present and future generations will fare and even how many people there will be in the future. Similar observations apply to many other policies.

---

* This chapter draws heavily on: Nicole, Hassoun. 2020. "Aiding the Poor in Present and Future Generations: Some Reflections on a Simple Model." *Oxford Handbook on Global Justice*, ed. Thom Brooks. Oxford: Oxford University Press and Nicole, Hassoun. 2024. "Global Health Impact: Human Rights, Access to Medicines, and Measurement." *Developing World Bioethics* 24 (1): 37–48.

For simplicity, and because the arguments in this portion of the book may well apply irrespective of one's account of the threshold for a basic minimum, this chapter will refer to the help we might provide people in securing what they need for a basic minimum as *aid*. Moreover, it will suppose that individuals' levels of *need* correspond to how far they fall below the threshold and assume full interpersonal comparisons of these needs.[1] Finally, it will refer to the things people require to fulfill needs—e.g. institutions, capabilities, opportunities and resources—etc. as *goods*.

It is worth pausing here, however, to consider how researchers might arrive at concrete, measurable indicators of individuals' life quality using the minimally good life account that would let us see how far below the threshold different people fall. How researchers should construct an index likely depends on their purpose and required degree of accuracy (Pogge, 2009; Subramanian, 1997, Subramanian, 2002; Subramanian, 2006). In some cases, it may suffice to ask people what kinds of lives, in general, they would contently live. For a more accurate measure, researchers may have to ask people to consider whether a broader range of different lives qualify as minimally good. In other cases, we must do further philosophical, as well as empirical, work to develop good measures of individuals' ability to live minimally well. Even if I am right that relationships, pleasures, knowledge, appreciation, and worthwhile activities benefit most individuals, we must consider how each affects individuals' ability to live minimally well (Hassoun, 2020a). What kinds of relationships and pleasures matter?[2] How should we evaluate their quality? What constitutes knowledge, valuable achievement, worthwhile activity, and so forth? Moreover, researchers must explain how to compare each of the things that contribute to individuals' ability to live minimally well to generate an index that measures how people generally fare overall. There is a lot of room for future research, but I set these questions aside here and simply suppose that we might eventually arrive at a good enough approximation for allocating aid based on the principles defended below.

This chapter argues that in present generations we should both prioritize the least well-off and try to help a greater number of people, but in future generations we only have to help as many people as possible (whenever doing

---

[1] For one way of doing this see Hare (1981). Some work on theory of mind may add to Hare's account by helping to explicate the process by which such comparisons are made. See Goldman (1993); Gopnik and Wellman (1992). In any case, I leave it to future research to determine whether this chapter's conclusions can be weakened considering whatever incomparability might remain.

[2] Some suggest pleasure is just desire fulfillment, others that it is a felt evaluation, and yet others that it is a simple unanalyzable feature of experience that makes the experience attractive (Heathwood, 2006).

so does not require sacrificing our own ability to live well enough—though, hereafter, I leave this constraint implicit throughout) (Hassoun, 2009, 259–260).[3] Unlike many consequentialist theories, I just aim here to provide some guidance for choosing between policies for aiding those in present and future generations where we can only do a limited amount of good for people who require assistance in living minimally good lives. Principles for arbitrating between such policies need not help us decide between all possible policies that impact such people. They are not supposed to answer questions about potentially impermissible tradeoffs like: Can we sacrifice one person's ability to live minimally well to help those who can already live well enough? Can we allow one person to remain below the threshold to stop several others from falling below it?

Even questions like "Should we choose a policy that helps some people in present generations live minimally well or one under which people in the future would do better?" may be otiose when there is enough for all. For the failure to live minimally well is, presumably, a bad thing we should eliminate if we can.[4] As the next chapter suggests, we often assume too quickly that we have to make hard choices that keep some from getting what they need to live well enough.[5] Still, if there is not enough for all, this chapter argues that there is reason to prioritize the least well-off in all generations and help as many as possible in present generations.

2. Principles for Aiding Those in Present Generations

Although some principles that might guide aid distribution are deontological (Kamm, 2006), the best-known accounts of how we should help people in present and future generations are consequentialist. Maximizing consequentialists might suggest that we should just distribute aid most efficiently. That is, assuming a single unit of aid alleviates a single unit of need for all people, we should provide as much aid as possible, it does not matter how this aid is distributed. Prioritarians on the other hand believe that it matters that we help those who are less well-off. However, prioritarian principles often do not

---

[3] For further defense see Hassoun (2009). For discussion of how we should help those in future generations see Hassoun (2020d).
[4] Those who think some need is acceptable can limit their attention to desperate, involuntary deprivation.
[5] There is some evidence in behavioral economics that we fail to search long enough in looking for solutions to all kinds of problems (Bearden et al., 2005).

just prioritize alleviating needs in proportion to their weight, they give more than proportional weight to helping the less well-off. Others suggest different principles for distribution (Benbaji, 2006; Shields, 2018; Huseby, 2020). Some introduce multiple different thresholds and prioritize weighted need alleviation only among those below each threshold level or give equal weight to alleviating all needs.[6]

Consider one prioritarian argument against utilitarianism—Thomas Nagel's famous thought experiment. This thought experiment illustrates the prioritarian intuition that it is better to enable less well-off people to secure necessary goods: Barring threshold effects, Nagel suggests that parents should decide to help their sick child over their healthy one, even if the healthy child will benefit more from what his or her parents can do (Nagel, 1995). If prioritarianism is correct, it would suggest pursuing those policies that have the best consequences for those who are less well-off. It might, for instance, suggest doing more scientific research on those genetic diseases that impact the least well-off the most. In any case, many sufficientarians endorse prioritarianism (Benbaji, 2006).

Roger Crisp defends prioritarianism this way: He says that an impartial compassionate spectator would care not only about how much welfare (or good) exists but also about its distribution. The spectator would be motivated by concern for individuals and put herself into the shoes of all affected. So, Crisp claims that the spectator would be most concerned with the least well-off. After some sufficiency threshold, however, this concern would give out. Concern for others' headaches would count as mere benevolence on Crisp's account. Though, he also says that compassion extends beyond fulfilling even non-basic (e.g. resource) needs (Crisp, 2006, 258–259). More precisely, after considering potential distributions in a wide range of cases, Crisp endorses:

The Compassion Principle: absolute priority is to be given to benefits to those below the threshold at which compassion enters. Below the threshold, benefiting people matters more the worse off those people are, the more of those people there are, and the greater the size of the benefit in question. Above the threshold, or in cases concerning only trivial benefits below the threshold, no priority is to be given. (Crisp, 2006, 258)

---

[6] Nielsen and Axelsen specify, for instance, that we should ensure that everyone secures *equal* social and political capabilities. They also explain why we should limit inequality in capabilities that affect agency. Finally, they argue that people require different amounts of the things that ensure capabilities to fulfill needs (Nielsen and Axelsen, 2016, 12). Although this does not quite tell us how we should prioritize helping people below the various thresholds, it goes some way towards doing so.

Below the threshold, I believe Crisp intends to adopt a prioritarian principle.

Arguments for prioritarianism are most compelling when there are no special entitlements in the cases at hand. Many hold that parents have special obligations to their offspring that, for instance, allow them to neglect some impartial reasons in favor of helping others' sick children first. Similarly, some believe people have stronger obligations to compatriots than outsiders (Blake, 2001; Brock, 2009). Still, when there are no such special obligations in play, and we are just concerned to evaluate policies insofar as they aid those in need, prioritarianism is plausible.[7]

I have argued elsewhere, however, that prioritarianism should be modified so that it also considers the fact that it matters how many people we help in present generations (Hassoun, 2009). Although I will not make the case in great detail here, the problem with prioritarianism, when it is specified in the usual ways, is roughly this: It suggests it can be acceptable to ignore an arbitrarily large amount of need for an arbitrarily large number of better-off people to help the least well-off. To illustrate why this is unintuitive, suppose the prioritarian adopts some particular weighting schema. Suppose, for instance, that the prioritarian thinks we should allocate in proportion to need and one unit of necessary good alleviates one unit of need. Suppose, further, that the weight given to fulfilling a unit of need for a person equals the number of units the person needs before receiving the unit. So, for instance, giving a person three units below the threshold three units of necessary good yields a score of six—three points for alleviating the first unit, two points for alleviating the second unit, and one point for alleviating the third unit of need. Here is a diagram to illustrate how the weighting system works where the dotted line is the minimally good life threshold; the height of the boxes indicates the amount of goods the person has and the distance from the threshold indicates their need.

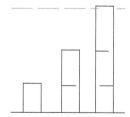

Fig. 1 Good and needs

---

[7] Prioritarianism is a kind of egalitarian concern that should be distinguished from concern for inequality. On inequality see Temkin (1993).

104 A MINIMALLY GOOD LIFE

Now suppose that we must choose how to allocate 100 units of necessary good between 200 people. Finally, suppose that 199 people need only one unit of necessary good but the last person needs 100 units. Here the width of the box is proportional to the number of people, the height to their goods, and the distance below the threshold to their needs.

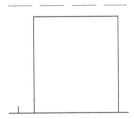

Fig. 2 Helping many

The problem is that alleviating the first unit of the last person's need is 100 times as good as completely alleviating any other person's need (100*1 = 100(1*1)). So, helping the least well-off person secure a single unit would be better than helping 99 other people secure a single unit each.[8] If the prioritarian does not think this is unintuitive, it is possible to create similar cases where this weighting schema suggests neglecting the needs of thousands or millions to help a single (much more) poorly-off person just a bit. Simply by multiplying the needs in the example above by any constant, we can also make the amount that the better-off need in the example arbitrarily large.

It should be easy for the reader to demonstrate that similar problems arise for other seemingly intuitive weighting schemas, so it is plausible that triage is sometimes required even when it does not alleviate the greatest amount of weighted need. Triage requires helping those who have great needs but not those who need the most first (even if the neediest could be helped). One way to justify policies that effectively require triage is by appealing to this principle: We should try to help *as many people as possible* meet their needs even if we cannot alleviate them completely.[9] In some situations, it is better to help a greater number than to help the least well-off, *even if helping the least well-off*

---

[8] This does, of course, presume that there is some significance to the threshold for need drawn on resources, welfare, or whatnot—that it matters if some cannot secure what they need. The case is not like a choice between giving the least well-off a little bit of food and giving 99 other people a bit of dessert.

[9] Again, need is supposed to be significant here, we are not concerned with helping people attain luxuries but with helping them avoid severe deprivation that, undermines their ability to live even minimally well.

is better on a prioritarian weighting schema. This principle expresses a concern for the separateness of persons. If each person matters, we should not just care about fulfilling as much (even appropriately weighted) need as possible; we should care about helping each person.[10] The fact that some have greater (even appropriately weighted) needs cannot always trump the fact that there are others in need. People merit respect as separate individuals.[11] Consider: it seems plausible that it is not the existence of necessary goods (welfare, capabilities, or whatnot) per se that matters. It matters that people have necessary goods (welfare, capabilities, or whatever). Similarly: the idea here is not that helping a greater number of people is better for that reason. Rather, the idea is that each person matters and, since people matter equally, we should try to help as many people as possible.

One might object that prioritarianism already includes a concern for helping a greater number of people. One might argue that the best way of looking at the prioritarian weighting system, it balances the number of people helped versus the amount of need people have.

This is simply not the case. Prioritarianism just tells us to weight individuals' needs and then minimize the sum of weighted need.[12] The number helped does not enter into this equation. It should be clear that the number of people helped does not matter on prioritarianism when one reflects on the fact that,

---

[10] Though, the account of the separateness of persons at issue is different than the account implicit in views which give everyone a veto over alternative distributions. Still, caring about the number of people affected does not preclude other moral concerns (for groups as well as individuals).

[11] This is obviously not the end of the debate on this issue. There are many potential ways of understanding the separateness of persons. Here I suppose prioritarians, like utilitarians, provide just "a principle for weighing individuals' claims one against the other (Segall, 2019, 146). It is the exclusive focus on *claims* as opposed to *persons* that is problematic and that makes it difficult for these theories to distinguish between interpersonal and intrapersonal tradeoffs (where intuitively many think we cannot weight claims the same way because in interpersonal cases we are deciding between different people's claims). Utilitarians normally say that everyone counts for one and none for more than one on their view, but that is not strictly true. "On utilitarianism *everyone's welfare* counts for one" (emphasis added) (Segall, 2019, 146). Similarly, prioritarians will likely reply that their theory does account for the separateness of persons because each person counts for one and no one for more than one, but again people do not count at all on the theory. It is only their needs that count. The pure aggregative aspect of prioritarianism—even below the threshold—simply maximize the satisfaction of weighted need no matter how it is distributed. Giving some weight to numbers helped is one way of making sure that people count and including some concern for the separateness of persons in a distributive principle. At a minimum, concern for the separateness of persons requires helping a greater number when choosing between situations with an equal total amount of appropriately weighted need alleviated. Though I have argued that numbers should count in other circumstances too, note that if we give weight to helping a greater number only in cases where the total appropriately weighted need alleviated is the same, prioritarians will not object to the principle. Note, also, that if this is how one weights helping a greater number, one will choose to help some people less to help a greater number, but not at the cost of alleviating less weighted need.

[12] On standard construals of prioritarianism, the weighting function must be strictly decreasing and strictly convex in capabilities, welfare, or whatnot. For a detailed discussion of prioritarian weighting and value functions, see Lumer (2005).

holding weighted need constant, prioritarinaism will never say it is better to help a greater number of people. This is so even in choosing between a policy that alleviates a great amount of need for one person and another that alleviates the same amount of weighted need but helps many still quite poorly-off people.[13]

If these arguments are correct (for further defense, see Hassoun (2009)), at least in a single (present) generation (with a constant size population), there is reason to temper prioritarianism with a concern for helping a greater number of people and endorse what I call the *effectiveness principle* (Hassoun, 2009).[14]

On the *effectiveness principle*, we should (1) rank distributions by how much prioritarian weighted need they alleviate (as Crisp does), but we should also rank them by how many people they help. Finally, we weight (1) alleviating prioritarian weighted need and (2) helping a greater number against each other to arrive at an overall evaluation. On my view, one might reasonably give different weight to (1) and (2), or at least we must reflect further to arrive at plausible weights.[15] Still, on the effectiveness principle, we must alleviate prioritarian weighted need and try to help a greater number of people (Hassoun, 2009, 259–260).[16]

I believe that we must care about helping as many as possible to respect the separateness of persons—helping each person must at least count for something (Hassoun, 2009), but David Miller and Gillian Brock critique the

---

[13] Nor should one object that it is only the size of the loss to an individual that matters, not numbers helped (Taurek, 1977). Even if we could not compare the size of losses between people, we can easily compare the number of people with losses. Moreover, we can suppose that the losses people below the threshold experience that affect their ability to live minimally well have significance. So, we should care about preventing or redressing each because we should care about the loss to each person. This, I propose, is a better way of accounting for the intuition that "persons should be regarded as persons, rather than objects" than by suggesting that the number of people helped does not count (though I also happen to think we can compare the amount of good we can do for each person and that that matters too) (Sanders, 1988). People are not mere vessels for goods.

[14] Some sufficientarians also suppose that prioritarianism does express concern for the number of people helped. For instance, Huseby (2020) cares about helping as many people as possible and about helping the worst-off and, like many prioritarians, he seems to think prioritarianism expresses concern for both the numbers helped and helping the worst-off. I have demonstrated that prioritarianism does not include concern for the number of people helped and have offered a theory that does so.

[15] The two propositions that make up the effectiveness principle can conflict. Sometimes we must choose between helping a greater number of people and helping those who are worse-off and, on any plausible way of specifying prioritarianism, we also need to specify how much priority we should give to the worse-off. This, however, is not a problem for present purposes. Rather, it is part of the reason this chapter's conclusions are so significant. As Appendix III demonstrates, even from such incomplete and underspecified principles (the effectiveness principle and a few others suggested in the literature), we can still arrive at a significant partial ranking over all potential policies in the simple model it lays out.

[16] I think the principle is appropriate for guiding how we should help people below the threshold for a minimally good life in present generations. For further defense see Hassoun (2009). For further discussion of how we should help those in future generations see Hassoun (2020d).

effectiveness principle by pointing out that it may make matters worse in one of the cases that motivate Crisp to propose his new alternative: A needs threshold focused on addressing the urgent needs of underserved populations first and foremost before excess resources are allocated to the luxuries demanded by those better-off, based on the weighted priority principle (Brock and Miller, 2019). If "enough people can have minor headaches relieved at the cost of denying someone a kidney transplant, the principle will advocate doing that" (Miller, 2020b). As they put it:

> Where the weighted priority principle can be faulted for allowing many relatively minor need claims to outweigh the more serious claims of a few badly-off people, adding in a component that gives credit simply for the number of people who are aided only adds to the problem. (Brock and Miller, 2019)

So, Miller and Brock do not believe the effectiveness principle improves over the weighted priority principle.

I do not believe the effectiveness principle falls prey to the worry Miller and Brock highlight (recall that the needs at issue are significant as we are only considering how to aid those below the threshold) but, even if it does, we might overcome the objection.[17] Crisp responds by excluding trivial needs from the equation he proposes. The effectiveness principle's weighted needs calculation plausibly includes this restriction too. Only needs that impact individuals' ability to live well enough count.[18] After all, we are considering aiding only those who cannot live even a minimally good life, not helping some get caviar and plover's eggs. Still, helping a great number of people live well enough could trump concern for helping a few very poorly-off individuals on the effectiveness principle just because helping a greater number matters even in some cases where we will alleviate more weighted need by helping fewer worse-off people (Widerquist, 2010; Knight, 2021b).[19] I believe we should endorse this result as one way of showing "respect for a person [is] to attend practically to their needs, even if only in a small way" (Brock and Miller, 2019). Sometimes we must help a greater number because each individual matters.

---

[17] Also see Fleurbaey and Tungodden (2010) on the tyranny of aggregation vs. the tyranny of non-aggregation.
[18] Although people may need many small pleasures to live well enough overall, something must have significant value for it alone to have an appreciable impact on overall life quality.
[19] Like Crisp's alternative, even the effectiveness principle's first part is not straightforwardly utilitarian as those with greater needs merit more weight.

Miller and Brock ask, however, if we can respect people if "everyone's claims are properly *considered* by whoever is performing an allocation, even if the end result is that some people get nothing because whatever claim[s] they might have ... [are] justifiably outweighed by the stronger claims of other people" (Brock and Miller, 2019). Moreover, they say "one might question whether the numbers being aided has the deeper significance that ... [I suggest], as opposed merely to providing evidence that no-one's claim has been overlooked" (Brock and Miller, 2019).

I believe we should give some weight to helping each person who cannot live minimally well, even when we should give much more weight to helping the worse-off. Often doing so will mean we should give each person something even if we cannot give them much because many have greater needs. Consider an illustration. Suppose an aid worker is tasked with delivering extra blankets to a local hospital in a war zone. Only the worst-off people are hospitalized but many people around the hospital are severely wounded. The mother of one such child asks for a blanket. It seems the aid worker should give the mother the blanket even though that will delay their arrival by a few minutes and might mean someone who is even worse-off does not receive help as quickly.[20] In these cases, we cannot just say we have considered helping someone and decided that others need more. We have given the person in need nothing that satisfies their need unless they need recognition.

I believe respecting the separateness of persons requires trying to help each individual (who has unmet needs) and not just fulfilling needs qua needs. Consider how some population ethicists say we should make people happy, not make happy people. People are not just vessels for welfare or life quality (Narveson, 1967). At least those who share this intuition should agree that we should not just look at people's needs for a similar reason (doing so treats people as mere vessels for needs satisfaction). We can avoid that problem if we give helping each person some independent weight in our calculations. This may *explain* the empirical evidence showing people "favour allocations that are inclusive in the sense that each recipient gets *something* even though their claims are in other ways quite different" (Miller, 2020b).[21] There is also

---

[20] Of course, if providing the blanket meant letting someone else die, the aid worker could refuse; but each person matters, and we should give some weight to helping each even when we are choosing how to distribute scarce goods to people who are all below the threshold.

[21] I did not intend the idea that "institutions should try to help as many people as possible meet their needs" (Hassoun, 2009, 258) to mean "meet their needs in full" (Miller, 2020b). I attach no special importance to helping people fully satisfy their needs for living a good enough life as opposed to helping those further below the threshold come closer to reaching it (rather I give more weight to helping those further below the threshold). Furthermore, I believe the effectiveness principle is better

empirical evidence that people sometimes favor helping a greater number over alternative distributions that fulfill more need (Hassoun, 2009). One can disagree and accept the minimally good life account of what we owe and can reasonably demand while endorsing a different theory of how we should help people below the threshold. Still, in what follows, I will suppose the effectiveness principle is correct as far as it goes.

3. Choosing Policies for Aiding People in Future Generations

Most of the work on intergenerational ethics focuses on whether or not it makes sense to talk about the interests, or rights, of future people. Some deny that it makes sense to consider the interests, or rights, of future people because they accept the so-called *non-identity problem* (Parfit, 1984). The basic worry is that if people in future generations cannot be harmed by our actions, it is not clear in what sense they can have interests or rights. It is, moreover, not possible to harm future people. Their very existence depends on present generations' actions. Different people will be born as a result of many of the things present generations do. So, whoever comes into existence who would not have existed but for their action has not been harmed by it.

There are many ways of responding to this problem. Some say that people are harmed if someone brings them into existence in a bad state or below some threshold (Shiffrin, 1999, 120–135; Harman, 2004, 92–93 and 107; Harman, 2009, 139; Rivera-Lopez, 2009, 337). Others argue that there is impersonal value in ensuring that whoever comes into existence does well (Temkin, 1993, 221–227; see also Broome (1992) and Feldman (1995)). Some say we can wrong people whom we have not harmed or point to the importance of acting with due caution or concern (Kavka, 1982, 97 and 104–105; Wasserman, 2005, 132–152). Yet others point out that the notion of harm at issue may be de dicto harm—the idea is that the people who come into existence, whoever they are, can be harmed by present generations' actions (Hare, 2007, 512–523).

Some object to the idea that future people can have rights, or interests, based simply on the fact that they will only exist in the future or on the fact

---

than a principle David Miller considers elsewhere that focuses on (possibly weighted) needs and the proportion of needs alleviated (Hassoun, 2009). It is, of course, important to explain the relative weight of meeting greater needs and helping more people to operationalize the effectiveness principle and in considering its merits and disadvantages.

that their existence is contingent (De George, 1981, 161; see also Macklin (1981), 151–152). Perhaps we should not say people can have rights or interests if they might not even exist or when they do not exist.

The above objections should not limit the scope of our concern for people in future generations. The objections are only compelling insofar as what is at issue is whether future people have interests or rights now. But, when these people come into existence, they will have interests and rights. So, we should consider all our policies' potential impacts on these interests and rights. Moreover, it makes sense to ensure that people's rights to what they need for a minimally good life are fulfilled when they come into existence (Wasserman, 2008, 529–533).

Some try to leverage the non-identity problem to defend their views about whether we should consider the size or composition of future generations in decision-making. David Benatar argues, for instance, that bringing people into existence in the future is wrong given that many people today are not living even minimally good lives. Benatar believes that we do nothing wrong by refraining from bringing people into existence who will have good lives (we do not deny people who exist any pleasure). However, we should not bring people into existence who will suffer (or we wrongly cause suffering). He also argues that most lives are not worth living (Benatar, 2006). Others claim that it is neither better nor worse to bring someone into existence given the non-identity problem because then existence and non-existence are non-comparable. The question of whether either judgment is sound from a "personal point of view" is difficult (Roberts, 2009).[22]

So, although I think there are good ways to overcome the non-identity problem, to avoid a few of these difficulties, the rest of this chapter takes an impersonal perspective. It illustrates how focusing on aiding people below the threshold can help us avoid some of the difficulties in dealing with "different number cases" where what we do will influence the number of people as well as the amount of goods people have (Parfit, 1984). Finally, it will offer some new arguments for how we should think about helping people live minimally good lives in present and future generations. It is impossible to resolve all the debates about these issues in what follows. So, Appendix III contains a model that should be useful for testing different principles, no matter their resolution.

---

[22] Some also consider whether we should only bring into existence the best people and there is a large literature on how to respond to historical injustice (Boonin, 2011). This chapter will not consider either of these issues.

The Number in Existence in Future Generations

It should be clear from the preceding discussion that, to arrive at well-justified principles for arbitrating between policies that do different amounts of good for people in future (as well as present) generations, we do not only need to know how good it is to help people with different levels of need. We also need to know whether the number of people in a population matters. Different policies, from investing in solar research to offering genetic counseling or therapies, may change future population size. So, what follows will, first, consider whether the number of people in a population matters. The next section will, then, consider how we should think about helping a greater number of future people and how we should think about meeting their needs.

First, it may be reasonable to treat existing and future people differently (this, itself, should be a surprising and interesting conclusion). Recall, that falling below the minimally good life threshold is, presumably, a bad thing. This fact has some pretty straightforward implications for how we should think about bringing more people into future generations below the threshold— there is at least one reason not to do so—those people will be below the threshold for living even a minimally good life. On the other hand, we cannot affect the birth of existing people (and it is rarely, if ever, possible to reduce the number of existing people in a morally acceptable way). If this reasoning is sound, there is reason to accept:

(1) No Mere Addition of the Poorly-Off: As long as there will be some people, it can be worse to add people who do not live minimally good lives to a population.[23]

This proposition does not imply that the relevant people's lives are not worth living. Rather, even some of those who cannot live minimally good lives can live quite valuable lives once they exist.

Nor does No Mere Addition of the Poorly-Off entail that we should prevent people who cannot live minimally good lives from reproducing, or even prevent people from reproducing who would have children who would not live minimally well. Doing so would, presumably, violate existing individuals'

---

[23] This principle is much weaker than the claim that we should be neutral about "making happy people" (Broome, 2005, 401). However, I am not convinced of his argument against this claim; see Broome (2005).

112 A MINIMALLY GOOD LIFE

rights (Sen, 1999). We might, instead, implement other policies to ensure that whoever comes into existence lives well enough (Sen, 1999).

Moreover, a stronger claim that it is not always better to bring people into future generations seems plausible. It seems hard to deny that—as long as there will be some people in future generations—it is not always better, it may even be worse, to have a greater number of people in a population (Rolston, 2008). Presumably, it would be better to have more people in some situations. Perhaps we will need to increase our population size at some point to maintain a decent standard of living for all. Sometimes, however, it is worse to have more people—people will fare worse if we overpopulate the planet (Hardin, 2002).[24] So, we might accept this axiom:

(2) No Mere Addition: As long as there will be some people, it can be *worse* to add some (even sufficiently well-off) people to a population.

We might also use a version of Parfit's paradox (using goods rather than welfare, in particular) to motivate the No Mere Addition axiom (Parfit, 1984). Consider three populations:

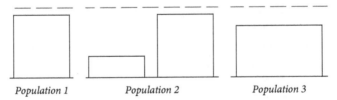

Population 1   Population 2   Population 3

Fig. 3 Parfit's paradox

Again the dotted line is the minimally good life threshold, the width of the boxes indicates the size of that segment of the population, and the height indicates the amount of goods that segment of the population has.[25] Population 1 might have

---

[24] Note that population seems to matter in both cases just because of how it impacts how people will fare. I doubt this will always be the case—perhaps our population size matters for environmental reasons.

[25] Looking at these diagrams one might wonder how to measure needs—even for a single person at a time and over time. Recall that, on the minimally good life view, it matters how people fare at particular times in their lives as well as over time. We are located in the present and although we can often affect how some individuals' lives go overall and compensate some people for deprivations in the past, we often care about how people are faring right now irrespective of how they may have fared in the past or might fare in the further future. At a time, we might simply look at deprivation from the minimally good life threshold. Of course, how deprived a particular person is will be a complicated value judgment on my view and it may be informed, but not determined, by resource limitations (whether others have enough effects how much it is reasonable for me to claim, for instance) as well as a

to choose between two policies—say Free Trade in which case Population 2 will result, and Constrained Trade in which case Population 3 may result.

Suppose one rejects No Mere Addition and accepts:

(3) Mere Addition: The mere addition of people with lives worth living is not worse (other things equal), than failing to bring these people into existence.

It follows from this axiom that Population 2 is not worse than Population 1 (Population 2 merely contains some additional people with lives worth living, though they are below the threshold for a minimally good life). Next, one might suggest that Population 3 is better than Population 2 and, hence, better than Population 1. For Population 3 is the same size as Population 2 but everyone is equal and has at least the average amount of goods in Population 2, maybe more. So, by transitivity, Population 3 is better than Population 1. If one has trouble seeing why Population 3 is better than Population 2, compare:

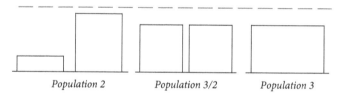

Fig. 4 Parfit's paradox elaborated

Population 3/2 is better than Population 2 because it has the same number of people in it and they are, on average, better-off. But Population 3/2 is equal to

---

person's psychology, circumstances, and history. But it seems that, for a single individual, we might arrive at an evaluation of how someone fares by putting ourselves into her shoes and considering whether we would now be content to live her life. Perhaps we could also do so counter-factually for her life at other times. And, if not, we might consider how far below the threshold the person falls (what we would need to be content to live her life at that time). We might arrive at similar overall evaluations of life quality. But what is the relationship between these judgments? Some people assume additivity in estimating total life quality (over one's complete life) compared to an ideal threshold. If this is right, and if we suppose that total life quality is not something different from life quality at all the times in one's life (because we do not want to double count total life quality and life quality at different times in one's life), we might end up with a measure of the quality of their life over time and total deprivation relative to the threshold from judgments of how people fare at all particular times in their life. But life quality might not be additive in this way. Perhaps we need to weight effects on total life quality of momentary life quality at different times differently or consider how life quality at some times affects life quality at others. Here I set aside these questions in considering how to prioritize helping different people who might fall further below the threshold than others at different points of time assuming we have a good way of understanding their lifetime need.

Population 3—the merging of the two sub-populations in moving from 3/2 to 3 makes no difference to our evaluation of these populations. So, a situation with a greater number of people but fewer necessary goods can be better than a situation with fewer people who all have more necessary goods. One can follow Parfit in iterating the example to arrive at the repugnant conclusion. Namely, that a situation with many people whose lives are barely worth living is better than a situation with a modest population containing only people with much better lives—or who are, at least, a lot better-off (Parfit, 1984). One might take this as a reason to reject the innocuous-sounding Mere Addition axiom. One way of avoiding Mere Addition just is to accept No Mere Addition.[26]

Of course, this argument is not definitive (though it is compelling). One could also avoid Parfit's paradox by denying that Population 3/2 is equal to 3 or that 3/2 (or 3) is better than Population 2 (and one cannot avoid Parfit's paradox if one is an average utilitarian). It is very hard to see how one could reject the claim that Population 3/2 is equal to Population 3. One might argue that neither Population 3/2 nor Population 3 is better than Population 2 even though people in 3/2 and 3 are, on average, better-off than people in 2 (and all of these populations have the same number of people). It is not clear whether this move will work. Perhaps one could refuse to endorse the claim that Population 3/2 and Population 3 are better than Population 2 because it requires one to endorse what may be impermissible tradeoffs. This would be quite plausible if 3 and 3/2 came from 2 (by making some better-off and others worse-off). But this need not be the case.[27] They could be the populations of two completely isolated islands.

---

[26] Alternately, one can accept a stronger principle like Population Neutrality: As long as there will be some people, the number of people in future generations does not matter intrinsically (non-instrumentally). Though, numbers can impact how people fare, so numbers matter instrumentally. We have reason to care about those who will be around when they are around, but there may be no non-instrumental reason to bring them into existence. This may not allow one to avoid Parfit's paradox, however. Further, see Broome (2005).

[27] There may be an impartial sense in which 3 and 3/2 are better than 2 without it necessarily being permissible to move from 2 to 3/2 or 3. If one who took this line did endorse Mere Addition one would say that a repugnant world is better than a world like 2 but would not have to say that we should, therefore, choose a repugnant world over a world like 2 (there may be a better alternative). Since this still seems quite implausible, however, there is reason to reject Mere Addition and accept No Mere Addition. Moreover, it is especially hard to see why 3/2 and 3 would be impartially better than 2. Further argument is necessary for No Mere Addition, however, as one could suggest that there is a threshold distinct from the threshold below which people's lives are very bad but still worth living and it is at that level at which No Mere Addition is true. This debate hangs on the nature of deprivation about which this chapter is attempting to stay relatively neutral.

One need not accept No Mere Addition in what follows, this chapter will just assume that No Mere Addition of Poorly-Off is defensible. To accept No Mere Addition, of the Poorly-Off one need not endorse any complete axiological theory—though some theories, like critical-level utilitarianism may entail the falsity of the view (Blackorby et al., 1995, 1303–1320). On critical level utilitarianism, there is a single level (of welfare or life quality) at which the addition of a person is neutral, below that level it is worse to add people to the population and above that level it is better. If people are above the critical level even though they cannot live minimally well, critical level utilitarianism provides a reason to reject No Mere Addition of Poorly-Off but if the threshold captures individuals' ability to live minimally well, critical level utilitarians can endorse my arguments. Critical level utilitarianism is, however, subject to a version of the repugnant conclusion above the critical level threshold and those who accept No Mere Addition of the Poorly-Off need not necessarily endorse critical level utilitarianism.[28]

One might object to No Mere Addition of the Poorly-Off by arguing that there *is* something intrinsically better about adding a poorly-off person to a population. To do so, one might adapt Gustaf Arrhenius' argument for the conclusion that it is always better to exist (especially if an existing person has some positive amount of goods). Arrhenius's argument proceeds primarily by criticizing the alternatives—that it is worse to exist or that existence and non-existence are equally valuable or incommensurable.

There is an important ambiguity in each of these statements, however. It can be better or worse *if* a person exists (in an impersonal sense) for reasons that may have nothing to do with how that person fares. Alternatively, it can be better or worse *for* that person if they exist (in a personal sense).[29] I do not believe that it is generally worse *for* (even very poorly-off) people to exist in a personal sense—they can have lives worth living.[30] The claim that there is nothing better about (or that there is a reason against) bringing some (poorly-off) people into existence does *not* imply that it is, normally, worse *for* these

---

[28] Critical-level utilitarianism may fall prey to a version of what Gustaf Arrhenius calls the *sadistic conclusion* on which it can be better to bring a few people into existence well below the threshold than to bring a greater number into existence just below the threshold (Arrhenius, 2020; Subramanian, 2023).

[29] To see the distinction, consider a case where adding someone to a population who will fare well enough strains the environment's capacity to provide more than a basic minimum for all. If this person's only alternative is non-existence, it is not worse for them to exist though it may be better for everyone else (and overall) not to bring them into existence.

[30] It is also not clearly worse if poor people exist—No Mere Addition of Poorly-Off is about the value of actions—it is generally worse to bring poor people into existence without reason.

people to exist; it does not imply that these peoples' welfare (e.g.) is lower, nor too low, if they exist. So, let us grant that it is *not* generally worse *for* (even very poorly-off) people to exist and consider whether Arrhenius' argument can establish that it is better to exist by showing that existence and non-existence are not equally valuable or all things considered incommensurable (in an impersonal sense).[31]

Granting that it is not generally worse *for* (even very poorly-off) people to exist, if existence and non-existence are not equally valuable or incommensurable, on Arrhenius' view, it is supposed to follow that it is better to exist (irrespective of a person's need). Arrhenius says that the view that existence and non-existence are equally valuable or incommensurable yields a few radically implausible conclusions when combined with what he calls the Person Affecting Restriction (also see Temkin (1993) and Boonin (2011)).

The Person Affecting Restriction says:

(a) If outcome A is better (worse) than B, then A is better (worse) than B for at least one individual.
(b) If outcome A is better (worse) than B for someone but worse (better) for no one, then A is better (worse) than B. (Arrhenius, 2011, 160)

Arrhenius says the Person Affecting Restriction and the idea that existence and non-existence are incommensurable (or, presumably, equally valuable) yield Strict Comparativism. Strict Comparativism (put here in terms of need rather than welfare) is the idea that only the needs of those who exist in all of the situations we are considering matter. We do not have to consider the needs of those who exist in only some situations (Arrhenius, 2011, 164). Arrhenius thinks Strict Comparativism is implausible. To see why, consider Future Bliss and Future Hell—we can suppose everyone is below the needs threshold in this diagram but only the x people exist in both outcomes, the y and z people are potential future people:

---

[31] Though I believe Arrhenius is primarily concerned with the latter type of claim in this section of his book, he does consider the *if* claim in examining what he calls asymmetrical views (Arrhenius, 2011, 167–168). On these views, it is only worse if those with negative welfare (or life quality) exist but neutral whether those with positive welfare (or life quality) exist. I do not believe anything this chapter says commits its proponents to this view. So, I will not discuss the issue at length due to space constraints (for some discussion, see the note below). However, even if one believes this chapter's argument commits us to a corresponding kind of (need) asymmetry (on which it is normally neutral if those not in need are brought into existence but bad if needy people are brought into existence), I do not think that the problems Arrhenius raises for asymmetrical views will plague this view.

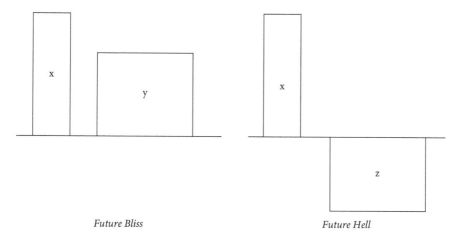

Fig. 5 Future Bliss and Future Hell

Since only the x people exist in both outcomes, Future Bliss is as good as Future Hell on Strict Comparativism (the x people's needs are equal in both situations and Strict Comparativism says only these people's needs count) (Arrhenius, 2011, 166). Arrhenius says this is implausible. Strict Comparativism also requires rejecting a principle Arrhenius believes is quite compelling:

> The Egalitarian Weak Dominance Principle: If population A is a perfectly equal population of the same size as population B and every person in A has at least as high welfare as every person in B, and some people in A have higher welfare than some people in B, then A is better than B, other things being equal. (Arrhenius, 2011, 165)

So, Arrhenius says, it is not the case that existence and non-existence are equally valuable or incommensurable. Arrhenius concludes that existence is better than non-existence.

Note, first, that even if Future Bliss and Future Hell are *future* situations, the principles this chapter endorses would suggest choosing Future Bliss over Future Hell if we had to decide between them (assuming all are below the threshold).[32] There is no immediate tension between this conclusion and the view that it is not better that a greater number of poorly-off people exist.

---

[32] Assume here that we represent everything in positive (though potentially very whole small numbers) as negative numbers and fractions can yield odd answers in population ethics.

The relevant principles sufficient to support this conclusion might be conditional ones like this: if more future people exist, it is better if they have less need rather than more. So, there is reason to believe that there is a problem with Arrhenius' argument.[33] This problem may stem from the ambiguity in Arrhenius' claims that it is better or worse to exist or that existence and non-existence are equally valuable or incommensurable. As noted above, the claim that there is nothing better about (or that there is a reason against) bringing some (poorly-off) people into existence does *not* imply that it is, normally, *worse for* these people to exist (that is, that these people fare worse if they exist). Nor does it imply that existence and non-existence are equally valuable or incommensurable *for* these people. Saying that there is nothing better about (or that there is a reason against) bringing some (poorly-off) people into existence (everything considered) is compatible with it being better for these people if they exist. The necessary claim for this chapter's argument is a ceteris paribus claim about what kind of future we should choose, not a claim about how individuals will (or would) fare. That said, if Arrhenius' argument is correct, it does pose a challenge to the conclusion that there is nothing better about (or that there is a reason against) bringing some (poorly-off) people into existence. It provides a reason to think bringing more poorly-off people into existence is a good thing—it is better for these people to exist. However, to make his case Arrhenius' simply assumes the Person Affecting Restriction.[34]

---

[33] Consider Broome's argument against this proposal. Broome considers a version of the Mere Addition Paradox where most of the individuals in A have 4 units of good and one has 5. He then considers an otherwise identical situation, B, where the individual with 5 has 6 and there is an additional person who has 1 unit of good. Finally, C is the same as B but the person with 5 only has 4 and the person with 1 also has 4. He says that A is equally as good as B and C for the last person (who does not exist in A). B is better than A for the second to last person (who has 6 rather than 5) and A is better than C for that person (who has 5 rather than 4). So B is overall better than A, which is better than C. This, however, violates transitivity of betterness. We can represent the situations this way:

A = (4,4, . . . 4,5,*)
B = (4,4, . . . 4,6,1)
C = (4,4, . . . 4,4,4)

The problem with this argument is that it is not clearly the case that A is equally as good as B and C for the last person (who does not exist in A). It is true that A is neither better nor worse for that person than B and A is neither better nor worse for that person than C. But this tells us nothing about how B and C compare to each other. If either B or C will be the case, it is better for the last person to be in C than in B. So C is impersonally better than C in one respect—because the last person will be better-off in C than in B. A is incomparable with B and C for the last person. Nevertheless, C is clearly better than B for that person and better impersonally in one respect. That is, C>B for the last person. So even though B>A>C for the second to last person, it is not clearly the case that B>A>C all things considered.

[34] Moreover, even setting worries about semantic coherence aside, it does seem odd to say I am better-off existing since there is nothing to compare my state to if I do not exist (or, more precisely, if it is not the case that there is an I that exists).

It seems to me that there is no reason to accept this Restriction. The Person Affecting Restriction rules out views on which more than humans matter, for instance. It is also incompatible with impersonal values like peace or equality—insofar as those things do not impact how individuals fare.[35] If one rejects the Person Affecting Restriction, then one can avoid the conclusions Arrhenius believes are radically implausible and yet hold that it is not always better that poorly-off people exist. Rather, there is some reason against bringing more poorly-off people into existence since need is bad and there is reason to reduce it.[36]

Similarly, one cannot object that it would be better to bring a person into existence who would be below the minimally good life threshold for some short period than not to bring that person into existence at all. It is not clear why it would be a good thing to create this kind of need even for a short period.[37] There is at least one reason against bringing a person into existence who would be below the minimally good life threshold for some short period—that would increase deprivation. This point can be put in different ways. If people have a right against being below the threshold, for instance, then one might say this person's right would be violated for at least some period.[38] The next section considers these arguments' consequences for how we should aid those in future generations.

The Number Helped in Future Generations

Consider, then, what we should say about helping people in future generations (again, focusing only on those in need). Most surprisingly, in future generations, it seems nothing is gained by helping a greater number of people—or even one person—if it is possible not to bring them into existence

---

[35] Arrhenius admits this in a note.
[36] Incidentally I am not particularly concerned about the provision of only partial and incomplete principles. Arrhenius is trying to find a complete, consistent population axiology and I am not sure whether that is possible; but perhaps the piece-meal approach demonstrated in this chapter will get us as close as possible.
[37] The concern for separate persons might be used to justify some analogue to concern for numbers here—where each time a person is brought into existence deprived (assuming it could be prevented), that would be a separate mark against a policy. This would seem to provide additional reason against bringing people in need into existence, however. Further, if a policy wrongly brings extra people in need into existence, it would generally be better to help more of those people.
[38] Perhaps this kind of argument would not be successful if entailed by a complete population axiology that had other implausible consequences. Since, however, this chapter does not attempt to provide such an axiology, this form of argument is entirely reasonable (and the fact that this argument form is a good one is a good reason to accept this chapter's methodological approach).

at all.[39] For then, that person, or those people, will be in need for some time until they are helped. Intuitively, it would be better if they did not have to suffer from a lack of necessary goods for that amount of time. It would be better if they just came into existence with those goods. Tradeoffs may be appropriate, however, if we must choose between preventing a person from coming into existence with some need and alleviating a greater amount of need for a person who will come into existence (when s/he does).

One cannot use the preceding observations to argue against helping a greater number in present generations, though a similar argument suggests a distinction between what we should do for existing people from an ex-ante and ex-post perspective. It would be great were there no one we could help in present generations at all because everyone came into existence with whatever we could give them. Nevertheless, we can often help people in present generations (whether that is due to our mistakes in the past or not). So, right now, there is (ceteris paribus) reason to help as many people as possible in present generations.

Finally, note one interesting implication of acknowledging the rights of people in future generations to a basic minimum whenever they come into existence. Contra many so-called *longtermists*, doing so arguably entails that we should not prioritize preventing tragedies that could afflict many in far future generations who need not come into existence at great cost to those in present and near-future generations (e.g. if doing so requires allowing mass starvation, devastation due to climate change, etc.) (see e.g. Ord, 2020). Rather, barring tragic conflicts, we should both prioritize helping the global poor now and ensure everyone who comes into existence in the future has a basic minimum.

Summing Up: How to Think about Numbers in Future Generations

To sum up: Insofar as we can implement policies that affect whether people come into existence in the future with what we could instead give them once they are around, we should:

---

[39] Should we arrive at the same judgments about people who will come into existence relative to different baselines and those who merely might come into existence? And which baselines matter? We can consider, for example, who will exist but for our action or who will exist but for major changes in economic, social, or political conditions. Alternatively, we can consider who will likely exist or what is metaphysically possible. Here I assume that to properly judge individual actions, we should consider what would happen but for our individual decisions (where we can affect the existence of very few people). On the other hand, what policymakers could change easily enough seems to be in play when we are considering decisions at the societal level (where many more different people may be possible or actual).

(4) Minimize Prioritarian-Weighted Need in Future Generations: Given that being below the minimally good life threshold is bad there is, ceteris paribus, a reason to just minimize weighted need in future generations (rather than, say, embrace the Effectiveness Principle for future generations).

For, if neither numbers in existence nor numbers helped matters and there are no special entitlements, it is intuitive that it is only the amount of weighted need poorly-off individuals have that matters.[40]

4. Conclusion

Combining (1) with (4), it should be clear that this chapter has provided some preliminary defense for the following principle for choosing between policies that differentially aid (but do not harm) the poorly-off in present and future generations:

(A) Use resources to minimize weighted need in the future and to reduce weighted need and increase the number helped in the present.

---

[40] This way of putting the point actually goes some ways beyond what this chapter has established in favor of the neutrality assumption even with respect to poorly-off people. If, however, it can be worse to add poorly-off people to a population and allowing that tradeoffs may make it permissible to do so, the idea that we should be neutral about numbers seems like a reasonable background presumption. Moreover, at least insofar as we are certain of our policies' impact on future generations, it is quite plausible that we should minimize weighted need. For, as I hope will become clear upon reading Appendix III, we are making the same kinds of decisions about situations like A and B (below) that we would make for present generations if there were no initial situation (and hence, no number who could be helped).

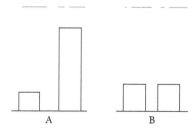

Situation A may be worse than B, though there is less need, because the worse-off are worse-off. There may be 6 units of unmet need in A and 8 in B. The prioritarian intuition is reasonable when there are no differences between situations in terms of the number who could be helped and everyone's claims are equal. Again, see Appendix III for clarification on the basic model supposed here.

That is, in the future, we should have a prioritarian concern for alleviating need and, in the present, we should also consider the number helped. Recall that (1) said we should use resources to reduce weighted need and increase the number helped in present generations and (4) said use resources to minimize weighted need in the future.

This does not provide a complete account of how we should arbitrate between policies that aid the poorly-off, never mind a complete account of intergenerational justice. This principle does not explain the exact weight we should give to minimizing weighted need in present nor future generations. Nor does it explain how either should be weighed against helping a greater number of people in present generations. Some other principles for meeting need are vague. Prioritarianism, for instance, does not tell us *how much* weight to give to helping less well-off people. Unlike prioritarianism, however, the different parts of this chapter's principle might conflict. Nevertheless, I will not attempt to precisify this account of how we should aid the poor further here; rather I refer interested readers to Appendix III where I explain how even such an incomplete account can provide significant guidance for choosing between policies that affect present and future generations in different ways. Further research on how we should choose between policies that impact the poor in present and future generations is pressing and important. To get more guidance, we must answer harder questions about how to deal with tradeoffs between present and future generations and other things that matter. The next chapter turns to these questions.

6
Hope and the Virtue of Creative Resolve

1. Introduction

How can we help people everywhere live minimally good lives in our imperfect world? Vast swaths of humanity live in desperate poverty.* Many suffer from oppression, terrible violence, and disease. Moreover, everyone remains incredibly vulnerable to natural and anthropogenic threats like climate change and pandemics. So, some may deny we should try to help people live minimally well because doing so seems hopeless. Others may worry that, in trying to help others, we will risk our own ability to live well enough. How should we respond to such apparent tragedy?

This chapter argues that by cultivating a new virtue that I call *creative resolve* we can help many people live at least minimally good lives and overcome apparent tragedy together. In a phrase, creative resolve is the disposition to commit, imagine, and act to help people secure the things they need to live well enough insofar as necessary, possible, and otherwise morally permissible (and it can also help us secure other significant moral goods). Even in our tragic world, where millions suffer from desperate poverty, oppression, and violence and we all face existential health and environmental threats, creative resolve helps us secure these goods. Those who have the virtue (1) question limits to the possibility of helping people live minimally well (and securing other significant moral goods). They also (2) seek out creative ways of securing (or better securing) these goods and (3) try to secure them. Of course, if we cannot permissibly help people live well enough, creative resolve does not require us to do so. Nevertheless, this chapter suggests, we should not be too quick to conclude that we cannot help each other live well enough. Rather, hope supports the obligation to have creative resolve and find good ways of overcoming apparent tragedies when we can.

---

* This chapter draws upon the material from Hassoun, Nicole. 2022. "Responding to the Tragedies of Our Time - The Human Right to Health and the Virtue of Creative Resolve." *Global Justice: Theory Practice Rhetoric* 13 (2): 41–59 CC BY 2.0 and Hassoun, Nicole. 2020a. *Global Health Impact: Extending Access on Essential Medicines for The Poor*. Oxford: Oxford University Press. https://www.theglobaljusticenetwork.org/index.php/gjn/article/view/256

Although creative resolve does not appear on canonical lists of the virtues, this chapter explains how the character trait can enhance our lives' value and help us ensure that others live well enough in the face of the terrible problems we face in the twenty-first century—from major pandemics to climate change. To make this case, I argue that when people have the right kind of hope, they *should* have creative resolve and that the virtue embodies a particularly important kind of hope. Doing so helps explain why hope has so much value in human affairs (Bovens, 1999; Moellendorf, 2006; Milona, 2017a; Milona, 2017b; Stockdale, 2021). It helps us respond effectively to complacency, disaffection, and other vices that threaten the very fabric of our relations with others in this rapidly changing world (Bovens, 1999; Walker, 2006; Chignell, 2014; Milona, 2017a; Milona, 2017b). Moreover, I explain how the virtue can help us make progress in securing the things we need to live well enough together.

I will primarily focus on examples of creative resolve in promoting access to basic healthcare throughout for two reasons. First, the COVID-19 pandemic laid bare the myriad ways that health problems can threaten individuals' ability to live well enough. Second, it embodied the kind of tragic collective action problem humanity will have to overcome this century if we hope to help everyone live even minimally good lives. Finally, because I hope that those with different conceptions of virtue ethics can embrace creative resolve, I will try to stay as neutral as I can between different conceptions of virtue in what follows (Hurka, 2003; Swanton, 2013).[1] Those with different conceptions might modify the interpretation of the virtue I offer slightly throughout.

2. Creative Resolve

Before explaining the virtue of creative resolve at more length, let me start with an example: Consider how civil society organizations have fostered hope—exercising the virtue of creative resolve in the face of the global AIDS crisis. By the late 1990s, many people in rich countries could live long, productive lives with HIV due to antiretroviral therapy, but treatment cost

---

[1] Though I agree that virtue concepts must just figure centrally in a theory for it to qualify as a virtue ethics, my conception of virtue ethics is even broader than Christine Swanton's proposal as I would not rule out of court conceptions of the virtue along the lines of Thomas Hurka's virtue consequentialism (Hurka, 2003). For this reason, I offer some consequentialist arguments for the virtue. I also argue that it is often partly constitutive of the (minimally) good life.

US$12,000/per patient per year (Hassoun, 2020a). At the same time, millions died every year from AIDS in Sub-Saharan Africa (Hassoun, 2020a). Civil society organizations, like South Africa's Treatment Access Campaign (TAC), refused to accept pharmaceutical companies' claim that they could not lower prices (Heywood, 2008). Instead, activists came up with, and implemented, innovative ways of educating patients and, linking "information about health... to rights, empowered marginalized people who began to assume both a public voice and a visibility" and demand access to treatment (Heywood, 2008). The costs of first-line medicines fell to approximately $1000/year and the protests they organized allowed generic companies to enter the fray (t'Hoen et al., 2011; Jewell, 2016). By 2001, a generic company, CIPLA, offered first-line antiretrovirals (ARVs) for less than $350/per year. Because civil society organizations exercised the virtue of creative resolve, millions of people eventually secured the treatment they needed to survive and flourish (t'Hoen et al., 2011, 4).[2]

Creative resolve is a disposition that inclines us to (1) question limits to the possibility of helping people live minimally well (and securing other significant moral goods); (2) seek out creative ways of securing (or better securing) these goods; and (3) try to secure them.[3] The virtue includes abiding by the proviso that we must only try to fulfill these conditions insofar as necessary and where possible and otherwise morally permissible. Finally, although I believe creative resolve can help us secure many moral goods, even beyond helping individuals flourish, I will focus on what helps people live well enough in what follows.

To fulfill the first condition for creative resolve, we must question limits to the possibility of helping people live minimally well. We must question the assertion that we cannot do so as well as our beliefs and background assumptions about what we can do. What questions we must raise depends on the nature of the assertion or assumptions. We might question their reliability, source, or purported implications. Sometimes we must question the claim that helping people live minimally well infeasibly demands too much. We must also consider whether common ways of trying to help people live minimally well will succeed and consider alternative approaches. We cannot simply suppose that others will take care of the problems people face in living

---

[2] CIPLA's CEO's commitment to fulfilling rights and producing drugs for the poor at reasonable cost was the basis for his move to lower prices (t'Hoen et al., 2011).

[3] Although people will typically fulfill the conditions for creative resolve in this order, that need not always be the case. In some cases, for instance, we may have to question the limits to possibility after coming up with creative new means of trying to secure important goods.

minimally good lives. Without sufficient (and accurate) evidence that we cannot help people flourish, we must fulfill the other conditions for creative resolve.

Consider how Jonathan Mann questioned the evidence against the possibility of helping people secure the healthcare they needed to live minimally well during the AIDS crisis. Mann, the former director of the WHO Global Program on AIDS, advocated for a human rights-driven approach to fighting back AIDS that fought not only the virus but also the inequality, poverty, oppression, and gender-based violence easing its spread. Mann forced the world to take responsibility for this global problem because he challenged the status quo whenever he encountered roadblocks. In 1990, he resigned as the director for the WHO Global Program on AIDS and accused the WHO's director-general, Hiroshi Nakajima, of failing in the fight against the virus. In 1994, speaking at the President's Advisory Council on AIDS, he accused the National Institutes of Health of violating human rights because it did not do enough to support research on an AIDS vaccine (Hassoun, 2020c). Because he questioned the status quo, Mann not only helped people around the world access care for HIV but inspired a generation of scholars and activists committed to fighting for global health equity (Marks, 2001).

To fulfill the second condition for the virtue, we must seek out creative ways of helping people live minimally well, even when we do not know how to do so. We must consider all the options on the table and exercise our imagination to come up with new ones. Our ideas cannot be prosaic, trite, unexceptional, uninteresting, or uninspired. Often, we must be resourceful, innovative, original, and bold. We can fail to possess the virtue of creative resolve because we lack imagination or because custom or convention bind us too strongly. We must have the energy necessary to set goals and come up with plans to achieve them (Snyder, 2000).

Consider how Raj Panjabi, a Liberian doctor responded when he realized that many people simply could not get to his hospital on time because they would have to take a day-long journey to do so. Dr. Panjabi thought outside of the box and created a system of community health workers to provide care for people in their villages. When the idea worked, he created the non-profit Last Mile Health to provide community health workers for "the poor, the vulnerable, and the most marginalized" around the world (Last Mile Health, 2020). Today Last Mile Health partners with governments in Ethiopia, Uganda, and Malawi and, in Liberia, their community health workers help 746,000 people in fourteen districts (Gifford and Edmondo, 2019; Skoll, 2021).

To fulfill the final condition for creative resolve, we must actively try to overcome barriers to helping people live minimally well. We often have to act in the absence of complete knowledge and understanding. We must persist in trying to help people live well enough in the face of uncertainty. We must demonstrate commitment, resolution, determination, grit, will, and tenacity. Often fulfilling this condition for creative resolve requires working in solidarity with others (Atuire and Hassoun, 2023).

The global fight to eradicate polio exemplifies this feature of creative resolve, which the WHO African Region eradicated on August 25 of 2020. The fight against polio was a truly grassroots endeavor from the start, but a major problem was and continues to be reaching remote locations. To overcome this, the polio eradication campaign engaged in micro-planning, using satellite maps to ensure that every house, even in the most remote communities, received the vaccine, tracked transit communities, and marked fingers (Kawachi and Kennedy, 2006; WHO, 2018). In some communities, lack of engagement or hostility from minority groups towards the government posed problems. To get vaccinations to children, polio workers have done everything from writing messages on brick kilns to sending mobile workers to nomadic populations. They even put vaccination posts up at bus stations. Vaccinators would walk between houses marking them with chalk and the children with indelible ink. They tracked the virus with biological assay surveys and environmental surveillance to decide if wild polio caused individual cases or they came from the vaccine itself (some vaccine types produce a very small percentage of infections). In India, for instance, they essentially created a national shadow health system of more than 900,000 workers (Bartlett, 2014).[4] Vaccinators were so creative and persistent that they employed town criers to walk through the streets and tell people about the vaccine, had parades in the middle of villages to let people know they were there, and gave children in Afghanistan their polio vaccinations at the circus (Kawachi and Kennedy, 2006).

The proviso that we must only try to fulfill the conditions for creative resolve insofar as necessary and where possible and otherwise morally permissible constrains these conditions' application. While we can, and often should, question the apparently necessary, possible, and permissible.

---

[4] It is important, however, to integrate new initiatives sustainably into existing health systems and neither replicate efforts nor divert resources from such systems to vertical programs (Hassoun, 2020a). So, with creative resolve those directing the campaign might have done even more to support existing health systems and help people live minimally good lives.

The facts of the case determine the virtue's limits. This proviso helps ensure that the virtue lies at a mean between the extremes of recklessness and complacency in the face of apparent tragedy.[5] We must question limits to the possibility of helping people live minimally well, search for ways of doing so, and act absent sufficient evidence that we cannot do so in an acceptable way.[6] What counts as sufficient evidence depends on the stakes. If we lose little by trying hard to secure something very important, creative resolve requires we persist in doing so even given significant evidence against the possibility of success. But, even if we lose something very important, we cannot persist when the weight of evidence (that actually exists)[7] suggests we will lose more than we will gain. Sometimes we do not even have to question evidence against the possibility of helping people live well enough. Sometimes no such evidence exists or we cannot raise such questions. In other cases, we should not come up with alternatives or act given the evidence. No one should plot revolution, for example, if that will just hurt people. Though, in such cases, we may still have to seek out creative ways of helping people live minimally well and try to help them in other ways—for example, through civil disobedience if it can change illegitimate rules. Creative resolve assists us in finding good ways to overcome apparent tragedy *when possible*.

The virtue of creative resolve embodies a kind of practical wisdom.[8] When individuals' ability to live minimally good lives is at stake, and we should try to help them, we should resolve to exercise our imagination in doing so. In other words, if we should help people live minimally good lives, we should try to do so insofar as necessary and where possible and permissible. Even in the face of apparent tragedy (where it appears impossible to help everyone live well enough), we should not fail to help people on the assumption that we

---

[5] Though, as I discuss below, just as courage tends more towards rashness than cowardice, creative resolve may not lie at the exact midpoint between these vices.

[6] Sometimes we must hope against the evidence that we actually possess and, as I explain below, the virtue is quasi-objective. So, there can be evidence that one does not possess and the relevant focus here is on the evidence that actually exists (whether or not one has access to that evidence). Of course, one may not be blameworthy for acting in accordance with all the evidence one possesses if one has done everything one should in trying to secure sufficient evidence.

[7] See preceding note.

[8] Saying that creative resolve cannot require people to do the impossible, or impermissible, does not mean that those with creative resolve lack all vice (though they might if some versions of the unity of the virtues thesis prove true). The selfish, impatient, brash, or tactless may often fail to set the right moral ends. But if their vices do not undermine their ability to commit, imagine, and act to help people live well enough (or require them to try so hard that they sacrifice yet more important things), they can have creative resolve. That said, the ability to figure out what morality requires seems essential for creative resolve and some argue that it is this kind of phronesis that unifies the virtues. See below for a few reflections on how creative resolve relates to phronesis.

cannot do so. So, we should cultivate a disposition to exercise our imagination, in trying to do so, even if we do not always succeed.

We should not pursue some ways of trying to help people live minimally well, so creative resolve cannot require us to employ them. Mao's revolution was a failure of creative resolve, not an illustration. Even if Mao was well motivated and creatively tried to help people live better lives, he failed to respect basic rights causing immense suffering. Some of those advancing imperialism, and even slavery, seem to have genuinely believed in the rightness of their cause. Yet, they lacked the virtue because they did not *actually* help people live well enough in an effective way (within the limits of possibility and moral permissibility).[9]

I do not want to discount the difficulty of knowing whether a particular attempt to question, think creatively, and act to help people live minimally good lives qualifies as virtuous. We often make mistakes of empirical, as well as moral, judgment. Human life is radically contingent; our greatest tragedies may radically transform our lives in positive ways just as our greatest successes can ultimately prove our downfall. Even those who try hard and succeed in helping people live minimally well may lack the virtue. The merely reckless or hopelessly utopian do not have it.[10] Some sacrifice their families and futures for goods so unlikely attainable that even if their great luck compensates for their irresponsibility, it cannot save their virtue.

Still, we should try hard to help people live minimally well within the virtue's limits given that people often fail morally because they do not question their assumptions.[11] Significant psychological evidence shows that we generally fail to consider enough alternatives in making decisions (Bearden, Murphy, and Rapoport, 2005). Alternately, people may lack moral imagination because they take a much too narrow view of feasibility—assuming tight time frames and financial constraints (Brennan and Pettit, 2005). Some people also seem to have a very pessimistic view of possibility (Goodin, 1995, 40). Moreover, when we imagine ourselves succeeding in tasks, we will more likely do so—perhaps because fantasies, "Calhoun's 'imaginative projections'...

---

[9] On a different conception of the virtue of creative resolve that is not itself limited by the constraints of possibility and permissibility, one might assert that this is really a case where people had creative resolve but failed to have other virtues—e.g. fairness, temperance, etc. I prefer a conception of the virtues on which they do not conflict but contain internal constraints limiting the possibility of such conflicts. I discuss below why I prefer a quasi-objective conception of the virtue and how alternative, more subjective and objective, interpretations are possible.

[10] See preceding note.

[11] It is worth reflecting on what is too much to ask of oneself versus others though I suppose here that we must all help people live minimally well when doing so does not require sacrificing our own ability to live well enough.

[influence our] ... sense of agency" (Martin, 2013, 86). Hope can energize us to set goals and act on plans to achieve them (Snyder, 2000). For all these reasons, we should often look for alternatives even to apparent tragic dilemmas.[12]

Creative resolve's distinctive contribution lies in the fact that it provides an appropriate response to apparent tragedy. To make this case, the rest of this section first argues that perseverance and creativity alone do not suffice for creative resolve and explains how even creative perseverance may lead us astray. Second, it argues that creative resolve is not simply a combination of other virtues. Third, it explains how the virtue provides an appropriate response to apparent tragedy and clarifies its nature. Finally, it suggests that we can best contrast creative resolve with conservativism expressed in the vice of complacency.

One should not try to equate creative resolve with perseverance, but it does require something like it. Nathan King (2014) defines perseverance as persistence with serious effort in the face of obstacles. This is the resolve component of creative resolve. Those with creative resolve do not capitulate or compromise too quickly in the face of adversity. On the other hand, those with creative resolve do not commit so strongly to helping people live minimally good lives, that they become dogmatic, stubborn, pigheaded, obstinate, opinionated, inflexible, or unyielding and sacrifice things of greater value. They must acknowledge the constraints of the given. To have the virtue, one must possess a measure of flexibility and openness to new information and evidence. One must act reasonably. Though perseverance does not require any particular way of acting, creative resolve specifically requires one to question assumptions, beliefs, and assertions to the effect that one cannot help people live well enough, to think creatively about how to do so, and to try.[13] Moreover, the virtue only requires us to do these things insofar as necessary and where possible and permissible.

Similarly, one should not try to reduce creative resolve to simple creativity, though it requires a certain kind of creativity (Boden, 2004; Kieran, 2014). According to Matthew Kieran, creativity requires purposively and non-accidentally realizing the "new and worthwhile in a given domain," which requires the character and dispositions of mind necessary for acquiring and

---

[12] This paragraph draws heavily on Hassoun (2020a).

[13] Partly because it involves a kind of perseverance, creative resolve is often necessary for other virtues like courage, industriousness, and patience, and creative resolve often requires these things as well. One must overcome fear, laziness, frustration, and ossified ways of thinking to persevere, and one must persevere in the face of these obstacles to have courage, industriousness, patience, and creativity (King, 2014).

deploying knowledge, capacities, and skills (Kieran, 2014, 205). He suggests that we need many other things for creativity: perseverance, courage, humility, self-knowledge, resilience, patience, curiosity, passion, enjoyment of the activity for its own sake, and aspiration (Kieran, 2014). However, even with all these virtues (and many others), we might not have creative resolve. We might not try to help people live minimally well nor secure other significant moral goods; we might only try to realize something else new and worthwhile.[14] Creative resolve, on the other hand, requires a particular kind of creativity—creativity directed at helping people live minimally well (or securing other significant moral goods). We must think outside of the box in questioning the constraints of possibility and reveal options we may have neglected to consider. At the same time, our creativity must respect the constraints of empirical reality. We cannot imagine that we have found a way of helping people live well enough or securing other important moral ends when we have not. A prisoner might find some kind of freedom within her chains by reconceptualizing their import but does not, thereby, get rid of them. Our creativity should take us to, but only succeeds within the bounds of, the possible.

We can even have both creativity and perseverance but not creative resolve. We may persevere and have creativity but fail to use our creativity in persevering.[15] Alternatively, we may employ the wrong kinds of creativity or persevere in pursuit of the wrong ends. Often we cannot merely persist creatively to help people live well enough or secure other significant moral goods; we need the wisdom to question, imagine, and act effectively.

Other virtues not strictly required for creative resolve often help us possess the virtue as much as creativity and perseverance, but I do not believe one can reduce creative resolve to these virtues either.[16] We must honestly

---

[14] Some argue that creativity need not generate anything new but is a form of expression that involves inventiveness, originality, and ingeniousness, and that the creative products satisfy requirements of a practice (e.g. literature, science, or art) (Swanton, 2003).

[15] Partly because creative resolve has many dimensions, it is not just the mean between two extremes. Resolve, or perseverance, falls between the extremes of apathy and over-commitment, but it requires more commitment rather than less. Similarly, creative resolve tends more towards the extreme of excessive creativity than its lack.

[16] Creative resolve is a moral, as well as epistemic, virtue. It requires more than practical wisdom in gathering, considering, *and acting* on the evidence appropriately. Creative resolve is a particular way of, and a kind of excellence in, considering, gathering, and responding to evidence. Moreover, as I argue below, it partly constitutes a minimally good life for many people. It directs us to question the existing options and exercise our imagination to come up with new ones insofar as necessary, possible, and otherwise permissible. Creative resolve is arguably part of phronesis, which requires much more than just creative resolve. However, there are different conceptions of phronesis in the literature—some requiring wise political judgment, others something more like general prudence—so it is not possible to say exactly how the virtue relates to phronesis in general.

question our assumptions and courageously question the evidence others provide against the possibility of helping people live minimally well (Curzer, 2021). But honesty and courage do not guarantee creative resolve. We need understanding, flexibility, and insight to know when and how to approach problems from a new direction. We need tenacity, commitment, and independence to try to help people. But even those with understanding, flexibility, insightfulness, tenacity, commitment, *and* independence may lack creative resolve.[17] So, I do not think we can reduce creative resolve to a combination of other virtues or a conceptual framework that helps us understand them; I believe it is a stand-alone virtue.[18]

Creative resolve comprises a distinctively valuable component of human flourishing for many people because it can help us address apparent tragedy. The virtue's elements have an important synergy. Moreover, we have reason to cultivate this particular combination of traits (not just some of the virtue's constituents) to respond well to apparent tragic dilemmas. Creative resolve can help us ensure people live well enough as we struggle to address the most pressing challenges of our time (I will make this case at greater length below). The virtue requires us to go to the limits of permissibility and possibility in trying to overcome apparent tragedy (though the risks of tragedy determine these limits).

Creative resolve opposes conservatism in the personal, rather than political sense, but it limits radicalism with realism. As Michael Oakeshott puts it, "to be conservative ... is to prefer the familiar to the unknown, to prefer ... the actual to the possible, the limited to the unbounded, the near to the distant, the sufficient to the superabundant, the convenient to the perfect, present

---

[17] Creative resolve also requires more than what some have termed *practical imagination* insofar as it requires us to reflect on options that norms governing our narrative identities do not allow, or require, us to consider. Though some work on practical imagination may be helpful, e.g. in specifying the nature of options in general and the ways in which we can exercise our imagination creatively (Rorty, 2009; Smith, 2010). Creative resolve may even require us to reflect on what some have called "the unthinkable" (Smith, 2010).

[18] At least creative resolve is no more *obviously* reducible to a combination of other virtues than many canonical virtues. The virtue's interdependence is not unique—most virtues involve many others. One might argue that courage is persistence in the face of danger and perseverance persistence in the face of obstacles and ask whether there is anything more there than just persistence. Alternatively, one might argue that benevolence is generosity and compassion, leniency is generosity and mercy, and kindness is generosity and gentleness and suggest that, ultimately, we do not need these composite virtues at all. Even if what I will continue to call "creative resolve" is, ultimately, reducible to a combination of more primitive virtues or is better characterized as a cluster of virtues, however, I believe it is still important to examine the cluster. It helps us understand a significant, neglected feature of virtuous agency. The particular combination of components creative resolve involves is important for allowing us to overcome apparent tragedy (and, again, that is what I think makes it its own distinctive, stand alone, virtue). We need to understand how virtuous agents creatively resolve such problems, even if the virtue of creative resolve is not fundamental.

laughter to utopian bliss" (Oakeshott, 1962, 408). Rather than striving for the best possible results, conservatives embrace the status quo; they believe the status quo has mere existence value independent of whatever more substantive value it may have. Those who have creative resolve reject this status quo bias; they will call the status quo into question whenever doing so helps people live minimally well and does not sacrifice anything as significant.[19] Moreover, creative resolve requires the integrity necessary not only to find ways of helping people live well enough but, also, to follow through in doing so. That said, those who have the virtue will not radically change the status quo without paying attention to the facts on the ground. They safeguard other things that matter. They only reject the status quo with good reason.

We might best contrast creative resolve with complacency. Those with creative resolve can be content but not complacent. The complacent do not strive to help people live better lives or secure other important moral ends even where good reasons to do so exist. Instead, complacency replaces aspiration with a sense of mild dissatisfaction at best and often with apathy if not misplaced satisfaction. Often complacency sets in when people do not think they can help others (or secure other morally significant ends). Weakness, cowardice, or indecisiveness can undermine the virtue. Some care too much about pleasing people or fulfilling social expectations.

However, other vices can also undermine the virtue. Some let themselves become overwhelmed into inaction.[20] Others simply fail to consider the possibility of addressing difficult problems. Some refuse to acknowledge the possibility of making progress in helping others live minimally well because they focus on the worst possibilities. So, the virtue lets us resist apathy, close-mindedness, and pessimism as well as complacency when we confront apparent tragedy.

What should we say, however, about a case where a responsible agent would not reach the conclusions necessary to help people live minimally good lives? The person may not act viciously, but we can say that they fail to act virtuously. Even the responsible, I believe, can fail to act virtuously if the world does not cooperate. If the evidence does not actually point the way a responsible person thinks it does, they may fail to act virtuously, even if they lack culpability for doing so. Similarly, some may simply lack the resources necessary to secure the requisite evidence or to cultivate the necessary character.

---

[19] We cannot sacrifice life or limb in doing so (or our own ability to live well enough).
[20] I would like to thank Liam Shields for discussion here.

I think the preceding analysis makes the correct understanding of creative resolve quasi-objective. The virtue is a settled disposition that helps one act virtuously. Moreover, if the world generally cooperates, one can have the virtue because the disposition to act virtuously generally means one does. However, it seems, the virtue requires more than responsibility—it requires luck (Nelkin, 2013).[21] More precisely, to have creative resolve, the world must generally comply so that if one acts responsibly, one can help others live minimally good lives. Though, again, some fail to have the virtue due to bad luck not viciousness. Those who would deny this might accept a completely subjective, or objective, conception of the virtue. Perhaps, to have the virtue, one must only act responsibly or acting responsibly must always help people live minimally good lives. Someone who never has to try hard to help others can have creative resolve in some sense; they may have enough resolve to help others and the disposition to overcome challenges should they arise.[22] However, I believe those who do not ever have to try hard to help people in the actual world, often lack the virtue. They do not have the chance to cultivate the disposition. Similarly, it seems, we can have the virtue of creative resolve even if it does not always help us help others. Those who disagree can modify the conception of the virtue I offer accordingly throughout.

3. The Argument for the Virtue

How does creative resolve contribute to flourishing?[23] What follows argues that all the conditions for creative resolve help promote flourishing even though we can sometimes promote flourishing without creative resolve. To make its case, this section assumes that we should promote our own flourishing as well as contribute to others' flourishing when that does not require sacrificing our own ability to live well enough. It argues that the duty to help people live minimally well generates a duty to cultivate the virtue before explaining how the virtue contributes to the intrinsic value, or quality, of individuals' lives.

---

[21] For discussion of relevant kinds of luck in the moral domain, see Nelkin (2013). Also see Williams (1981) and Nussbaum (1986).

[22] It is also possible that those with the virtue will rarely have to exercise it.

[23] I focus on flourishing that may go well beyond the basic minimum here as I do not think the virtue's value is exhausted by its contribution to individuals' ability to live minimally well. In what follows, I aim first to establish that the virtue has great instrumental value. I then argue that it has significant intrinsic value as well.

Consider how each of the conditions for creative resolve promote flourishing. The first, questioning, condition for creative resolve promotes flourishing for this reason: If we accept that we cannot help people flourish without sufficient evidence, we will probably not exercise our (moral) imagination or try very hard to help them. The second, creativity, condition for the virtue promotes flourishing because it helps people secure the significant goods that help people flourish. We often need to find creative ways of securing these things to overcome barriers to doing so. The final, action, condition for creative resolve promotes flourishing because we cannot just come up with good ways of securing the things that help people flourish. We must often act to secure them to flourish and help others do so.

Creative resolve often helps people flourish because if we do not think we can promote flourishing, fail to come up with good ways of doing so, or simply do not try, we will probably not succeed. Consider a concrete example. People often fail to aid the poor because they do not believe aid helps, despite the strong evidence that supports many aid programs' efficacy (Hassoun, 2010; Hassoun, 2012).[24] People may lack this data or generalize inappropriately (and unreflectively) from evidence that aid is sometimes ineffective and conclude that all aid is counter-productive. They may not think very hard about how to locate good aid programs (e.g. using charity navigators that consider program evaluations) or come up with new ways of getting effective aid to people who need it. Moreover, even when people believe aid can help and do know what to do, they may simply not try hard enough to help.[25]

The preceding arguments establish that creative resolve has great instrumental value, but the virtue has intrinsic value as well. The instrumental arguments provide a ready response to the worry that creative resolve fails to track the bearers of value; we have reason to cultivate the virtue, in part, because it can help us secure important goods. However, creative resolve involves more than just doing the right thing, it displays excellence in doing so—often the virtue helps constitute flourishing and contributes to our lives' value.

---

[24] As previous chapters suggested, failing to aid may also be a failure of justice, beneficence, or even basic human decency, but creative resolve can help people come up with ways of improving aid programs significantly in a way that justice, beneficence, and decency alone cannot.

[25] Some may worry that we should not inculcate the virtue too widely and that there may be limits to some individuals' natural capacities that will limit their ability to secure creative resolve. These are both questions that merit empirical inquiry, but understanding the ways in which the virtue is limited will address some of the concerns here. Moreover, we can foster creativity and resolve at least in young children and I doubt any natural limits to this virtue are more extensive than to others like courage or humility, though it may be somewhat difficult to cultivate (and hence creative resolve constitutes an excellence of character).

Creative resolve partly constitutes flourishing; it orients us directly at flourishing and expresses our commitment to worthy ends including helping people live well enough.[26] (I suggest below that we can turn to some accounts of the hope that justifies creative resolve for an explanation of how this happens.) Creative resolve provides a good way of trying to help people live well enough; it involves the right kind of commitment, imagination, and action and can contribute significantly to the quality of one's life. Creative resolve displays a fitting attitude toward helping people flourish. People often find it hard to promote flourishing and those with creative resolve possess excellence in doing so. We admire those who do not give up too easily, can think outside of the box, and act to advance flourishing as long as they recognize the true limits of possibility and permissibility because they are better moral agents.[27] The persistence, commitment, creativity, inventiveness, originality, and boldness creative resolve involves partly constitute flourishing. The vices that undermine creative resolve also explain how those who lack the virtue lead less admirable lives. The unreflective, gullible, ignorant, unimaginative, apathetic, pessimistic, close-minded, conservative, or complacent often lack creative resolve. At the other extreme, the smug, arrogant, thick-headed, or hopelessly utopian often lack the virtue. One should exercise one's imagination to achieve cognitive contact with both actuality and possibility and doing so helps develop and constitute one's human potential. In light of its instrumental effects, we should have creative resolve. Independently of these effects, in our tragic world, we must often try hard to promote flourishing.[28]

Some may worry that creative resolve hinders flourishing's pursuit, but creative resolve contains an internal constraint that limits its tendency towards excess. One should try hard to come up with and implement creative ways to help people live well enough but only insofar as necessary and where possible and morally *permissible*.[29] When the costs of trying to help others exceed the gains, one should not persist in doing so.[30] Just as creative resolve can require

---

[26] Though, again, creative resolve is one among many virtues and people may flourish without it. Liam Shields raises an interesting question about creative resolve that may apply to many other virtues as well. As more and more people act with creative resolve, it seems less impressive when someone exercises the virtue. Perhaps people will have to have more and more creativity and resolve to qualify as excellent. Of course, there may be limits to the possibility and it is possible to understand excellence in different ways (it need not be statistically rare).

[27] We may even admire people with the virtue more when helping others live minimally well comes at some (e.g. personal) cost, so long as the sacrifice is not excessive (e.g. it may often be impermissible to sacrifice close personal relationships even to achieve very important ends).

[28] I would like to thank Nicholas Smith for extensive discussion.

[29] Here I am not focusing on legal permissibility—doing so may well require civil disobedience to change illegitimate laws.

[30] Creative resolve motivates us to pursue flourishing only insofar as necessary and when doing so is possible and permissible.

the bold virtues of courage, persistence, assertiveness, determination, and confidence, it can require the patient virtues of acceptance, humility, tolerance, understanding, and contentment.

I only stress creative resolve's positive—or commitment—side here because I believe that we desperately need more creativity and resolve rather than less in our world to ensure that everyone can live minimally well. Millions suffer in abject poverty, for instance, and few even consider, never mind address, the problem. Those with the virtue will try to help people in new, and more effective, ways when doing so does not require sacrificing things of greater value. And, when we have the internal and external resources necessary to do so, we should cultivate the virtue so that acting appropriately within its limits becomes part of our nature.

Still, one *lacks* creative resolve if one tries so hard to help others that one's efforts come at the expense of anything more significant things or one's own ability to live well enough. One should maintain a sense of proportion or balance and creative resolve should not threaten peace or harmony. Sometimes we best help others when we simply reflect, appreciate, or wait patiently. Those who try to change the world when they do not have to often live less good lives than those who simply appreciate it. Often charging ahead does not promote flourishing because we just end up hurting others or ourselves. We should not expend useless effort or waste resources that we might effectively employ in better ways. We should consider the risks of action as well as inaction. We should not persist in trying to help people in the face of impossibility or when doing so comes at the expense of more important goods. Creative resolve recognizes all of this. To have the virtue, we should persist only insofar as necessary and where possible *and permissible.*

4. Hope and the Virtue of Creative Resolve

This section argues that when people have the right kind of hope, they *should* have creative resolve and the virtue embodies a particularly important kind of hope. Doing so will help explain and support the claim that we should have the virtue.[31]

---

[31] Exploring the virtue's connection with moral emotions and other cognitive states may also help to explain and justify the virtue. It may turn out, for instance, that appropriately directed passion also supports the virtue—anger can motivate us, for instance, but it may be destructive without hope (Nussbaum, 2016; Srinivasan, 2017). I do not have the space here to adequately explore this possibility, however.

First, note that people can have many kinds of hope and yet lack creative resolve. On the orthodox definition, hope just requires desiring an end one believes possible but not certain (Bovens, 1999). On sophisticated versions of the standard account, the desire component of hope can vary along several dimensions: having more or less motivational power, effect on attention, ability to occupy the mind, and felt power, not only at a time but also over time (Milona, 2017a; Milona, 2017b). Some specify that hope requires taking the desire for an end as a reason (perhaps in addition to the probability information and the end itself) and adopting a stance towards the probability that justifies this (Martin, 2013, 61–62). Others maintain, "hoping for an outcome means being disposed to fantasize about it" (Bovens, 1999; Martin, 2013, 86). Yet others suggest hope requires acting as if the hoped-for end will come about (Pettit, 2004, 152). If people do not believe they can help others live minimally well, they will not generally try very hard to do so. But when hope inclines one to strive for the hoped-for end insofar as necessary, and where possible and permissible, it supports creative resolve. For hope to give rise to creative resolve, it must provide a reason for people to actively search for good ways of helping people live well enough and to try to do so. Moreover, hope must help us question limits to the possibility of helping people and do so.

Victoria McGeer and Margaret Urban Walker's work best explains the kind of hope that *should* give rise to creative resolve and that can help *justify* it: When one wants to secure a morally significant end and employs one's creativity in trying to do so, one has the relevant kind of hope (McGeer, 2004; Walker, 2006, ch. 2; McGeer, 2008). This hope goes beyond "imaginatively exploring what we can and cannot do in the world" to trying to achieve one's hoped-for end (McGeer, 2004, 104). So, *when one hopes in this way to help people live minimally well, one should have creative resolve.* (Though one might still fail to have creative resolve because justified hope does not entail that one will act correctly.) Still, in the absence of sufficient evidence that we should not try to help people live well enough, the relevant kind of hope supports the virtue. In some cases, we should not even fantasize about achieving a hoped-for outcome. We may hope for morally impermissible things. However, when we hope to help people live minimally good lives, and we should do so for all we know, we should have creative resolve.[32]

---

[32] Again, creative resolve can help us secure other important moral ends as well, though I believe it is particularly important for helping people live minimally well. The vices creative resolve counters are prominent when there are many countervailing considerations, moral claims have indeterminate implication, our actions have remote effects, and their significance remains hard to decipher. See, also, Hassoun (2020a).

Moreover, creative resolve *embodies* a kind of radical hope; even when we do not know how to help people live well enough, we have reason to find ways of doing so (Lear, 2008). As Kant put it:

> It does not matter how many doubts may be raised against my hopes from history, which, if they were proved, could move me to desist from a task so apparently futile; as long as these doubts cannot be made quite certain I cannot exchange the duty for the rule of prudence not to attempt the impracticable. (Kant, 1793, 8:309)[33]

We may need "moral improvisation" to come up with acceptable ways of helping people live minimally well (Herman, 2007, ch. 12).

Radical hope differs from faith. People have faith when the good they desire provides a reason for action and they believe they must try to secure the desired good *even when all the evidence suggests they are wrong*. Faith is often blind. The hope that gives rise to creative resolve helps us resist the bald assertion of terrible tragedy, but it does not allow us to ignore its existence (Nussbaum, 2000a). Sometimes radical hope will go beyond the evidence, but we should not ignore, and must sometimes actively seek, evidence that undermines hope. Sometimes we should not try to help others. However, we should persist in trying to help people live at least minimally good lives insofar as possible and otherwise permissible.

Moreover, to support the virtue, the hope creative resolve embodies must itself be virtuous.[34] If we focus too much on the possibility of securing what we desire, we may try too hard to secure the desired good. Those who ignore empirical reality may not only fare poorly themselves but also hurt others. Virtuous hopes, like creative resolve, help us secure important goods within the limits of possibility and permissibility. Virtuous hope helps us survive and

---

[33] Johnathan Lear's story about how the Crow responded to the end of civilization as they knew it illustrates radical hope. The Crow originally equated courage with bravery in conflict, but when their nomadic way of life ended, they demonstrated remarkable intelligence, flexibility, and restraint in reconceiving the virtue of courage to go beyond the martial courage with which they were familiar. They courageously refused to fight the onslaught of tragic history. They eventually aligned themselves with the US against its traditional enemies, the Sioux and the Blackfoot Nations, to defend their landholdings against the US. As Johnathan Lear put it, hope gave them "the sustenance . . . [to] hold onto this core commitment through the storm" (Lear, 2008, 121–122). Of course, radical hope may lack virtue (as I discuss below).

[34] Pettit seems to neglect this point. To explain how his account of hope is not irrational, Pettit says that when we estimate the expected utility of a desired end, we can adjust our estimate of its value as well as our probability estimate. Doing so, he thinks, requires no irrationality. I am not convinced. I believe not only that the evidence should dictate our credence in the likelihood of a desired end materializing but that even the way that we value things should depend on the nature of the value.

flourish and motivates our pursuit of significant moral ends (Bovens, 1999; McGeer, 2004; McGeer, 2008). Some people hope too much or too little to help everyone live well enough (Snow, 2013, 156). Still, virtuous hope, limited by moral and empirical reality, aids us in helping people live minimally well, in part, because it supports creative resolve: It motivates us to try hard to help others flourish insofar as necessary and where possible and permissible.

5. Creative Resolve, Hope, and Possibility

Creative resolve constitutes an important personal, as well as political, virtue. Those who struggle valiantly to help themselves and those around them live good enough lives often display the virtue. A child overcoming a learning disability, a young woman struggling for self-esteem, an adult trying to conquer depression, a politician implementing innovative programs to combat hunger in a community, a community organizer fighting to end violence against women in a nation, and national leaders forging agreements to promote international peace all exercise creative resolve when they persist, imagine, and act to help people live well enough.

Moreover, we often best acquire, and exercise, creative resolve by hoping and working together with others.[35] Because the virtue of creative resolve can help us address some of the most pressing challenges of our time, the hope that justifies the virtue and the hope it embodies can help strengthen our relationships to others and preserve the conditions for mutual flourishing.

Consider a final example of how working together with creative resolve nations collaborated to protect global health during the cold war: Smallpox was eradicated by the mid-1960s in the Americas when the Soviet Union proposed a global eradication campaign and an American led the campaign to eliminate it. It took incredible creativity and resolve to reach people even in the remotest corners of the earth and it required building one of the largest United Nations campaigns ever. When mass vaccination did not stop the virus, the campaign pioneered "ring vaccinations" a contact tracing-based immunization strategy that eventually let them conquer the disease (Hassoun, 2020a). The fact that we eliminated smallpox, one of the greatest pandemics of all time, during the Cold War shows that—with creative resolve—we can work together and help everyone survive and flourish.

---

[35] In some cases, this hope may even involve collective action and amount to a collective virtue—-e.g. when everyone intends to work together to secure flourishing and every individual's action is necessary for doing so (Bratman, 1992).

Working together with creative resolve, we can aid people around the world in overcoming the violence, oppression, and hardship that threaten their ability to live minimally good lives and secure the food, water, shelter, education, health care, and other things they need to flourish. By assisting us in combating oppression, disaffection, and protecting basic rights, creative resolve, and the hope it embodies, contribute to our moral character. By helping us acquire the things we need to live at least minimally well and overcome barriers to doing so, creative resolve helps us secure the significant moral goods at which we aim. With creative resolve, we can overcome apparent tragedy by investing hope in others. Working together with creative resolve, we can act with solidarity to can build our social world and help people around the world flourish.

6. Conclusion

This chapter argued that we should embrace creative resolve—a new virtue that can help us overcome some of the most pressing problems of the twenty-first century. This virtue requires us to try hard to find new ways of helping people live good (enough) lives. Although creative resolve does not appear on canonical lists of virtues, it can help us overcome apparent tragedy. Varieties of hope not only support creative resolve, but creative resolve embodies radical hope. Creative resolve can help us to respond effectively to the vices that threaten the very fabric of our relations with others in this rapidly changing world. Moreover, creative resolve constitutes a deeply personal virtue. It lies at the foundation for our greatest successes in our most private struggles. It helps build character and promotes flourishing. The virtue of creative resolve, and the hope it embodies, can help us ensure that people everywhere flourish.

Conclusion—Beyond a Basic Minimum

Is A Minimally Good Life Really Good Enough?

1. Beyond Solidarity

A Minimally Good Life set out a new account of the basic minimum we must provide for others and can claim as a matter of basic justice. It argued that most alternative accounts of what people owe to each other as a basic minimum demand too much in some respects and do not demand enough in others. *A Minimally Good Life* suggested that we should put ourselves into others' shoes to decide what people need to live good enough lives. It, then, argued that we must provide this minimum for others out of concern for our common humanity whenever doing so does not require sacrificing our own ability to live well enough. Moreover, *A Minimally Good Life* argued that this amounts to a political, or human rights, obligation. Many maintain that global justice and respect for human rights require everyone to have whatever will let them live minimally good lives (Nickel, 2007; Brock, 2009; Hassoun, 2020a). However, *A Minimally Good Life* concluded that we must often help people live at least minimally well in our personal, as well as political, lives.

2. Reprise

A Minimally Good Life's first chapter sketched an account of the minimally good life on which people need an adequate range of the fundamental conditions for securing relationships, pleasures, knowledge, appreciation, worthwhile activities, and other life improving goods. Specifically, it argued that we must secure those goods a reasonable, caring, free person would (in conversation with others) set as a minimal standard of justifiable aspiration/basic right. As reasonable, caring, free people, we should put ourselves in others' shoes and consider whether we would now be content to live their lives in trying to determine what they need to live minimally well. On this account, people need many different things to live well enough, though everyone needs adequate resources, opportunities, and capabilities. Once we put ourselves in others' shoes and seriously consider what they need to live well enough, deliberation and debate can help resolve disagreements about what a minimally good life requires.

The second chapter argued that the minimally good life account of the basic minimum has some advantages over several competing accounts. The alternative accounts either fail to provide some of the things people need to secure a basic minimum or require we provide people with things that they do not need to do so. The chapter argued that the minimally good life account, unlike the main alternatives, plausibly provides a necessary and sufficient standard of minimum provision (one that gives each person all and only what they need). It better accounts for all of the things each person needs to reach a basic minimum without suggesting people need things they do not.

The third chapter considered what we owe to others *simply out of concern or respect for our common humanity*. The chapter argued that people must at least help each other live minimally good lives when that does not require sacrificing their own ability to live well enough. Individuals' common humanity demands this kind of respect.[1] Global justice and respect for human rights require ensuring that everyone can live minimally well. Moreover, no one should subject others to a system of coercive rules under which they would not be content to live as others do. Legitimate political societies, that have a right to rule, must ensure that their subjects can live at least minimally good lives. Finally, concern for our common humanity plausibly requires helping others flourish in our personal, as well as political, lives.

The fourth chapter argued that the main alternative accounts of basic justice either demand too much, not enough, or both. Unlike the main competitors, the minimally good life account leaves significant room for charity or altruism, while acknowledging the importance of freedom, rights, and responsibility. We should have sufficient freedom to care for others and ourselves. Moreover, the minimally good life account treats everyone equally. It specifies that we must only help others live well enough when we can without sacrificing our own ability to do so. It ensures that everyone can demand the assistance they need to secure this much when others need not sacrifice so much to help them.

The fifth chapter considered how to help people live minimally good lives in present and future generations. In present generations, it argued that we

---

[1] This is so even though more than welfare, or how people fare, plausibly matters for basic justice, never mind justice more broadly. We cannot account for environmental justice within the confines of a welfarist theory, e.g., if it requires respect for non-sentient life (Hassoun, 2011a).

should prioritize the least well-off but also consider the numbers helped. In future generations, the chapter claimed that we need not prioritize the least well-off when we can ensure that whoever comes into existence lives a minimally good life. Otherwise some people will preventably fail to live minimally well for some period of time. Since everyone should secure a basic minimum whenever they come into existence, we should not generally bring people into existence who will not have their rights fulfilled (barring tragic choices) and we can reject the repugnant conclusion. Finally, the chapter argued that we should help everyone in present generations live minimally well before creating greater numbers in future generations We cannot focus on helping those in the far future who need not come into existence (e.g. by preventing potential asteroid impacts) at great cost to those in present and near-future generations (by allowing mass starvation, climate change to proceed unchecked, or millions to die due to non-anthropogenic natural disasters, etc.). Barring tragic conflicts, we can both aid those below the threshold for a minimally good life now and ensure everyone who comes into existence in the future has this basic minimum.

The final chapter considered how we should respond to the apparently tragic state of our world—where helping everyone live even minimally well seems impossible. It defended a new virtue that I call *creative resolve* that gives us a response to apparent tragedy in motivating us to try hard to overcome it. Creative resolve is the disposition to commit, imagine, and act to help people secure the things they need to live well enough insofar as necessary, possible, and otherwise permissible. Those with creative resolve (1) question limits to the possibility of helping people live minimally well (and securing other significant moral goods); (2) seek out creative ways of securing (or better securing) these goods; and (3) try to secure them. Moreover, the final chapter argued that when people have the right kind of hope, they *should* have creative resolve and that the virtue embodies a particularly important kind of radical hope; even when we do not know how to help people live minimally good lives, we have reason to find ways of doing so. This helps explains hope's value. Hope and creative resolve help us flourish in our rapidly changing world.

3. Good Enough in Practice as Well as Theory

A Minimally Good Life provides a substantial, and deep, account of how to think about the basic minimum each and every person needs for a minimally good life that can help us in practice as well as theory. Informed by empirical work on what people need to live well enough, it provides a basis for further research on the factors that contribute to minimally good lives (and the connection between such lives and other things that matter) (Graham, 2009). We need to understand what, at a minimum, we owe to others to create just societies. We cannot create good indicators or measure performance in respecting, protecting, and fulfilling claims if we do not really understand what basic minimum we must provide.

This book's method for figuring out what people need to live minimally good lives can help us promote flourishing. It can help caring, reasonable, free decision-makers understand their constituents' interests in living minimally good lives. And, when facing particular individuals with complaints, it can help policymakers better evaluate their justification. Individuals can also employ the account in considering what they owe to others in their personal, as well as political, lives. In short, *A Minimally Good Life*'s mechanism for deciding what people need to live minimally well can help guide those who care for others who fall below this threshold and policymakers working to ensure that people rise above it.

Some argue that we cannot just ensure that everyone lives minimally good lives (Casal, 2007; Moyn, 2018). Critics claim that those striving for sufficiency often neglect the pressing problem of promoting equality (Moyn, 2018). These critics can agree that we should not strive for equal suffering, affliction, or impoverishment and acknowledge that calls for equality often come tinged with envy. Nevertheless, they contend that we should strive for something more inspiring than a basic minimum (Casal, 2007). Some even claim that concern for protecting the human rights of all has created a morality of depths, diverting our attention from the nobler, and more aspirational, ideals of the French enlightenment (Moyn, 2018). Even basic justice, never mind justice and morality more generally, may require many things besides helping others live minimally well.

Although we should not focus on inequality among the rich before sufficiency for the poor, helping people live minimally well would do a great deal to promote equality (Huseby, 2020). Even in rich countries, greater inequality correlates with worse mental and physical health, drug abuse, violence, lower social mobility, poorer child wellbeing and education, and greater rates of teen pregnancy (Wilkinson and Pickett, 2011). Inequality may also erode trust and community life, increase anxiety and sickness, and lead to excess consumption (Wilkinson and Pickett, 2011). It would take an incredible amount of resources to help everyone live even minimally flourishing lives.

Providing these resources would almost certainly reduce inequality greatly. Of course, even eliminating extreme monetary poverty will not ensure that everyone stands in relations of free, reasonable care with one another and can contentedly live life in each other's shoes. Great inequality in opportunities can, for instance, undermine our relationships with others around the world as well as our compatriots. Moreover, we must ensure that the wealthy and powerful cannot exert undue influence on political processes to promote their own interests at the expense of others' ability to live well enough. This may require limiting individuals' ability to inherit capital and corporate influence on politics (Picketty, 2014; Hassoun, 2017). Furthermore, inequalities can undermine individuals' ability to live well enough if the inequalities influence social standing or undermine our dignity or common humanity (Anderson, 1999). For all of these reasons, human rights, international development, and basic social safety nets for all aid the global struggle for greater equality and do not detract from it.

Even if we must do much more than provide everyone with a basic minimum, the claim that we should help everyone live good enough lives is not only wildly aspirational but also inspirational (Hassoun, 2020b). It requires putting basic health care systems in place for all and ensuring that people can secure adequate food, water, shelter, and education among many other things (Hassoun, 2020b).

Moreover, the minimally good life account of the basis for human rights that protect everyone's ability to secure a basic minimum requires each of us to stand behind the commitment to fulfilling these rights (Hassoun, 2020b). This commitment may seem futile in our quickly changing world where—with the rise of nationalism, deregulated international capital, and democratic decline—we face terrible threats to human progress and development from the unraveling of social safety nets to climate change and pandemics. But we must overcome these seemingly insurmountable problems together (Hassoun, 2020b).

Whereas in previous ages human rights were the morality of depths not the heights of moral progress, and that may always be so, today we lack even basic human decency. That is what the minimally good life account can offer—a way of relating to each other that can help us all flourish. It constitutes a minimal, but demanding, commitment to decency or what I call our common humanity. So, when institutions fail, individuals should commit to fixing them or at least helping each other find a bed for the night (Reiff, 2002, Hassoun, 2012, Hassoun, 2014).[2]

---

[2] More precisely, when institutions fail, we must help others secure the basic minimum when that does not require sacrificing our own ability to do so.

There is a way of seeing human rights as brakes, or constraints, on free enterprise and democratic decision making just as there is a way of seeing democratic decision making as mere preference aggregation, but both fail to capture the relevant values at stake. Just as genuine democratic discourse and processes help constitute a wiser society, taking responsibility for human rights and ensuring a minimally good life for all enriches our relationships to compatriots and other members of the international community. This commitment is *part* of what it means to live a minimally good life in solidarity with others (Atuire and Hassoun, 2021).

To achieve basic justice and help people attain even a basic minimum, we must come up with creative ways of combating the poverty, oppression, and violence that threaten our relationships with others—our common humanity—in this rapidly changing world. To ensure that people live minimally good lives, we must persist in the struggle to protect human rights and fulfill basic needs. To help everyone live well enough, we must exercise creative resolve.

Appendix I

This appendix argues that legitimate rulers—who have a justification right to rule—must at least ensure that those they subject to coercive rules live minimally well.[1] Where, I suppose, coercive rules carry with them sanctions—punishments or penalties—for those violating their dictates.[2] More precisely, this appendix argues that cooperating members of political systems exercising coercive force over one another must help each other live minimally good lives when that does not require sacrificing their own ability to do likewise. Even if we do not bear responsibility for the fact that some cannot live such lives without assistance, we bear responsibility for how we respond to others' needs. There plausibly exist other conditions for legitimacy and, again, full justice and morality certainly require more than helping our compatriots live minimally good lives.[3] Still, if the arguments below go through, members of political societies exercising coercive rule over one another must ensure that their compatriots live minimally good lives. Otherwise, they rule illegitimately.[4]

Consider, first, why cooperating members of political systems exercising coercive force over one another must at least help each other live minimally good lives when that does not require sacrificing their own ability to do likewise: Otherwise, they fail to respect individuals' common humanity. As humans, everyone has an equal claim to freedom, but also to reasonable care and concern under coercive rule. For rulers to justifiably subject people to coercive rules, they must exercise appropriate impartiality and only create rules for others under which they would contently live.

Again, one might try to ground the claim to respect for common humanity in different ways, but I believe that its ground lies, in part, in the fact that we stand in important relationships of care and concern to others participating in our uniquely human moral community. As humans, we all benefit significantly from care and concern over the course of our lives. Without these things, we simply could not survive, never mind develop or flourish. Recall, moreover, that most people must live under coercive rules over which they exercise limited control. So, the relationships at issue include political relations.[5]

---

[1] Here I am not concerned with individuals' perceptions of governmental authority. I have said nothing to rule out the possibility that a government justifiably exercises political authority despite the fact that its subjects do not believe it is legitimate. Moreover, I am interested in the justification of coercion, in general, not indexed to a particular political system like liberal democracy.

[2] Usually, the coerced have no good alternative but to abide by the rules because someone threatens them with sanctions. Typically, coercion also undermines autonomy, to at least some extent, by limiting options and engaging the coerced person's will; but, as I use the term, coercion can include exercises of brute force or violence (Fowler, 1982, 329–355; Frankfurt, 1988, 104–116).

[3] I do not think rulers can legitimately say they do not have to provide protection against common threats to individuals' ability to live minimally good lives because people do not need such protection to live well enough. At least, rulers cannot just say someone is lucky not to need so much to justify the failure to provide such a basic minimum when there is enough to provide it to all. Here, however, I only defend the weaker claim that each person must have enough.

[4] I do not provide an account of how it is acceptable to respond to illegitimate rules but see Chapters 5 and 6 and Appendix III for some discussion of how we should help people live minimally well in our tragic world.

[5] These institutions are justified, in part, by the ways in which they help us live well enough together; they promote the common good and help us solve collective action problems.

Consider, then, why coercive rulers must respect individuals' common humanity and why this requires ensuring that all their subjects live at least minimally well. Respect for individual freedom requires that people at least be able to object, if not consent, to coercive rule (which I take to include the threat, as well as exercise, of brute force). So, coercive rulers must make sure that their subjects can secure sufficient autonomy to object (or consent) to that rule.[6] More precisely, if someone requires assistance to secure this autonomy and no one else is providing it, coercive rulers must do so on pain of illegitimacy (Hassoun and Brock, 2012). But legitimate rulers must do more than ensure that their subjects can consent to their subjection. Their rule must be *worthy* of consent; legitimate rulers treat people as equals (impartially), with compassion or empathy. As humans, everyone can equally claim not only freedom but also reasonable care and concern under coercive rule (the kinds of flourishing relationships that support and help constitute our common humanity). For rulers to justifiably subject people to coercive rules, they must create rules for others under which they would contently live (as others do). They must create conditions under which people will lead morally (and otherwise) decent lives. They must respond to others' needs and claims to decent treatment.[7] To ensure individuals live minimally well, those subjecting them to coercive rules must take responsibility for ensuring that they can secure the capacities, resources, and institutions that they need. When people require assistance to live minimally good lives, and no one else is providing this assistance, coercive rulers must do so, on pain of illegitimacy. At least, rulers who respect individuals' common humanity must provide this assistance when doing so does not require sacrificing their own ability to live well enough. Hence cooperating members of political systems (citizens) who exercise coercive force over one another must at least help each other live minimally good lives when that does not require sacrificing their own ability to do likewise.

Let me explain why respect for common humanity requires coercive rulers to ensure that all their subjects live at least minimally well in a different way. Legitimate rulers (who have a justification right to rule) must equally consider their subjects' interests in a way that respects their common humanity.[8] So legitimate rulers cannot subject others to rules only the coerced or constrained could reasonably accept. Moreover, legitimate rulers have to exercise impartial, reasonable, care, ensuring that their subjects have everything they need to be reasonably content under these rules. Legitimate rulers must employ the free, reasonable, care standard for deciding what people need under coercive rule. They should put themselves in their subjects' shoes deciding with free, reasonable care what basic minimum others require (Hassoun, 2020a; Hassoun, 2020b). And, at least in democratic societies, compatriots (co-rulers) ultimately bear the responsibilities that come with this governance.[9] Moreover, if these arguments go through, the minimally good life account may apply well beyond national borders (to whatever coercive international institutions exist) (Hassoun and Brock, 2012). All coercive institutions have to help their subjects live minimally good lives.

---

[6] For discussion of coercion, and its compatibility with consent, see Hassoun (2012).
[7] As I explain in Chapter 3, I think justice requires this much even of those not subjecting people to coercive rule. Individuals' claims, and our obligations to them, only grow stronger when we subject them to coercive rules.
[8] I set aside other questions about legitimacy here, e.g. whether legitimacy requires democratic rule.
[9] I do not consider the obligations of compatriots under autocratic or dictatorial regimes. However, in Chapter 3, I argue at some length that the reasons common humanity demands respect from rulers apply much more generally beyond borders and in our personal as well as political lives.

Appendix II

Liam Murphy's (2000) fair shares view, in *The Moral Demands of Affluence*, may also let people do almost nothing for others while leaving great needs unmet or require some to sacrifice everything for others. Murphy does not provide a first order account of what constitutes one's fair share, so his view may not require people to give up anything significant to help others, and it may also require them to give up everything to assist in our non-ideal world—depending on what first order account he endorses.

Murphy considers versions of these worries in examining some apparent counterexamples to his view. Specifically, he imagines a case where two potential rescuers are standing near a shallow pond in which two children are drowning. He thinks potential rescuers should each do their part and save one child. But, if one decides not to help, Murphy says the other need not rescue the second child on her own. Moreover, Murphy says that his view might not even require rescue in the standard case where there is only one baby to save. If there is something else a potential rescuer could do to help more people without excessive cost (like give money to Oxfam), Murphy thinks that is required. He notes that his view is sensitive to the number of potential rescuers, but the fact of non-compliance does not change our obligations. Moreover, Murphy says that other principles do not issue more intuitive verdicts about rescue cases. For instance, optimizing principles like Singer's require us to do whatever best promotes welfare or utility and that may require neglecting to rescue some to help many others. Murphy thinks his view is more plausible than the competitors' views because it recognizes the importance of a fair distribution of burdens. He suggests that "our strong negative reaction to failures to rescue is based not so much on a sense that the agent acted terribly wrongly but on a sense that his emotional indifference to the victim's plight shows him to have an appalling character" (Murphy, 2000, 133). On the other hand, Murphy explicitly endorses the idea that in some extraordinary cases we must sacrifice our lives or limbs for others.

I do not believe any of these replies succeed. Murphy appears to have missed the point of the worry that his view does not require enough: It is not that there is something special about immediate rescue when many others are suffering and one person cannot help everyone. Rather, the problem is that his principle does not require rescue *even when nothing else important is at stake*—simply because others are not doing their part. Moreover, the fact that others *could* help, that some *other* principles fare poorly, and that other things *could* be at stake cannot address the key concern that if others are *not helping, the relevant fair shares principles* may require us to do next to nothing to help others in desperate need when nothing else *is* at stake. Nor can an appeal to fairness explain why someone does not have to rescue another person when nothing else significant is at stake. One who neglects to rescue in such circumstances acts wrongly precisely because they have failed to do what they should and rescue an innocent human being. We do not have to explain why we think people who fail to rescue others in such circumstances are moral monsters by pointing to their "emotional indifference" (Murphy, 2000, 133). After all, some of those who neglect to rescue others may feel terribly bad about doing what they think they ought to do. The issue with Murphy's reply to the claim that fair shares views may require too much is this: Even if some extraordinary cases where people must sacrifice life or limb for others exist, Murphy says that they need not generally do so. Normally no one must sacrifice so much. But Murphy's theory offers no grounds for ruling many such sacrifices out.

Murphy also considers some other potential counterexamples to his view that seem pertinent to consider here. He acknowledges, for instance, that in non-ideal situations where people are not complying with their obligations, his principle would not require us to do our part to rectify the failures—e.g. by contributing to a campaign to help refugees in a war-torn region. The problem is that his view of what we must give is insensitive to how much aid people need. Murphy replies that although non-compliance increases the need for aid, that "does not increase the level of required sacrifice for complying agents" (Murphy, 2000, 125). He says that it is only unintuitive because there is a deontic constraint against doing harm. It is worth quoting him at length at this point:

> The mistake here is to transfer the sense that noncompliers act more wrongly when they do harm than when they allow harm to the question of what complying third parties are responsible for. If the question is whether A can legitimately fail to sustain sacrifice for the sake of benefiting B, it does not matter whether B's foreseeable needs are due to C foreseeably doing harm or allowing harm.* A's concern is with the effects of C not doing what she is required to do, not with the seriousness of C's wrongdoing. In any case, when thought about directly, it is not clear why responsibility should *more* easily transfer from C to A. the *more* wrong C's noncompliance (Murphy, 2000, 126).

I agree that there is a difference between the blameworthiness of those who create additional need and how demanding the obligation to fulfill need becomes, but Murphy's response to the counterexamples above does not work. Those who believe that our obligations should track the amount of need in a situation may not even endorse the doing allowing distinction. Even if they do, they can hold both that it is worse to cause harm and that one's obligations to aid grow in situations with greater needs. This point is, in principle, compatible with the view that non-compliance, in increasing the need for aid, "does not increase the level of required sacrifice for complying agents" (Murphy, 2000, 125). Rather, it may be increasing need *alone* that increases the required sacrifice of all agents. It may increase the required sacrifice so much that even when some do not comply, others must provide the requisite assistance. In short, even if Murphy's principle was sustainable, it does not show that the level of required sacrifice does not track need. However, if sacrifice must track need, this opens the potential for conflict between the tracking requirement and the claim that we never need to pick up the slack. In such cases, Murphy has not provided any reason to think his principle should always trump.

Appendix III

This appendix presents a simple model for choosing between policies that affect present and future generations in different ways.[1] Recall first, that Chapter 5 argued that we should:

(A) Use resources to minimize weighted need in the future and to reduce weighted need and increase the number helped in the present.

What follows will argue that this principle provides significant guidance in this model if one also accepts the following, almost uncontroversial, principle:

(B) When two policies have the same impact on present generations, they should be judged solely based on their impact on future generations. When two policies have the same impact on future generations, they should be judged solely based on their impact on present generations.

I then suggest that, to get further guidance about what policies to pursue, one must answer harder questions about how to deal with tradeoffs between aiding those in present and future generations.

The model below should, moreover, provide fruitful avenues for further inquiry. Researchers can use it to explore rankings of situations specifying some of the missing parameters in the principles I have proposed for aiding the poor in present and future generations in different ways. They can also consider, for instance, how including a discount rate will impact judgments about situations with people with more or less need in the present and future and with different numbers of people in the future. Alternately, if researchers provide a fully cashed out account of how we should arbitrate between policies that impact those below the threshold, the model may also allow them to consider whether the resulting ranking is, ultimately, plausible. One may find that the proposed ranking conflicts with some other plausible principles of global, or intergenerational, justice.

Consider the model's basic components. First, the model supposes that each person can have one of three levels of good below the threshold in the initial, present, and future situations. (The initial situation shows what the case is in the present before we give aid.) The model will use H, M, and L to represent high, medium, and low levels of good and vectors to represent a situation profile with the same two people in the initial and present situations and up to two additional people in the future. The number 0 will be used to represent the lack of a person in the future. So, for instance, the situation profile below would be: (M,L;M,H;H,0).[2]

---

[1] In variable population situations generations overlap. Here I will, however, only consider what we should say about two generations that do not overlap.
[2] It should be easy to see how to extend the model so that it can be used to consider impacts on different future generations. One can also incorporate uncertainty into the model.

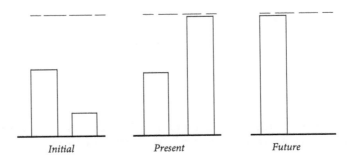

Fig. 6 Relevant possibilities

The model also assumes anonymity—that a person's particular identity does not matter. So it need not consider, for instance, both (L,M;H,L;M,0) and (M,L;L,H;0,M). It supposes our judgments about these two situation profiles will be the same.

Furthermore, let us suppose that when a person has H they have no need, so we do not need to represent situation profiles where there are no future people or only one future person. That is, suppose the "scores" in the situation profiles where a future person has H will be the same as the scores in the otherwise equivalent situation profiles where the future person does not exist. So (L,L;L,L;H,H) receives the same score as (L,L;L,L;0,0), for instance. Whether this is plausible depends on exactly how one thinks about the significance of adding people who are above the threshold to a population. This assumes that preventing a person in need from coming into existence is as good as bringing someone who is not in need into existence.[3] However, this assumption just simplifies the representation of possibilities below. If preventing a needy person from coming into existence is better (or worse) than bringing someone who is not needy into existence, the ranking of possible situations *might* not be *as* extensive, but the ranking of at least 1/2 of these situations would be the same. So, the assumption that preventing a needy person from coming into existence is as good as bringing someone who is not needy into existence does not challenge the conclusion that the principles his paper relies upon can yield an *extensive* ordering of possible situations.

One way of representing the relevant possibilities where there are (up to) two people in the future is this:[4]

---

[3] It would, presumably, be better to bring a person into existence with more rather than less goods. So, there is a sense in which it is better to bring someone into existence at or above the threshold than to prevent that person from coming into existence poorly-off (that is to bring the person into existence below the threshold). But there is another sense in which this is not clearly true. It is not clearly better to bring someone into existence with a lot of goods than to prevent that (or a different) person from coming into existence at all because they would be poorly-off if they came into existence.

[4] To construct the rows, start from (L,L;L,L;L,L) then increase the amount the people in future generations have along each row as follows: (L,M), (L,H), (M,M), (M,H), (H,H). In each of the first six columns increase the amount in the present and then the initial situation in the same way. For each increment in the initial situation, e.g. when it is (L,M), repeat the process in the present and future situations to generate new rows and fill in columns. That is, this method will yield this diagram if one also considers the exceptions discussed below.

(L, L; L, L; L, L)	(L, L; L, L; L, M)	(L, L; L, L; L, H)	(L, L; L, L; M, M)	(L, L; L, L; M, H)	(L, L; L, L; H, H)
(L, L; L, M; L, L)	(L, L; L, M; L, M)	(L, L; L, M; L, H)	(L, L; L, M; M, M)	(L, L; L, M; M, H)	(L, L; L, M; H, H)
(L, L; L, H; L, L)	(L, L; L, H; L, M)	(L, L; L, H; L, H)	(L, L; L, H; M, M)	(L, L; L, H; M, H)	(L, L; L, H; H, H)
(L, L; M, M; L, L)	(L, L; M, M; L, M)	(L, L; M, M; L, H)	(L, L; M, M; M, M)	(L, L; M, M; M, H)	(L, L; M, M; H, H)
(L, L; M, H; L, L)	(L, L; M, H; L, M)	(L, L; M, H; L, H)	(L, L; M, H; M, M)	(L, L; M, H; M, H)	(L, L; M, H; H, H)
(L, L; H, H; L, L)	(L, L; H, H; L, M)	(L, L; H, H; L, H)	(L, L; H, H; M, M)	(L, L; H, H; M, H)	(L, L; H, H; H, H)

Fig. 7 Levels of goods across time

The model increments the amount those in future generations have going across each row and increments the amount those in present generations have going down each column (in the same way).

This diagram does not include boxes where the amount in the present is less than the amount in the initial situation.[5] For, recall that the principles defended in the text do not allow us to judge those. They only govern how we should aid those in need.

It is not necessary to consider anything beyond the first six rows (represented above) in what follows. (Subsequent rows would be added by incrementing the amount in the initial situation in the same way.) The reason why it is not necessary to show all the rows in the above model is that the scores the improvements from the initial situation to the present receive in subsequent boxes are the same as the scores improvements from the initial situation to the present receive in some of the cases above. (L,M;M,M;0,0) = (L,L;L,M;0,0), for instance. To see this, recall our principles:

(A) Use resources to minimize weighted need in the future and to reduce weighted need and increase the number helped in the present.

(B) When two policies have the same impact on present generations, they should be judged solely based on their impact on future generations. When two policies have the same impact on future generations, they should be judged solely based on their impact on present generations.

These principles do not require us to consider how much need there is to begin with. They just require us to look at the amount of need fulfilled in present and future generations and the number helped in present generations.[6] Of course, one might argue that we should accept additional principles that focus on the amount of need in a situation. It is plausible, for instance, that the world would be better if there were never any need at all.[7] If we consider the amount of need in the initial situation, we would have to consider the remaining rows beyond the sixth. Recall, however, that we cannot do anything about the need in the initial situation right now—though we might have been able to do something about it in the past—and we are only evaluating policies we might implement now. That said, the principles above should suffice for illustrating the advantages of this book's model for arbitrating between a wide range of possible policies.

---

[5] So, when the initial situation is (L,M), the first row with a present situation has (L,M) as well.
[6] Moreover, suppose that changes in situations that we are evaluating are due to our actions.
[7] So (L,M;L,M;H,0) would be better, rather than worse, than (L,L;L,M;H,0), for instance. For, there is less total need in (L,M;L,M;H,0) than (L,L;L,M;H,0) and it would not be better to help a greater number (because the person helped could otherwise have had less total need over the course of their life).

Let us employ the following representation of rankings between situation profiles: (L,L;L,M;H,0) < (L,L;M,M;H,0) means that (L,L;L,M;H,0) is ranked lower than (L,L;M,M;H,0) on the appropriate principle. Recall that, in the future, we should have a prioritarian concern for alleviating need and, in the present, we should also consider the number helped. Given (B) it follows that (L,L;L,L;L,L) < (L,L;L,L;L,M) < (L,L;L,L;L,H) and (L,L;L,L;L,L) < (L,L;L,M;L,L) < (L,L;M,M;L,L), for instance.

With two exceptions, each box below another or to the right of it in the diagram above is ranked higher than the preceding box. The first exception is this: Sometimes the boxes in the third row are ranked higher than the corresponding boxes in the fourth row and vice versa. That is (L,L;L,H;L,L) may be better than (L,L;M,M:L,L), (L,L;L,H;L,M) may be better than (L,L;M,M;L,M), and so on (or vice versa). Which is ranked higher depends on the relative weighting of needs and numbers helped in present generations.[8] The second exception is this: Sometimes the boxes in the third column are ranked higher than the corresponding boxes in the fourth and vice versa. Which is ranked higher depends on whether bringing one person into existence with H is better than bringing two people into existence with M (though this will be decided once the numerical value of M and H are known—that is, if $M > 1/2H$ then the fourth column is ranked higher than the third, if $1/2H > M$ then the third column is ranked higher than the fourth, and if $M = 1/2H$ the scores in the third and fourth columns will be equal).[9]

Since the ranking of rows is determined by what happens in present generations alone, and the ranking of columns is determined by what happens in future generations alone, the overall ranking will not change in other ways. We can know, for instance, that (L,L;M,M;M,H) < (L,L;M,H;H,H). Since (L,L;M,M;M,H) < (L,L;M,H;M,H) by the second part of (A) (or (1)) irrespective of the order of the third and fourth rows,

---

[8] Consider a case where the third row is higher than the fourth row. The ranking of rows is determined by what happens in present generations alone. So suppose, for instance, that in present generations moving a person from L to M is worth 2 points in present generations, moving a person from M to H is worth 1 point, and moving a person from L to H is worth 3 points. Further, suppose that in present generations helping each person gets 1 point. In present generations the score for the first row = 0, the second row = 3, the third row = 4, the fourth row = 6, the fifth row = 7, and the sixth row = 8. The score increases along each row. A similar pattern holds (in all cases) for future generations—the score increases within each group of six situation profiles. Suppose, for instance, that in future generations if a person with L is in the population one receives no credit, if a person with M is in the population one receives 2 points and if a person with H is in the population one receives 3 points. So (L,L;L,L;L,L) = 0, (L,L;L,L;L,M) = 2, (L,L;L,L;L,H) = 3, (L,L;L,L;M,M) = 4, (L,L;L,L;M,H) = 5, (L,L;L,L;H,H) = 6. That is, things get better on this paper's suggested principles as we move to the right across rows and down each column.

[9] Consider a case where the fourth row is higher than the third row. Suppose, for instance, that alleviating the first unit of a person's need is worth 10 points in present generations, alleviating the second unit of a person's need is worth 9 points, and alleviating the third unit is worth 8 points. Suppose further that someone with L has no units of necessary good, someone with M has one unit of necessary good, and someone with H has three units of necessary good. So, alleviating the first unit of a person's need moves them from L to M but one must alleviate the second and third unit of a person's need to move them from M to H. Finally, suppose helping a single person is worth only 1 point. The score in present generations for the first row = 0, the second row = 11, the third row = 28, the fourth row = 22, the fifth row = 39, and the sixth row = 56. The reason the fourth row is higher (has less need) than the third row is that more weighted need is alleviated in helping someone move from M to H than in moving two people from L to M. This pushes in the opposite direction as numbers. So, if helping a person was worth 10 points rather than 1, the ranking of the third and fourth rows would be reversed. The score in present generations for the first row would = 0, the second row would = 20, the third row would = 37, the fourth row would = 40, the fifth row would = 47, and the sixth row would = 74.

and (L,L:M,H:M,H) < (L,L;M,H;H,H) by the first part of (A) (or (4)) irrespective of the order of the third and fourth columns, (L,L;M,M;M,H) < (L,L;M,H;H,H) by the kind of transitivity specified in (B). That such incomplete and underspecified principles (A) and (B) allow us to arrive at such a complete ranking in this model is remarkable. What is interesting about this is that we did not have to decide how to treat present generations compared with future generations to rank many of the situation profiles in the model above where both present and future situations are different. Nor did we need to decide exactly how much weight to give fulfilling need in present or future generations. Nor did we have to decide how to compare helping a greater number in present generations to either of these things. Of course, we would have to make all of these decisions to get a full ranking over all possible situations. Still, that we can know so much about the ranking of possible situations using such incomplete principles is fantastic.

To see how this model can help us evaluate the impact of many policies, consider three possible responses to climate change—adaptation, mitigation, and geoengineering. Suppose that adaptation brings large gains to present people (it moves them from L to H) but ensures that those in the future have only a moderate amount of goods—M. Suppose mitigation brings modest gains to present people (it moves them from L to M) and also ensures that those in the future have a moderate amount of goods—M. Finally, suppose geoengineering has no impact on the present (so they will remain at L) but ensures that those in the future have no need—H. The box in the fourth column of the bottom row demonstrates the effect of adaptation if there are two people in the future (L,L;H,H;M,M). The box in the fourth column of the fourth row demonstrates the effect of mitigation with two people in the future (L,L;M,M;M,M). Geoengineering yields the final column on the right of the top row (L,L;L,L;H,H). So, adaptation is always better than mitigation in this example,[10] but the model does not tell us whether either should be preferred to geoengineering (or vice versa).[11] To answer that question, we would need to know the relative importance of helping present people vs. ensuring that (any) future people have more. The model does suggest, however, that if a policy could achieve (L,L;H,H;H,H), it would be better than all the alternatives (whether the policy ensures that all the people in the future are at or above the threshold—have H—or just refrains from creating poorly-off people in future generations).[12]

Consider a more complicated example to illustrate how it is possible to determine the score for boxes in rows beyond the sixth row in the model by considering the scores in one or more boxes in these first six rows. Looking only at initial and present situations it is reasonable to suppose, for instance, that (L,L;L,L) receives the same score as (L,M;L,M), (L,L;L,M) receives the same score as (L,M;M,M), and (L,L;L,H) receives the same score as (L,M;M,H). Further, it seems reasonable to suppose that, just with respect to the amount of need met, (L,L;M,H) should receive the same score as the sum of (L,M;M,M) and (L,M;M,H). In (L,L;M,H) the first person is moved from L to M and the second person is moved from L to H in transitioning from the initial situation to the present. Similarly, in (L,M;M,M) the first person is moved from L to M and in (L,M;M,H) the second person is moved from L to H in transitioning from the initial situation to the

---

[10] It does not matter what the relative weight of needs and numbers helped in present generations is or whether helping one person move from L is better than helping two people move from L to M.

[11] This ranking would not change if there were only one person in the future on adaptation. It does not tell us what to do if there are two people in the future on adaptation and only one person on mitigation.

[12] Assume, for simplicity, that some people will exist who are not affected by the policy.

present. Finally, concerning numbers helped (L,M;M,M) and (L,M;M,H) are the same as (L,M;M,H); they all help one person. So, aggregating the relevant components of the scores from (L,M;M,M) and (L,M;M,H) it is possible to arrive at the score for (L,L;M,H). I trust that, from these examples, one can work out the other equivalences between the first six and the remaining rows for the improvements between the initial situation and the present (for those inclined to generate the complete matrix).

In any case, the model and principles proposed here should provide fruitful avenues for further inquiry. We can use the model to explore rankings of situation profiles when the missing parameters in this chapter's proposed principles for choosing between policies that aid (but do not harm) the poor are specified in different ways. We can consider, for instance, how including a discount rate will impact judgments about situation profiles with people who are more or less poor in the present and future and different numbers of people in the future. The model can also be used to test principles for arbitrating between possible policies that impact the poor. We can use it to see if the ranking of situation profiles on these principles is, ultimately, plausible. Moreover, it is possible to see how this chapter's principles (or others) fare in similar, but more complicated, models (e.g. with more than two people in present or future generations). In any case, further research on how we should choose between policies that impact the poor in present and future generations is pressing and important.

References

Africa Check. 2019. "Factsheet: South Africa's Crime Statistics for 2018/19." Johannesburg, South Africa: University of the Witwatersrand. Updated April 12, 2019. Accessed October 5, 2019. Available online at: https://africacheck.org/fact-checks/factsheets/factsheet-south-africas-crime-statistics-201819.

Albertsen, Andreas. 2020. "Personal Responsibility in Health and Health Care: Luck Egalitarianism as a Plausible and Flexible Approach to Health." *Political Research Quarterly* 73 (3): 583–595.

Albertsen, Andreas, and Nielsen, Lasse. 2020. "What Is the Point of the Harshness Objection?" *Utilitas* 32 (4): 427–443.

Atuire, Caesar Alimsinya, and Hassoun, Nicole. 2023. "Rethinking Solidarity towards Equity in Global Health: African Views." *International Journal for Equity in Health* 22 (1): 52.

Alkire, Sabina. 2002. *Valuing Freedoms: Sen's Capability Approach and Poverty*. Oxford: Oxford University Press.

Ainsworth, Mary D. Salter. 1988. "On Security." From the *Proceedings of the State University of New York*. Stony Brook Conference on Attachment.

Ainsworth, Mary D. Salter. 2010. "Security and Attachment." In *The Secure Child: Timeless Lessons in Parenting and Childhood Education*, ed. Richard Volpe. Charlotte: Information Age Publishing.

Anderson, Elizabeth. 1999. "What Is the Point of Equality?" *Ethics* 109 (2): 287–337.

Anderson, Elizabeth. 2010. "The Fundamental Disagreement between Luck Egalitarians and Relational Egalitarians." *Canadian Journal of Philosophy* 40 (1): 1–23.

Angner, Erik. 2011. "Current Trends in Welfare Measurement." In *The Elgar Companion to Recent Economic Methodology*, ed. John B. Davis and D. Wade Hands, 121–154. Chelterham: Edward Elgar Publishing.

Annas, Julia. 1993. *The Morality of Happiness*. New York: Oxford University Press.

Arneson, Richard. 1999. "Human Flourishing Versus Desire Satisfaction." *Social Philosophy & Policy* 16 (1): 113–142.

Arneson, Richard. 2000. "Luck Egalitarianism and Prioritarianism." *Ethics* 110(2): 339–349.

Arneson, Richard. 2004. "Moral Limits on the Demands of Beneficence?" In *The Ethics of Assistance: Morality and the Distant Needy*, ed. Deen Chatterjee, 33–58. Cambridge: Cambridge University Press.

Arneson, Richard. 2005. "Distributive Justice and Basic Capability Equality: 'Good Enough' Is Not Good Enough." In *Capabilities Equality: Basic Issues and Problems*, ed. Alexander Kaufman, 17–38. London: Routledge.

Arneson, Richard. 2012. "Moral Limits on the Demands of Beneficence?" In *The Ethics of Assistance: Morality, Affluence, and the Distant Needy*, ed. Deen K. Chatterjee, 35–58. Cambridge: Cambridge University Press.

Arneson, Richard. 2013. "From Primary Goods to Capabilities to Well-Being." *Critical Review of International, Social, and Political Philosophy* 16 (2): 179–195.

Arthur, John. 2002. "Famine Relief and the Ideal Moral Code." In *Ethics: History, Theory and Contemporary Issues*, ed. Steven Cahn and Peter Markie. Oxford: Oxford University Press.

Arrhenius, Gustaf. 2011. *Population Ethics: The Challenge of Future Generations*. March Draft of Manuscript provisionally accepted by Oxford University Press.

Arrhenius, Gustaf. 2020. "Population Paradoxes without Transitivity," In *Oxford Handbook of Population Ethics*, ed. Gustaf Arrhenius, Bykvist Krister, Tim Campbell, and Elizabeth Finneron-Burns, 189–198. Oxford: Oxford University Press.

REFERENCES

Atuire, Caesar, and Hassoun, Nicole. 2021. "Rethinking Solidarity towards Equity in Global Health: African Views." *International Journal for Equity in Health* 22 (1): 52.

Axelsen, David, and Nielsen, Lasse. 2015. "Sufficiency as Freedom from Duress." *Journal of Political Philosophy* 23 (4): 406–426.

Baltussen, Rob, Sylla, Mariame, Frick, Kevin, and Mariotti, Silvio. 2005. "Cost-Effectiveness of Trachoma Control in Seven World Regions." *Ophthalmic Epidemiology* 12 (2): 91–101.

Bartlett, Karen. 2014. "Eradicating the Last 1% of Polio Is Deadly but Necessary." *Newsweek*. New York: Newsweek Incorporated. November 28. Accessed October 5, 2023. Available online at: https://www.newsweek.com/2014/12/05/last-stand-against-polio-287862.html#:~:text=When%2040%2Dyear%2Dold%20Liberian,West%20Africa's%20most%20populous%20city.

Barry, Nicholas. 2006. "Defending Luck Egalitarianism." *Journal of Applied Philosophy* 23(1): 89–107.

Bearden, Neil, Murphy, Ryan, and Rapoport, Amnon. 2005. "A Multi-attribute Extension of the Secretary Problem: Theory and Experiments." *Journal of Mathematical Psychology* 49: 410–425.

Begley, Charles, and Durgin, Tracy. 2015. "The Direct Cost of Epilepsy in the United States: A Systematic Review of Estimates." *Epilepsia* 56 (9): 1376–1387.

Beitz, Charles, and Goodin, Robert. 2009. *Global Basic Rights*. New York: Oxford University Press.

Benatar, David. 2006. *Better Never to Have Been: The Harm of Coming into Existence*. Oxford: Oxford University Press.

Benbaji, Yitzhak. 2005. "The Doctrine of Sufficiency: A Defence." *Utilitas* 17 (3): 310–332.

Benbaji, Yitzhak. 2006. "Sufficiency or Priority?" *European Journal of Philosophy* 14 (3): 327–348.

Birks, David. 2014. "Moral Status and the Wrongness of Paternalism." *Social Theory and Practice* 40 (3): 483–498.

Blackorby, Charles, Bossert, Walter, and Donaldson, David. 1995. "Intertemporal Population Ethics: Critical-Level Utilitarian Principles." *Econometrica* 63: 1303–1320.

Blake, Michael. 2001. "Distributive Justice, State Coercion, and Autonomy." *Philosophy and Public Affairs* 30 (3): 257–296.

Blake, Michael. 2013. *Justice and Foreign Policy*. Oxford: Oxford University Press.

Blatz, William. 1966. *Human Security: Some Reflections*. Toronto: University of Toronto Press.

Boden, Margaret. 2004. *The Creative Mind: Myths and Mechanisms*, 2nd edn. London: Routledge.

Boonin, David. 2011. *Should Race Matter?* Cambridge: Cambridge University Press.

Bovens, Luc. 1999. "The Value of Hope." *Philosophy and Phenomenological Research* 59 (3): 667–681.

Bowlby, John. 1969. *Attachment and Loss*. New York: Basic Books.

Bratman, Michael. 1992. "Shared Cooperative Activity." *Philosophical Review* 101 (2): 327–341.

Braybrooke, David. 1987. *Meeting Needs*. Princeton: Princeton University Press.

Brennan, Geoffrey. 2013. "Feasibility in Optimizing Ethics." *Social Philosophy and Policy* 30 (1–2): 314–329.

Brennan, Geoffrey, and Pettit, Philip. 2005. *The Economy of Esteem: An Essay on Civil and Political Society: An Essay on Civil and Political Society*. Oxford: Oxford University Press.

Brock, Gillian. 2009. *Global Justice: A Cosmopolitan Account*. Oxford: Oxford University Press.

Brock, Gillian. 2013. "Contemporary Cosmopolitanism: Some Current Issues." *Philosophy Compass* 8 (8): 689–698.

Brock, Gillian, and David Miller. 2019. "Needs in Moral and Political Philosophy." In *The Stanford Encyclopedia of Philosophy*, ed. Edward N. Zalta, https://plato.stanford.edu/archives/sum2019/entries/needs/.

Brock, Gillian and Nicole Hassoun. 2013. "Distance, Moral Relevance of." In *The International Encyclopedia of Ethics*, ed. Hugh LaFollette. New Jersey: Wiley-Blackwell.

Broome, John. 1992. *Counting the Cost of Global Warming*. Cambridge: The White Horse Press.

Broome, John. 2005. "Should We Value Population?" *Journal of Political Philosophy* 13 (4): 399–413.
Buchanan, Allen. 2013. *The Heart of Human Rights*. Oxford: Oxford University Press.
Caney, Simon. 2006. *Justice beyond Borders: A Global Political Theory*. Oxford: Oxford University Press.
Caney, Simon. 2009. "Ethics and Global Climate Change." In *Climate Ethics*, ed. Stephen Gardiner, Simon Caney, Dale Jamieson, Henry Shue, 10–15. Oxford: Oxford University Press.
Carey, Brian. 2020. "Provisional Sufficientarianism: Distributive Feasibility in Non-Ideal Theory." *Journal of Value Inquiry* 54 (4): 589–606.
Carter, Ian. 2014. "Is the Capability Approach Paternalist?" *Economics and Philosophy* (30): 75–98. Cambridge: Cambridge University Press.
Casal, Paula. 2007. "Why Sufficiency Is Not Enough." *Ethics* 117 (2): 296–327.
Chase, Elain, and Bantebya-Kyomuhendo, Grace. 2014. *Poverty and Shame: Global Experiences*. Oxford: Oxford University Press.
Chignell, Andrew. 2014. "Modal Motivations for Noumenal Ignorance: Knowledge, Cognition, and Coherence." *Kant-Studien* 105 (4): 573–597.
Claassen, Rutger. 2014. "Capability Paternalism." *Economics and Philosophy* 30 (1): 57–73.
Cohen, Gerald. 1989. "On the Currency of Egalitarian Justice." *Ethics* 99 (4): 906–944.
Collins, Stephanie. 2013. "Duties to Make Friends." *Ethical Theory and Moral Practice* 16 (5): 907–921.
Coplan, Amy, and Goldie, Peter. 2011. *Empathy: Philosophical and Psychological Perspectives*. Oxford: Oxford University Press.
Copp, David. 1998. "Equality, Justice, and the Basic Needs." In *Necessary Goods*, ed. Gillian Brock, 113–133. Lanham: Rowman and Littlefield.
Crisp, Roger. 2006. *Reasons and the Good*. Oxford: Clarendon Press.
Crisp, Roger. 2008. "Compassion and Beyond." *Ethical Theory and Moral Practice* 11 (3): 233–246.
Cruft, Rowan. 2015. "From a Good Life to Human Rights: Some Complications." In *Philosophical Foundations of Human Rights*, ed. Rowan Cruft, Matthew S. Liao, and Massimo Renzo. 101–116. Oxford: Oxford University Press.
Cullity, Garrett. 2004. *The Moral Demands of Affluence*. Oxford: Oxford University Press.
Culter, David, and Summers, Lawrence. 2020. "The COVID-19 Pandemic and the $16 Trillion Virus." *Journal of the American Medical Association* 324 (15): 1495–1496.
Curzer, Howard. 2012. "Courage and Continence (NE III.6-9)." In *Aristotle and the Virtues*, 19–64. Oxford: Oxford University Press.
Daemen, Maria A. 2022a. "Being Sure and Living Well: How Security Affects Human Flourishing." *Journal of Value Inquiry* 58 (1): 93–110.
Daemen, Maria A. 2022b. "Freedom, Security, and the COVID-19 Pandemic." *Critical Review of International Social and Political Philosophy*: 1–21. https://doi.org/10.1080/13698230.2022.2100961.
Darwall, Stephen. 2002. *Virtue Ethics*. New Jersey: Wiley-Blackwell.
Darwall, Stephen. 2006. *The Second Person Standpoint: Morality, Respect and Accountability*. Cambridge: Cambridge University Press.
De Cock, Nathalie, D'Haese, Marijke, Vink, Nick, Van Rooyen, Johan C., Staelens, Lotte, Schönfeldt, Hettie C., and D'Haese, Luc. 2013. "Food Security in Rural Areas of Limpopo Province." *South Africa Food Security* 5 (2): 269–282.
De George, Richard. 1981. "The Environment, Rights and Future Generations." In *Environmental Ethics*, ed. E. Partridge, 157–166. New York: Prometheus Books.
Dorsey, Dale. 2010. "Three Arguments for Perfectionism." *Noûs* 44 (1): 59–79.
Dorsey, Dale. 2012. *The Basic Minimum: A Welfarist Approach*. Cambridge: Cambridge University Press.
Dowling, John E. 2020. "Restoring Vision to the Blind." *Science* 368 (6493): 827–828.
Duflo, Esther, and Abhijit Banerjee. 2022. "Balancing Hope and Despair in Turbulent Times." *The New York Times*, December 1, 2022. Available online at: https://www.nytimes.com/2022/12/01/special-series/climate-change-covid-optimism.html.

Dumitru, A. 2017. "On the Moral Irrelevance of a Global Basic Structure: Prospects for a Satisficing Sufficientarian Theory of Global Justice." *Croatian Journal of Philosophy*, 17 (50): 233–264.
Dworkin, Ronald. 1978. *Taking Rights Seriously*. Cambridge, MA: Harvard University Press.
Dworkin, Ronald. 2000. *Sovereign Virtue*. Cambridge, MA: Harvard University Press.
Engster, Daniel. 2005. "Rethinking Care Theory: The Practice of Caring and the Obligation to Care." Hypatia 20 (3): 50–74.
Enoch, David. 2016. "II—What's Wrong with Paternalism: Autonomy, Belief, and Action." *Proceedings of the Aristotelian Society* 116(1): 21–48
Estlund, David. 2019. *Utopophobia: On the Limits (If Any) of Political Philosophy*. Princeton: Princeton University Press.
Etya'ale, Daniel. 2001. "Update on Onchocerciasis, Community Eye Health." *Vision* 14 (38): 19–21.
Feinberg, Joel. 1984. "The Moral and Legal Responsibility of the Bad Samaritan." *Criminal Justice Ethics* 3(1): 56–59.
Feldman, Fred. 1995. "Justice, Desert, and the Repugnant Conclusion." *Utilitas* 7: 567–585.
Feldman, Fred. 2004. *Pleasure and the Good Life: Concerning the Nature, Varieties, and Plausibility of Hedonism*. Oxford: Clarendon Press.
Fletcher, Guy. 2013. "A Fresh Start for the Objective-List Theory of Well-Being". *Utilitas* 25 (2): 206-20.
Finkelstein, Marni, Wamsely, Mark, and Miranda, Doreen. 2002. *What Keeps Children in Foster Care from Succeeding in School?* New York: Vera Institute of Justice.
Finkelstein, Claire. 2003. "Is Risk a Harm?" *University of Pennsylvania Law Review* 151: 963–1001.
Fleurbaey, Marc. 1995. "Equal Opportunity or Equal Social Outcome?" *Economics and Philosophy* 11 (1): 25–55.
Fleurbaey, Marc. 2008. *Fairness, Responsibility, and Welfare*. Oxford: Oxford University Press.
Fleurbaey, Marc, and Tungodden, Bertil. 2010. "The Tyranny of Non-aggregation versus the Tyranny of Aggregation in Social Choices: A Real Dilemma." *Economic Theory* 44: 399–414.
Fowler, Mark. 1982. "Coercion and Practical Reason." *Social Theory and Practice* 8: 329–355.
Frankfurt, Harry. 1987. "Equality as a Moral Ideal." *Ethics* 98: 21–43.
Frankfurt, Harry. 1988. "Necessity and Desire" and "Coercion and Moral Responsibility". In *The Importance of What We Care About*, ed. Ted Honderich, 80–116. Cambridge: Cambridge University Press.
Fraser, Nancy. 1989. "Talking about Needs: Interpretive Contests as Political Conflicts in Welfare-State Societies." *Ethics* 99 (2): 291–313.
Fried, Charles. 1976. "Equality and Rights in Medical Care." *The Hastings Center Report* 6 (1): 29–34.
Gaita, Raimond. 1999. *A Common Humanity: Thinking about Love and Truth and Justice*. London: Routledge Press.
Gallup, John, and Sachs, Jeffrey. 2001. "The Economic Burden of Malaria." *American Journal of Tropical Medicine and Hygiene* 64 (1–2): 85–96.
Gardiner, Stephen. 2010. :Ethics and Global Climate Change:, In *Climate Ethics: Essential Readings* Gardiner, Stephen, Caney, Simon, Jamieson, Dale, Shue, Henry eds. Oxford: Oxford University Press.
Gheaus, Anca. 2013. "The Feasibility Constraint on the Concept of Justice." *Philosophical Quarterly* 63 (252): 445–464.
Gifford, Rebecca, and Edmondo, Aimee. 2019. "2019 Annual Reports." *Last Mile Health*. Accessed October 5, 2023. https://2019-annual-report.lastmilehealth.org/.
Gilabert, Pablo. 2011. "Humanist and Political Perspectives on Human Rights." *Political Theory* 39 (4): 439–467.
Gilabert, Pablo. 2017. "Justice and Feasibility: A Dynamic Approach." In *Political Utopias: Contemporary Debates*, ed. Kevin Vallier and Michael Weber. Oxford: Oxford University Press.

REFERENCES 163

Gilabert, Pablo. 2019. *Human Dignity and Human Rights*. Oxford: Oxford University Press.

Gilabert, Pablo, and Lawford-Smith, Holly. 2012. "Political Feasibility: A Conceptual Exploration." *Political Studies* 60 (4): 809–825.

Goldman, Alvin. 1993. "The Psychology of Folk Psychology." *Behavioral and Brain Sciences* 16: 15–28.

Goodin, Robert. 1995. "Political Ideals and Political Practice." *British Journal of Political Science* 25 (1): 37–56.

Gopnik, Alison, and Wellman, Henry. 1992. "Why the Child's Theory of Mind Really Is a Theory." *Mind and Language* 7: 145–171.

Gough, Ian. 1994. "Economic Institutions and the Satisfaction of Human Needs." *Journal of Economic Issues* 28 (1): 25–66.

Graham, Carol. 2009. *Happiness around the World: The Paradox of Happy Peasants and Miserable Millionaires*. Oxford: Oxford University Press.

Griffin, James. 1986. *Well-Being: Its Meaning, Measurement, and Moral Importance*. Oxford: Oxford University Press.

Griffin, James. 2008. *On Human Rights*. New York: Oxford University Press.

Gupta, Sanjeev, Davoodi, Hamid, and Alonso-Terme, Rosa. 1998. "Does Corruption Affect Income Inequality and Poverty?" *IMF Working Paper*. Washington, DC: International Monetary Fund. Accessed October 5, 2023. https://papers.ssrn.com/sol3/papers.cfm?abstract_id=882360.

Hampton, Jean. 1993. "Selflessness and the Loss of Self." *Social Philosophy and Policy* 10 (1): 135–165.

Hanna, Jason. 2018. *In Our Best Interest: A Defense of Paternalism*. Oxford: Oxford University Press.

Hardin, Garrett. 2002. "The Tragedy of the Commons." In *Environmental Ethics What Really Matters, What Really Works*, ed. David Schmidtz and Elizabeth Willott. New York: Oxford University Press.

Hare, R.M. 1981. *Moral thinking: its levels, method, and point*. Clarendon Press. https://academic.oup.com/book/12440.

Hare, Casper. 2007. "Voices from Another World: Must We Respect the Interests of People Who Do Not, and Will Never, Exist?" *Ethics* 117: 498–523.

Harman, Elizabeth. 2004. "Can We Harm and Benefit in Creating?" *Philosophical Perspectives*. Vol 18: 89–113.

Harman, Elizabeth. 2009. "Harming as Causing Harm." *Harming Future Persons* 35: 137–154.

Hassoun, Nicole. 2008. "Free Trade, Poverty, and the Environment." *Public Affairs Quarterly* 22 (4): 353–380.

Hassoun, Nicole. 2009. "Meeting Need." *Utilitas* 21 (3): 250–275.

Hassoun, Nicole. 2010. Making the Case for Foreign Aid. *Public Affairs Quarterly* 24 (1): 1–20.

Hassoun, Nicole. 2011a. "The Anthropocentric Advantage? Environmental Ethics and Climate Change Policy." *Critical Review of International Social and Political Philosophy* 14 (2): 235–257.

Hassoun, Nicole. 2011b. "Raz on the Right to Autonomy." *European Journal of Philosophy* 22 (1): 96–109.

Hassoun, Nicole. 2012. *Globalization and Global Justice: Shrinking Distance, Expanding Obligations*. Cambridge: Cambridge University Press.

Hassoun, Nicole. 2013. "Human Rights and the Minimally Good Life." *Res Philosophica* 90 (3): 413–438.

Hassoun, Nicole. 2014. "New Institutionalism and Foreign Aid." *Global Justice: Theory, Practice, Rhetoric* 7: 12–27.

Hassoun, Nicole. 2015. "Coercion, Legitimacy, and Global Justice." *Journal of Social Philosophy* 46: 178–196.

Hassoun, Nicole. 2016. "Basic Needs." In *International Development and Human Aid: Principles, Norms, and Institutions for the Global Sphere*, ed. Paulo Barcelos and Gabriele De Angelis 51–71. Edinburgh: Edinburgh University Press.

Hassoun, Nicole. 2017. "The Evolution of Wealth; Democracy or Revolution?" In *Wealth: NOMOS LVIII*, ed. Jack Knight and Melissa Schwartzberg 125–145. New York: New York University Press.

Hassoun, Nicole. 2020a. *Global Health Impact: Extending Access to Essential Medicines for the Poor*. Oxford: Oxford University Press.
Nicole Hassoun, 2020b. "What Is a Minimally Good Life and Are You Prepared to Live It?" *Psyche*. Accessed May 6, 2021. Available online at: https://psyche.co/ideas/what-is-a-minimally-good-life-and-are-you-prepared-to-live-it.
Hassoun, Nicole. 2020c. "Jonathan Mann's Human Rights Blueprint for Global Health Must Guide COVID-19 Response." *The Hill*. September 2, 2020. Available online at: https://thehill.com/opinion/healthcare/514775-jonathan-manns-human-rights-blueprint-for-global-health-must-guide-covid.
Hassoun, Nicole. 2020d. "Aid and Future Generations," In *The Oxford Handbook of Global Justice*, ed. Thom Brooks. Oxford: Oxford University Press.
Hassoun, Nicole. 2021a. "Good Enough? The Minimally Good Life Account of the Basic Minimum." *Australasian Journal of Philosophy* 100 (2): 1–12.
Hassoun, Nicole. 2021b. "Sufficiency and the Minimally Good Life." *Utilitas* 33 (3): 321–336.
Hassoun, Nicole. 2022. "The Minimally Good Life Account of What We Owe to Others and What We Can Justifiably Demand." Special Issue on Basic Needs: Normative Perspectives, Lessico di Etica Pubblica 1 (2022): 107–126. http://www.eticapubblica.it/.
Nicole, Hassoun. 2024. "Solidarity and creative Resolve". UNDP. *Human Development Report 2023/2024 : Breaking the Gridlock - Reimagining Cooperation in a Polarized World*. Available online at: https://digitallibrary.un.org/record/4040333.
Hassoun, Nicole and Brock, Gillian. 2012. "Needs." In *International Encyclopedia of Ethics*, ed. Hugh LaFollete. New Jersey: Wiley-Blackwell.
Hassoun, Nicole, and Wong, David. 2015. "Conserving Nature; Preserving Identity: Conserving Nature." *Journal of Chinese Philosophy* 42 (1–2): 176–196. https://doi.org/10.1111/1540-6253.12189.
Haybron, Daniel. 2007. "Do We Know How Happy We Are?" *Noûs* 41 (3): 394–428.
Haybron, Daniel. 2008. *The Pursuit of Unhappiness*. Oxford: Clarendon Press.
Haybron, Daniel. 2013. *Happiness: A Very Short Introduction*. Oxford: Oxford University Press.
Haybron, Daniel. 2017. "Eudaimonism, Ancient and Modern." St. Louis University Working Paper. https://sites.google.com/site/danhaybron/happiness-and-well-being.
Heathwood, Chris. 2005. "The Problem of Defective Desires." *Australasian Journal of Philosophy* 83 (4): 487–504.
Heathwood, Chris. 2006. "Desire Satisfaction and Hedonism." *Philosophical Studies* 128 (3): 539–563.
Heathwood, Chris. 2014. "Subjective Theories of Well-Being." In *The Cambridge Companion to Utilitarianism*, ed. Ben Eggleston and Dale Miller. Cambridge: Cambridge University Press.
Helliwell, John, Huang, Haifang, Grover, Shawn, and Wang, Shun. 2018. "Empirical Linkages between Good Government and National Well-Being." *Journal of Comparative Economics* 46 (4): 1332–1346.
Herington, Jonathan. 2015. "The Contribution of Security to Well-Being." In *Security: Dialogue across Disciplines*, ed. Philippe Bourbeau, 22–44. Cambridge: Cambridge University Press.
Herlitz, Anders. 2018. "The Indispensability of Sufficientarianism." *Critical Review of International Social and Political Philosophy* 22: 929–942.
Herman, Barbara. 2007. *Moral Literacy*. Cambridge, MA: Harvard University Press.
Heywood, Mark. 2008. "Chapter Three: South Africa's Treatment Action Campaign (TAC): An Example of a Successful Human Rights Campaign for Health." *Treatment Action Campaign (TAC)*. Updated March 26, 2008. Accessed October 8, 2021. Available online at: https://www.tac.org.za/news/chapter-three-south-africas-treatment-action-campaign-tac-an-example-of-a-successful-human-rights-campaign-for-health-2/.
Hirose, Iwao. 2015. *Egalitarianism*. New York: Routledge Press.
Hurka, Thomas. 2003. *Virtue, Vice, and Value*. Oxford: Oxford University Press.
Huseby, Robert. 2010. "Sufficiency: Restated and Defended." *Journal of Political Philosophy* 18 (2): 178–197.

Huseby, Robert. 2020. "Sufficiency and the Threshold Question." *Journal of Ethics* 24: 207-223.
IPPC, 2007. "Summary for Policymakers." In *Climate Change 2007: Impacts, Adaptation, and Vulnerability. Contribution of Working Group II to the Fourth Assessment Report of the Intergovernmental Panel on Climate Change*, ed. M. L. Parry, O. F. Canziani, J. P. Palutikof, P. J. van der Linden, and C. E. Hanson. Cambridge: Cambridge University Press. Available online at: http://www.ipcc.ch/pdf/assessment-report/ar4/wg2/ar4-wg2-spm.pdf.
Jamieson, Dale, and Elliot, Robert. 2009. "Progressive Consequentialism." *Ethics* 23 (1): 241-251.
Jewell, Catherine. 2016. "Making Quality Medicines Affordable: An Interview with CIPLA." *World Intellectual Property Organization (WIPO) Magazine*. August. (4): 2-6.
John, Stephen. 2011. "Security, Knowledge and Well-Being." *Journal of Moral Philosophy* 8 (1): 68-91.
Jones, Karen. 2004. "Trust and Terror." In *Moral Psychology: Feminist Ethics and Social Theory*, ed. Peggy DesAutels and Margaret Urban Walker. Lanham: Rowman & Littlefield.
Jones, Karen. 2019. "Trust, Distrust, and Affective Looping." *Philosophical Studies* 176: 95-107.
Kagan, Shelly. 1994. "Me and My Life." *Proceedings of the Aristotelian Society* 94: 309-324.
Kagan, Shelly. 1998. *Normative Ethics*. Boulder: Westview Press.
Kant, Immanuel. 1785. *Foundations of the Metaphysics of Morals*. Indianapolis, IN: Bobbs-Merrill Company.
Kant, Immanuel. 1793. "On the Common Saying: This May Be True in Theory, But It Does Not Hold in Practice." In *Toward Perpetual Peace and Other Writings on Politics, Peace, and History*, ed. Pauline Kleingeld, 44-66. New Haven: Yale University Press, 2006.
Kamm, Frances. 2006. *Intricate Ethics: Rights, Responsibilities, and Permissible Harm*. Oxford: Oxford University Press.
Karnein, Anja. 2014. "Putting Fairness in Its Place: Why There Is a Duty to Take Up the Slack." *Journal of Philosophy* 111 (11): 593-607.
Kauppinen, Antti. 2013. "Empathy, Emotion Regulation, and Moral Judgment." Oxford: Oxford University Press.
Kavka, Gregory. 1982. "The Paradox of Future Individuals." *Philosophy & Public Affairs* 11: 93-112.
Kawachi, Ichiro, and Kennedy, Bruce P. 2006. *The Health of Nations: Why Inequality Is Harmful to Your Health*. New York: The New Press.
Keyes, Corey. 2002. "The Mental Health Continuum: From Languishing to Flourishing in Life." *Journal of Health and Social Behavior* 43 (2): 207-222.
Kieran, Matthew. 2014. *Creativity, Virtue, and the Challenges from Natural Talent, Ill-Being and Immortality*. Cambridge: Cambridge University Press.
Killmister, Suzy. 2016. "Dignity, Torture, and Human Rights." *Ethical Theory and Moral Practice* 19 (5): 1087-1101.
King, Nathan. 2014. "Perseverance as an Intellectual Virtue." *Synthese* 191 (15): 3501-3523.
Kittay, Eva. 2005. "At the Margins of Moral Personhood." *Ethics* 116 (1): 100.
Knight, Carl. 2005. "In Defence of Luck Egalitarianism." *Res Publica* 11 (1): 55-73.
Knight, Carl. 2013. "Luck Egalitarianism." *Philosophy Compass* 8 (10): 924-934.
Knight, Carl. 2015. "Abandoning the Abandonment Objection: Luck Egalitarian Arguments for Public Insurance." *Res Publica* 21 (2): 119-135.
Knight, Carl. 2021a. "An Argument for All-Luck Egalitarianism." *Philosophy and Public Affairs* 49 (4): 350-378.
Knight, Carl. 2021b. "Enough Is Too Much: The Excessiveness Objection to Sufficientarianism." *Economics & Philosophy* 38 (2): 275-299.
Kraut, Richard. 1994. "Desire and the Human Good." *Proceedings and Addresses of the American Philosophical Association* 63 (2): 39-54.
Kraut, Richard. 2007. "What Is Good and Why: The Ethics of Well-Being." Cambridge, MA: Harvard University Press.
Kreuder, Nick, and Hassoun, Nicole. Forthcoming. "Moral Status." *Public Affairs Quarterly*.
Last Mile Health. 2020. "Our Commitment to Anti-Racism." *Last Mile Health*, Accessed June 2, 2020. Available online at: https://lastmilehealth.org/2020/06/02/our-commitment-to-anti-racism/.

REFERENCES

Lear, Jonathan. 2008. "Radical Hope: Ethics in the Face of Cultural Devastation." Cambridge, MA: Harvard University Press.
Lelkes, Orsolya. 2006. "Knowing What Is Good for You: Empirical Analysis of Personal Preferences and the 'Objective Good.'" *The Journal of Socio-Economics, The Socio-Economics of Happiness* 35 (2): 285–307.
Liao, Matthew S. 2015. "Human Rights as Fundamental Conditions for a Good Life." In *Philosophical Foundations of Human Rights*, ed. Rowan Cruft, Matthew Liao, and Massimo Renzo, 79–100. Oxford: Oxford University Press.
Lichtenberg, Judith. 2010. "Negative Duties, Positive Duties, and the 'New Harms.'" *Ethics* 120 (3): 557–578.
Lichtenberg, Judith. 2013. *Distant Strangers: Ethics, Psychology, and Global Poverty*. Cambridge: Cambridge University Press.
Lippert-Rasmussen, Kasper. 2011. "Egalitarianism and Collective Responsibility." In *Egalitarianism and Responsibility*, ed. C. Knight and Z. Stemplowska, 98–114. Oxford: Oxford University Press.
Lippert-Rasmussen, Kasper. 2015. "Luck Egalitarianism." London: Bloomsbury.
Locke, John. 1689. *Two Treatises of Government*. Cambridge: Cambridge University Press.
Lumer, Christoph. 2005. "Prioritarian Welfare Functions—An Elaboration and Justification." In *Democracy and Welfare*, ed. Daniel Schoch, 43. Paderborn: Mentis.
Macklin, Ruth. 1981. "Can Future Generations Correctly Be Said to Have Rights?" In *Environmental Ethics*, ed. Ernest Partridge, 51–156. New York: Prometheus Books.
Marks, Stephen P. 2001. "Jonathan Mann's Legacy to the 21st Century: The Human Rights Imperative for Public Health." *Journal of Law, Medicine & Ethics* 29 (2): 131–138.
Martin, Adrienne. 2013. *How We Hope: A Moral Psychology*. Princeton: Princeton University Press.
Maslow, Abraham Harold. 1942. "The Dynamics of Psychological Security-Insecurity." *Journal of Personality* 10 (4): 331–344.
Mayell, Hillary. 2002. "Climate Studies Point to More Floods in this Century." *National Geographic*. January 30. Available online at: http://news.nationalgeographic.com/news/2002/01/0130_020130_greatfloods.html.
McGeer, Victoria. 2004. "The Art of Good Hope." *Annals of the American Academy of Political and Social Sciences* 592: 100–127.
McGeer, Victoria. 2008. "Trust, Hope and Empowerment." *Australasian Journal of Philosophy* 86 (2): 237–254.
Mikulincer, Mario, and Shaver, Phillip. 2015. "Boosting Attachment Security in Adulthood: The 'Broaden-and-Build' Effects of Security-Enhancing Mental Representations and Interpersonal Contexts." In *Attachment Theory and Research: New Directions and Emerging Themes*, ed. Jeffry Simpson and Steven Rhodes, 124–144. New York: The Guilford Press.
Mill, John S. 1863. *Utilitarianism*. London: Parker, Son and Bourn.
Miller, David. 2001. *Principles of Social Justice*. Cambridge, MA.: Harvard University Press.
Miller, David. 2019. "The Nature and Limits of the Duty of Rescue." *Journal of Moral Philosophy* 17 (3): 1–22.
Miller, Richard. 1998. "Cosmopolitan Respect and Patriotic Concern." *Philosophy & Public Affairs* 27 (3): 202–224.
Miller, David. 1999. *Principles of Social Justice*. Cambridge, MA.: Harvard University Press.
Miller, Richard. 2010. *Globalizing Justice: The Ethics of Poverty and Power*. New York: Oxford University Press.
Miller, Richard. 2015. "The Ethics of Social Democracy." Oxford Studies in Political Philosophy Conference. Syracuse, NY: Syracuse University.
Miller, David. 2020a. "Distribution According to Need: What Does It Mean?" In *Empirical Research and Normative Theory: Transdisciplinary Perspectives on Two Methodical Traditions between Separation and Interdependence*, ed. Alexander M. Bauer and Malte Meyerhuber, 35–74. Berlin: De Gruyter.
Miller, David. 2020b. "Needs Based Justice." In *Empirical Research and Normative Theory: Transdisciplinary Perspectives on Two Methodical Traditions between Separation and Interdependence*, ed. Alexander M. Bauer and Malte Meyerhuber. Berlin: De Gruyter.

Milona, Michael. 2017a. "Finding Hope." *Canadian Journal of Philosophy* 49 (5): 710–729.
Milona, Michael. 2017b. "Intellect versus Affect: Finding Leverage in an Old Debate." *Philosophical Studies* 174 (9): 2251–2276.
Moellendorf, Darrell. 2002. *Cosmopolitan Justice*. Boulder: Westview Press.
Moellendorf, Darrell. 2006. "Hope as a Political Virtue." *Philosophical Papers* 35 (3): 413–433.
Moellendorf, Darrel. 2014. *The Moral Challenge of Dangerous Climate Change: Values, Poverty, and Policy*. Cambridge: Cambridge University Press.
Moyn, Samuel. 2018. *Not Enough: Human Rights in an Unequal World*. Cambridge, MA: Belknap Press.
Murphy, Liam. 2000. *Moral Demands in Non-ideal Theory*. New York: Oxford University Press.
Nagel, Thomas. 1995. *Equality and Partiality*. Oxford: Oxford University Press.
Narveson, Jan. 1967. "Utilitarianism and New Generations." *Mind* 76 (301): 62–72.
National Academies of Sciences, Engineering, and Medicine. 2016. *Making Eye Health a Population Health Imperative: Vision for Tomorrow*. Washington, DC: The National Academies Press.
New York Times Editorial Board. 2020. "With Coronavirus, 'Health Care for Some' Is a Recipe for Disaster." *New York Times*. Updated March 6, 2020. Accessed January 5, 2023. https://www.nytimes.com/2020/03/06/opinion/coronavirus-immigrants-health.html.
Nickel, James. 2007. *Making Sense of Human Rights*. Oakland: University of California Press.
Nielsen, Lasse. 2020. "Sufficiency and Satiable Values." *Journal of Applied Philosophy* 36 (5): 800–816.
Nielsen, Lasse. 2016. "Sufficiency Grounded as Sufficiently Free: A Reply to Shlomi Segall." *Journal of Applied Philosophy* 33: 202–216.
Nielsen, Lasse, and Axelsen, David. 2016. "Capabilitarian Sufficiency: Capabilities and Social Justice." *Journal of Human Development and Capabilities* 18 (1): 46–59.
Nelkin, Dana. 2013. "Moral Luck." In *The Stanford Encyclopedia of Philosophy*, ed. Edward N. Zalta, https://plato.stanford.edu/entries/moral-luck/.
Noddings, Nel. 2002. *Starting at Home: Caring and Social Policy*. Oakland: University of California Press.
Nozick, Robert. 1974. *Anarchy State and Utopia*. New York: Basic Books.
Nussbaum, Martha 1986. "The Fragility of Goodness." *Journal of Philosophy* 85 (7): 376–383.
Nussbaum, Martha. 2000a. "The Costs of Tragedy: Some Moral Limits of Cost-Benefit Analysis." *Journal of Legal Studies* 29 (2): 1005–1036.
Nussbaum, Martha. 2000b. *Women and Human Development: The Capabilities Approach*. Cambridge: Cambridge University Press.
Nussbaum, Martha. 2006. *Frontiers of Justice: Disability, Nationality, Species Membership*. Cambridge, MA.: Harvard University Press.
Nussbaum, Martha. 2007. "Human Rights and Human Capabilities." *Harvard Human Rights Journal* 20 (21): 14.
Nussbaum, Martha. 2011. *Creating Capabilities*. Cambridge, MA: Harvard University Press.
Nussbaum, Martha. 2016. *Anger and Forgiveness: Resentment, Generosity, Justice*. Oxford: Oxford University Press.
Oakeshott, Michael. 1962. *Rationalism in Politics and Other Essays*. New York: Basic Books Pub. Co.
Oberdiek, John. 2012. "The Moral Significance of Risking." *Legal Theory* 18 (3): 339–356.
O'Dowd, Ornaith. 2016. "'Caring-about' and the Problem of Overwhelming Obligations." *Hypatia* 31 (4): 795–809.
Organization for Economic Co-operation and Development (OECD). 2019. "Education at a Glance 2019: Country Note South Africa, OECD Indicators." *Organization for Economic Co-operation and Development*. Accessed October 5, 2023. Available online at: https://www.oecd.org/education/education-at-a-glance/EAG2019_CN_ZAF.pdf.
O'Neill, Onora. 2005. "The Dark Side of Human Rights." *International Affairs* 81 (2): 427–439.
Ord, Toby. 2020. *The Precipice: Existential Risk and the Future of Humanity*. New York: Hachette Books.
Page, Scott. 2007. *The Difference: How the Power of Diversity Creates Better Groups, Firms, Schools, and Societies*. Princeton: Princeton University Press.

Parekh, Bhikhu. 1975. *Marx and the Whole Man: The Concept of Socialism*. Brookline, MA: Holmes & Meier Publishers.
Parfit, Derek. 1984. *Reasons and Persons*. Oxford: Clarendon Press.
Parfit, Derek. 2011. *On What Matters*, vol. 1, Oxford: Oxford University Press.
Pedersen, Viki, and Midtgaard, Soren. 2018. "Is Anti-Paternalism Enough?" Political Studies 66 (3): 771–785.
Pettit, Phillip. 2004. "Hope and Its Place in Mind." *Annals of the American Academy of Political and Social Science* 592 (1): 152–165.
Persson, Ingmar. 2013. "Prioritarianism." In *The International Encyclopedia of Ethics*, ed. Hugh LaFollette. Malden, MA: Wiley-Blackwell.
Perry, Stephen R. 1997. "Risk, Harm, and Responsibility." In *Philosophical Foundations of Tort Law*, ed. David G. Owen, 321–346. Oxford: Oxford University Press.
Philips, Jos. 2008. "A Critique of Three Recent Studies on Morality's Demands: Murphy, Mulgan, Cullity and the Issue of Cost." *Ethics. An International Journal for Moral Philosophy* 7 (1): 1–13.
Piketty, Thomas. 2014. "Capital in the Twenty-First Century: A Multidimensional Approach to the History of Capital and Social Classes". *British Journal of Sociology* 65(4): 736–747.
Placani, Adriana. 2016. "When the Risk of Harm." *Law and Philosophy* 36 (1): 77–100.
Pogge, Thomas. 2008. *World Poverty and Human Rights*. Cambridge: Polity Press.
Pogge, Thomas. 2009. "Developing Morally Plausible Indices of Poverty and Gender Equity: A Research Program." *Philosophical Topics* 37 (2): 199–221.
Pogge, Thomas W., and Pogge, Thomas C. 2002. "Can the Capability Approach Be Justified?" *Philosophical Topics* 30 (2): 167–228. Available online at: http://www.jstor.org/stable/43154399.
Popper, Karl. 1986. "Utopia and Violence." *World Affairs* 149 (1): 3–9.
Quong, Jonathan. 2010. *Liberalism without Perfection*. Oxford: Oxford University Press.
Railton, Peter. 1986. "Facts and Values." *Philosophical Topics* 14 (2): 5–31.
Rappoport, Angelo. 1924. *Dictionary of Socialism*. London: T. Fisher Unwin Ltd.
Rawls, John. 1971. *A Theory of Justice*. Cambridge, MA: Harvard University Press.
Rawls, John. 1980. "Kantian Constructivism in Moral Theory." *Journal of Philosophy* 77 (9): 515–572.
Rawls, John. 1999. *The Law of Peoples*. Cambridge, MA: Harvard University Press.
Raz, Joseph. 1986. *The Morality of Freedom*. Oxford: Clarendon Press.
Raz, Joseph. 2015. "Human Rights as Fundamental Conditions for a Good Life." In *Human Rights in the Emerging World Order*, ed. Rowan Cruft, Matthew S. Liao, and Massimo Renzo, 79–100. Oxford: Oxford University Press.
Reiff, David. 2002. *A Bed for the Night: Humanitarianism in Crisis*. New York: Simon and Schuster.
Risse, Mathias. 2012. *On Global Justice*. Princeton: Princeton University Press.
Rivera, Joseph. 1977. "A Structural Theory of the Emotions." *Psychological Issues* 10: 1–178.
Rivera-Lopez, Eduardo. 2009. "Individual Procreative Responsibility and the Non-identity Problem." *Pacific Philosophical Quarterly* 90: 99–118.
Roberts, Melinda. 2009. "The Nonidentity Problem." In *Stanford Encyclopedia of Philosophy*, ed. Edward N. Zalta, https://plato.stanford.edu/archives/fall2017/entries/nonidentity-problem/.
Robeyns, Ingrid. 2016. "The Capability Approach." In *Stanford Encyclopedia of Philosophy*, ed. Edward N. Zalta, https://plato.stanford.edu/entries/capability-approach/.
Robeyns, Ingrid. 2017. "Having Too Much." In *NOMOS LVI: Wealth. Yearbook of the American Society for Political and Legal Philosophy*, ed. Jack Knight and Melissa Schwartzberg. New York: New York University Press.
Robeyns, Ingrid. 2019. "What, if Anything, Is Wrong with Extreme Wealth?" *Journal of Human Development and Capabilities* 20 (3): 251–266.
Rolston III, Holmes. 2008. "Feeding People versus Saving Nature." In *The Ethics of the Environment*, ed. London: Routledge.
Rorty, Amelie. 2009. "Educating the Practical Imagination." In *The Oxford Handbook of Philosophy of Education*, ed. Harvey Siegel, 195–209. Oxford: Oxford University Press.

Rosati, Connie. 1995. "Persons, Perspectives, and Full Information Accounts of the Good." *Ethics* 105 (2): 296–325.
Ruger, Jennifer. 2010. *Health and Social Justice*. New York: Oxford University Press.
Sanders, John T. 1988. "Why the Numbers Should Sometimes Count." *Philosophy and Public Affairs* 17: 3–14.
Sandler, Lauren. 2020. "COVID-19's Body Count Will Go beyond Those Who Die from the Disease: It Didn't Have to Be This Way." *Time Magazine*. New York: Time Inc. 28 April. Accessed October 8, 2021. https://time.com/5828700/coronavirus-safety-net-poverty/.
Santos-Paulino, Amelia. 2012. "Trade, Income Distribution and Poverty in Developing Countries: A Survey." In *UNCTAD Discussion Papers from United Nations Conference on Trade and Development*. Geneva: UNCTAD.
Scanlon, Thomas. 1975. "Preference and Urgency." *Journal of Philosophy* 72 (19): 655–669.
Scheffler, Samuel. 1993. *Human Mortality*. Oxford: Oxford University Press.
Scheffler, Samuel. 1994. *The Rejection of Consequentialism: A Philosophical Investigation of the Considerations Underlying Rival Moral Conceptions*. Oxford University Press, Oxford.
Scheffler, Samuel. 2015. "The Practice of Equality." In *Social Equality: On What It Means to Be Equals*, ed. Carina Fourie, Fabian Schuppert, and Ivo Walliman-Helmer. New York: Oxford University Press.
Scheffler, Samuel. 2016. "Death and the Afterlife." In *Berkeley Tanner Lectures*, ed. Niko Kolodny. New York: Oxford University Press.
Scheffler, Samuel. 2018. *Why Worry about Future Generations?* New York: Oxford University Press.
Segall, Shlomi. 2010. *Health, Luck, and Justice*. Princeton: Princeton University Press.
Segall, Shlomi. 2014. "What Is the Point of Sufficiency?" *Journal of Applied Philosophy* 33 (1): 36–52.
Segall, Shlomi. 2019. "Sufficientarianism and the Separateness of Persons." *Philosophical Quarterly* 69 (274): 142–155.
Sen, Amartya. 1980. "Equality of What?" In *Tanner Lectures on Human Values*, ed. Sterling McMurrin. Cambridge: Cambridge University Press.
Sen, Amartya. 1999. *Development as Freedom*. New York: Anchor Books.
Sher, George. 2014. *Equality for Inegalitarians*. Cambridge: Cambridge University Press.
Shields, Liam. 2012. "The Prospects for Sufficientarianism." *Utilitas* 24 (1): 101–117.
Shields, Liam. 2016. "Sufficiency Principle." In *The International Encyclopedia of Ethics*, ed. Hugh LaFollette. New Jersey: Wiley. 1–8.
Shields, Liam. 2018. *Just Enough Sufficiency as a Demand of Justice*. Edinburgh: Edinburgh University Press.
Shields, L. 2020. "Sufficientarianism." *Philosophy Compass* 15 (11): 1–10.
Shiffrin, Seana. 1999. "Wrongful Life, Procreative Responsibility, and the Significance of Harm." *Legal Theory* 5: 117–148.
Shiffrin, S. V. 2000. "Paternalism, Unconscionability Doctrine, and Accommodation." *Philosophy and Public Affairs* (29): 205–250.
Sinnott-Armstrong, Walter. 2015. "Consequentialism." In *The Stanford Encyclopedia of Philosophy*, ed. Edward N. Zalta, https://plato.stanford.edu/entries/consequentialism/
Singer, Peter. 1972. "Famine, Affluence, and Morality." *Philosophy and Public Affairs* 1 (3): 229–243.
Skoll. 2021. "Last Mile Health." *Skoll Foundation*. Accessed January 5, 2023. https://skoll.org/organization/last-mile-health/#:~:text=Impact%20%26%20Accomplishments,14%20districts%20in%20the%20country.
Slote, Michael, and Pettit, Philip. 1984. "Satisficing Consequentialism." *Proceedings of the Aristotelian Society, Supplementary Volumes* 58 (1): 139–176.
Smith, Adam. 1904. *An Inquiry into the Nature and Causes of the Wealth of Nations*. 5th ed. New York: P. F. Collier & Son.
Smith, Adam, and Haakonssen, Knud. 2002. (Original work 1759). "The Theory of Moral Sentiments." In *Cambridge Texts in the History of Philosophy*, ed. Haakonssen, Knud, 7–16. New York: Cambridge University Press.

Smith, Matthew. 2010. "Practical Imagination and its Limits." *Philosophers' Imprint* 10 (3): 1–20.
Snow, Nancy. 2013. "Hope as an Intellectual Virtue." In *Virtues in Action: New Essays in Applied Virtue Ethics*, ed. Michael W. Austin, 153–170. London: Palgrave Macmillan.
Snyder, Charles. 2000. *Handbook of Hope: Theory, Measures and Applications*. San Diego: Academic Press.
Sobel, David. 1999. "Subjectivism and Idealization." *Ethics* 119 (2): 336–352.
Sorabji, Richard. 1980. *Necessity, Cause, and Blame Perspectives on Aristotle's Theory*. Ithaca: Cornell University Press.
South African Government. 2020. "Water and Sanitation." Pretoria: South African Government. https://www.gov.za/about-sa/water-affairs.
Srinivasan, Amia. 2017. "The Aptness of Anger." *Journal of Political Philosophy* 26 (2): 123–144.
Steiner, Hillel. 2009. "Left Libertarianism and the Ownership of Resources." *Public Reasons* 1(1): 1–8.
Stemplowska, Zofia. 2016. "Doing More Than One's Fair Share." *Critical Review of International Social and Political Philosophy* 19(5): 591–608.
Stemplowska, Zofia. 2019. "Coercing Compliers to Do More Than One's Fair Share." *Zeitschrift für Ethik und Moralphilosophie* 2: 147–160.
Steyl, Steven. 2020. "Caring Actions." *Hypatia* 35 (2): 279–297.
Stockdale, Katie. 2021. *Hope under Oppression*. Oxford: Oxford University Press.
Subramanian, Swamy. 1997. "Introduction: The Measurement of Inequality and Poverty." In *The Measurement of Inequality and Poverty*, ed. S. Subramanian, 1–13. Oxford: Oxford University Press.
Subramanian, Swamy. 2002. "Counting the Poor: An Elementary Difficulty in the Measurement of Poverty." *Economics and Philosophy* 18: 277–285.
Subramanian, Swamy. 2006. "Poverty Measurement and Theories of Beneficence." *Rights, Deprivation, and Disparity: Essays in Concepts and Measurement*. Delhi: Oxford University Press.
Subramanian, Sreenivasan. 2023. "The Repugnant, the Sadistic, and Two 'Despotic' Conclusions in Population Ethics." Wellington University of Victoria Working Paper. https://www.wgtn.ac.nz/cpf/publications/working-papers/2023-working-papers/WP01-2023-SRD-Conclusions.pdf.
Swanton, Christine. 2003. *Virtue Ethics: A Pluralistic View*. Oxford: Oxford University Press.
Swanton, Christine. 2013. "The Definition of Virtue Ethics." In *The Cambridge Companion to Virtue Ethics*, ed. Russell, Daniel, 315–338. Cambridge: Cambridge University Press.
Tan, Kok-Chor. 2004. *Justice without Borders*. Cambridge: Cambridge University Press.
Tan, Kok-Chor. 2012. *Justice, Institutions, and Luck: The Site, Ground, and Scope of Equality*. Oxford: Oxford University Press.
Tasioulas, John. 2013. "Human Dignity and the Foundations of Human Rights." In *Understanding Human Dignity*, ed. Christopher McCrudden, 293–314. Oxford: Oxford University Press.
Tasioulas, John. 2015. "Human Rights as Fundamental Conditions for a Good Life." In *Philosophical Foundations of Human Rights*, ed. Rowan Cruft, Matthew S. Liao, and Massimo Renzo, 79–100. Oxford: Oxford University Press.
Taurek, John M. 1977. "Should the Numbers Count?" *Philosophy & Public Affairs* 6(4): 293–316.
Temkin, Larry. 1993. *Inequality*. New York: Oxford University Press.
t'Hoen, Ellen, Berger, Jonathan, Calmy, Alexandra, and Moon, Suerie. 2011. "Driving a Decade of Change: HIV/AIDS, Patents and Access to Medicines for All." *Journal of the International AIDS Society* 14 (15): 1–12.
Thomson, Judith. 1976. "Property Acquisition." *Journal of Philosophy* 73 (18): 664–666.
Tiberius, Valerie. 2008. *The Reflective Life*. Oxford: Oxford University Press.
Timmer, Dick. 2021a. "Libertarianism: Pattern, Principle, or Presumption?" *Journal of Applied Philosophy* 29 (4): 271–288.
Timmer, Dick. 2021b. "Justice, Thresholds, and the Three Claims of Sufficientarianism." *Journal of Political Philosophy* 30 (3): 298–323.

Tungodden, Bertil, and Vallentyne, Peter. 2006. "Person-Affecting Paretian Egalitarianism with Variable Population Size." In *Intergenerational Equity and Sustainability*, ed. John Roemer and Kotaro Suzumura, 176–200. New York: Palgrave Macmillan.
Unger, Peter. 1996. *Living High and Letting Die: Our Illusion of Innocence*. New York: Oxford University Press.
US Department of Health and Human Services. 2019. "U.S. Department of Health and Human Services, Child Welfare Outcomes 2016: Report to Congress." *Children's Bureau*. Accessed October 8, 2021. https://www.acf.hhs.gov/cb/resource/cwo-2016.
Vallentyne, Peter. 2002. "Brute Luck, Option Luck, and Equality of Initial Opportunities." *Ethics* 112 (3): 529–557.
Vallentyne, Peter, and Steiner, Hillel. 2009. "Libertarian Theories of Intergenerational Justice." In *Intergeneration Justice*, ed. Axel Gosseries and Lukas H. Meyer, 50–76. Oxford: Oxford University Press.
Van Parijs, Philippe, and Vanderborght, Yannick. 2017. *Basic Income: A Radical Proposal for a Free Society and a Sane Economy*. Cambridge, MA: Harvard University Press.
Vandamme, P.-É. 2017. "Why Not More Equality? Sufficientarianism and Inequalities above the Threshold." *Law, Ethics and Philosophy*, 130–141.
Venkatapuram, Sridhar. 2011. *Health Justice*. Cambridge: Polity Press.
Voigt, Kristin. 2007. "The Harshness Objection: Is Luck Egalitarianism Too Harsh on the Victims of Option Luck?" *Ethical Theory and Moral Practice* 10(4): 389–407.
Waldron, Jeremy. 1999. *Law and Disagreement*. Oxford: Oxford University Press.
Walker, Margaret. 2006. *Moral Repair: Reconstructing Moral Relations after Wrongdoing*. New York: Cambridge University Press.
Wall, Steven. 1998. "Liberalism, Perfectionism and Restraint." Cambridge: Cambridge University Press.
Wall, Steven. 2017. 'Perfectionism in Moral and Political Philosophy'. In *The Stanford Encyclopedia of Philosophy*, ed. Edward N. Zalta, https://plato.stanford.edu/archives/fall2021/entries/perfectionism-moral/.
Waterman, Alan. 1993. "Two Conceptions of Happiness: Contrasts of Personal Expressiveness (Eudaimonia) and Hedonic Enjoyment." *Journal of Personality and Social Psychology* 64 (4): 678–691.
Wasserman, David. 2005. "The Nonidentity Problem, Disability, and the Role Morality of Prospective Parents." *Ethics* 116: 132–152.
Wasserman, David. 2008. "Hare on De Dicto Betterness and Prospective Parents." *Ethics* 118: 529–533.
Wendt, Fabian. 2017. "The Sufficiency Proviso." In *Routledge Handbook of Libertarianism*, ed. Jason Brennan, Bas Vann der Vossen, and David Schmitz, 138–153. London: Routledge.
Wertheimer, Richard. 2002. "Youth Who Age Out of Foster Care: Troubled Lives, Troubling Prospects." *Child TRENDS*. December 1. Available online at: https://www.childtrends.org/publications/youth-who-age-out-of-foster-care-troubled-lives-troubling-prospects. Accessed October 8, 2021.
WHO (World Health Organization). 2018. "Best Practices in Innovations in Microplanning for Polio Eradication." Geneva: World Health Organization. Accessed October 5, 2023. Available online at: https://polioeradication.org/wp-content/uploads/2018/12/Best-practices-in-innovations-in-mircoplanning-for-polio-eradication.pdf.
Williams, Bernard. 1985. *Ethics and the Limits of Philosophy*. London: Fontana.
Wilkinson, Richard, and Pickett, Kate. 2011. *The Spirit Level: Why Greater Equality Makes Societies Stronger*. New York: Bloomsbury Publishing.
Williams, Bernard. 1981. *Divine Commands and Morality*. Oxford: Oxford University Press.
Williams, Bernard. 2006. *Ethics and the Limits of Philosophy*. Abingdon: Routledge Press.
Widerquist, Karl. 2010. "How the Sufficiency Minimum Becomes a Social Maximum." *Utilitas* 22: 474–480.
Wolff, Jonathan, and de-Shalit, Avner. 2007. *Disadvantages*. Oxford: Oxford University Press.
Wolf, Susan. 1982. "Moral Saints." *Journal of Philosophy* 79 (8): 419–439.

Wonderly, Monique. 2019. "On the Affect of Security." *Philosophical Topics* 47 (2): 165–181.
World Bank. 2019. "The World Bank, Life Expectancy at Birth, Total (Years)—South Africa." Washington, DC: The World Bank. Available online at: https://data.worldbank.org/indicator/SP.DYN.LE00.IN.
Yontcheva, Boriana, and Masud, Nadia. 2005. "Does Foreign Aid Reduce Poverty? Empirical Evidence from Nongovernmental and Bilateral Aid." IMF Working Papers. Washington, DC: International Monetary Fund.

Index

Since the index has been created to work across multiple formats, indexed terms for which a page range is given (e.g., 52–53, 66–70, etc.) may occasionally appear only on some, but not all of the pages within the range.

Access to basic healthcare 24 n.39, 31, 38, 45–6, 72, 77, 124–6
Adaptive preferences 12–13, 23–5, 23 n.34, 28 n.52, 37–8, 40–2, 40 n.15, 44–5, 54, 62–3
Adequate account (of the basic minimum/ basic justice) 10–13, 36, 45–6, 56, 60, 72, 83–5
Adequate range 11–14, 18–19, 33 n.70, 36, 46–7, 62–5, 77, 142–3
Adequate resources 4–5, 14–16, 18, 24 n.35, 30, 34, 38, 45–7, 53–4, 56 n.51, 59–60, 73–4, 91–2, 142–3
Advantage(s) 6–7, 15–16, 34 n.2, 38–9, 39 n.11, 40 n.14, 44, 53, 55, 55 n.50, 57, 65 nn.12, 14, 78–9, 143, 155
Agency 13–14, 16, 40–2, 40 n.13, 45–6, 65 n.14, 82–3, 102 n.6, 132 n.18
Aid 7, 31, 31 n.62, 35, 36, 45–6, 58–60, 68–9, 69 n.22, 73 nn.33, 36, 77, 79–82, 84, 85 n.6, 86–98, 86 n.11, 87 n.14, 94 n.26, 95 n.30, 100–3, 107–8, 108 n.20, 119, 121–2, 135, 135 n.24, 141, 143–6, 152–3, 155, 158
  Aid distribution 101–2
AIDs 124–6
Appreciation 2, 5–6, 11–14, 16–19, 30–1, 36–7, 55 n.50, 62–4, 100, 142–3
Appropriate impartiality and compassion 4–5, 12–13, 22, 27–9, 37–8, 62–5, 70–1, 82–3, 149
  Compassion 3–5, 9, 19–20, 102, 132, 150
  Impartiality 4–5, 27–9, 61–2, 63 n.8, 70–1, 82–3, 102, 149

Autonomy 4–5, 10–11, 10 n.1, 14–18, 21, 29, 39 n.11, 40 nn.14, 15, 49 n.34, 51–2, 51 n.38, 55, 64, 67–8, 72, 72 n.28, 150
  Autonomy-promoting options 30–1
  Autonomy-undermining coercion and constraint 27–9, 69, 149 n.2

Basic freedom 6–7, 61, 65–8, 91–2
Basic minimum 1–13, 16, 18–22, 25–7, 29, 32–3, 58–9, 61–2, 64–5, 71–2, 75–98
  Plausible basic minimum 16 n.15, 19–20, 19 n.23, 35–6, 40, 42–4, 45 n.28, 47, 49–52, 49 n.34, 51 n.38, 55, 57, 92–3
Basic right 11–12, 17–27, 20 nn.25, 26, 36–8, 42–3, 57, 61–2, 64–5, 76–7
Beneficence 3, 6 n.10, 34, 61, 70, 72–4, 74 n.36, 82, 85 n.9, 86, 92–3, 135 n.24
  Imperfect duties of beneficence 74 n.36, 85 n.9
Bodily integrity 53, 55, 60–1, 64–5, 77, 84–5

Capability(ies) 3–4, 4 n.4, 6, 10 n.1, 13–14, 30, 34 n.2, 39 n.11, 40–4, 40 n.15, 50–5, 51 nn.39, 41, 54 n.49, 72 n.30, 74 n.37, 75–6, 81, 81 n.2, 100, 102, 102 n.6, 104–6, 142–3
  Basic capabilities/capacities 14, 22 n.31, 39 n.11, 40 n.15, 50–1, 64, 67–8, 72 n.30, 81 n.2
  Capability account 3–4, 38–9, 50–4, 57, 65 n.14
  Capability theory 4–6, 50–1
  Central capabilities 4 n.4, 51–2, 54

INDEX

Character and circumstance 16–17, 24–5
Charity 58, 61, 72, 79, 82, 92–3, 135, 143
Choice-worthy lives 61, 72, 81, 81 n.2
Climate change 7–9, 99, 120, 123–4, 143–4, 146, 157
Coercive 6–7, 12 n.6, 27–9, 40–2, 56, 62 n.7, 64 n.11, 66 n.17, 71, 72 n.28, 75 n.38, 77 n.43, 80–1, 86 n.10, 143, 149–50, 149 nn.1, 2, 150 nn.6, 7
Coherent preferences 40, 44–5
Coherentist 13 n.7, 60 n.4, 84
Collective action 66 n.17, 124, 140 n.35, 149 n.5
Common humanity 2–4, 9, 11–15, 17–20, 22, 24–5, 28–9, 32, 34–5, 37–8, 49, 54, 56, 59–72, 74–7, 80–3, 87–8, 91–2, 96–7, 143, 145–6, 149–50
  Respect for common humanity 1–2, 3 n.3, 6–7, 6 n.10, 9, 10 n.1, 11 n.3, 12 n.5, 20 n.25, 24 n.37, 28–9, 29 n.55, 59, 60 n.3, 65–8, 67 n.19, 68 n.20, 69 nn.23, 26, 71–2, 76–7, 80–3, 87–8, 91–5, 94 n.27, 96 n.31, 97, 149–50
  Concern for common humanity 6 n.10, 9, 28, 32–5, 47, 54 n.48, 56, 58–9, 60 n.4, 64–5, 67 nn.18, 19, 69 n.23, 80–1, 93–5, 142–3
Compatriots 68–9, 69 n.23, 96 n.31, 103, 145–7, 149–50, 150 n.9
Complacency 124, 127–8, 130, 133, 136
Conflict 1, 7–8, 32 n.68, 60 n.4, 106 n.15, 120, 122, 129 n.9, 139 n.33, 143–4, 152–3
Consequentialism 70–2, 75–6, 76 n.41, 85 n.9, 87 n.14, 88 n.15, 100–2, 107 n.19, 124 n.1
Conservatism 130, 132–3, 136
Constraint 6–7, 12–13, 19–22, 27–9, 34 n.52, 40 n.14, 42 n.20, 44–5, 44 n.22, 46 n.31, 49, 50 n.36, 56, 65–8, 71, 81 n.1, 91–2, 94, 95 n.28, 97, 100–1, 116, 116 n.31, 129–31, 129 n.9, 136–7, 147, 152
  Constraints of possibility 19–20, 129 n.9, 130–1
Contractualist 4–5, 10–11, 63, 74–5, 87 n.14

Cost 7–9, 11 n.2, 14–15, 20 n.26, 23–4, 24 nn.35, 37, 31–2, 38, 39 n.11, 43–4, 43 n.21, 48 n.32, 59, 62–4, 70, 73–6, 73 nn.33, 34, 74 n.36, 80–2, 84, 85 n.6, 86–91, 86 n.10, 88 n.17, 89 n.19, 93–4, 95 n.30, 97–8, 105–7, 105 n.11, 120, 124–5, 125 n.2, 136–7, 136 n.27, 143–4, 151
COVID-19 pandemic 9, 31, 124
Creative resolve 8–9, 123–41, 144, 147
Culture 18, 69, 91 n.23

Dale Dorsey 39–44, 39 n.12, 40 nn.13, 15, 41 nn.16, 17, 42 n.20
David Axelsen 3–4, 4 n.4, 53–4, 53 n.47, 55 n.50, 102 n.6
David Braybrooke 49 n.34
David Miller 86–9, 87 nn.12–14, 17, 93, 106–8, 108 n.21
Debate(s) 11–13, 31–2, 70 n.27, 105 n.11, 110, 114 n.27, 142–3
Decision-making capacity 89–90, 110, 145
Deliberation 5, 11–13, 11 n.4, 24 n.39, 27–8, 28 n.53, 29 n.58, 39–40, 55 n.50, 63, 64 n.10, 69 n.26, 90 n.20, 142–3
Demandingness 11 n.3, 60–1, 60 n.4, 82
  Demand too much/not enough 2–4, 7, 60–2, 64, 74 n.36, 77, 79, 81–3, 85, 85 n.6, 92, 96–8, 125–6, 142–3, 151–2
Democratic societies 58, 77–9, 77 n.44, 96, 96 n.31, 146–7, 149 n.1, 150, 150 n.8
Deontological 71–2, 74 n.36, 101–2, 152
Deprivation 5, 41 n.17, 48 n.32, 84, 101 n.4, 112 n.25, 114 n.27, 119
  Severe deprivation 77, 77 n.43, 104 n.9
Derek Parfit 112–14, 114 n.26
  Parfit's paradox 112–14, 114 n.26
  Repugnant Conclusion 7–8, 113–15, 143–4
Desideratum 59–62, 60 n.4, 77, 81, 83–5, 85 n.6
Dignity 2, 15, 17–18, 36–7, 41 n.17, 145–6
  Safeguard dignity 17–18, 36–7
Disadvantage(s) 8–9, 19–20, 44–5, 65 n.14, 108 n.21
Discrimination 17–18, 69, 81 n.2

INDEX   175

Disease 31, 47–9, 73–4, 99, 102, 123, 140
Distinctively human 2, 17–18, 21 n.27,
    65–7, 67 n.18, 80–1, 91–2, 132
Distributive equality 73–6, 78–9, 105 n.11
Doing allowing distinction 152

Easy rescue 70, 74 n.36, 84–5, 85 n.9, 97–8
Economic, social, or political conditions
    120 n.39
Effectiveness principle 106–8, 106 n.15,
    107 n.19, 108 n.21, 121, 129, 131,
    135, 137, 141
  Number helped 7–8, 100–1, 103–7,
    105 n.11, 106 nn.13–15, 111,
    119–22, 121 n.40
  Weighted need 101–8, 105 n.11, 107 n.19,
    108 nn.20, 21, 121–2, 121 n.40, 153,
    155–7, 156 n.9, 157 n.10
  Weighted Priority Principle 106–7
  Use resources to minimize weighted
    need in the future 101–5, 105 n.11,
    121–2, 121 n.40, 153, 155
Egalitarian 17–18, 32, 35, 51–2, 51 n.44,
    59 n.2, 65 n.14, 69–76, 73 nn.31, 32,
    74 n.37, 76 n.40, 81 n.2, 84, 89,
    103 n.7, 117, 145–6
  Luck egalitarianism 71–4,
    73 nn.31, 32, 34, 78–9
    Traditional luck egalitarian 58, 73–4
  Relational egalitarianism 74–5, 74 n.37
Empathy 12–13, 19–20, 19 n.23, 24–5,
    25 n.41, 87–8, 150
  Projective empathy 24–5, 37 n.8, 62 n.6
  Put ourselves into others' shoes 2, 5,
    13 n.7, 19, 21, 27 n.49, 28, 38–9,
    62 n.6, 63, 142–3
Empirical evidence 12 n.5, 13 n.9, 108
Entitlements 85, 85 n.8, 97–8, 103, 121
Equal claim to freedom 65, 67–8, 149
Ex-ante and ex-post perspective 16, 120
Exist 1, 10–11, 14, 18 n.20, 21–2, 29–31,
    34 n.2, 48 n.32, 49–50, 53–4, 55 n.50,
    59–61, 60 n.3, 64, 68, 77–8, 81, 87–8,
    95, 97, 102, 109–12, 116–17,
    118 nn.33, 34
  Bring people into existence 7–8, 109–13,
    110 n.22, 114 n.26, 115–20,
    115 nn.28–30, 116 n.31, 119 n.37,
    143–4, 154, 154 n.3, 156

Fair shares view 84–8, 85 n.8, 87 n.13,
    151–2
Famine 59–60, 99
First person perspective 12–13, 34 n.52,
    44–5
Freedom 4 n.5, 6–7, 12 n.6, 16–18, 23,
    27–9, 34 n.1, 37 n.9, 40 n.14, 53–5,
    58–9, 61, 65–8, 71–2, 79, 81 n.2,
    87–8, 91–2, 130–1, 143, 149–50
Full justice 59, 149
Fundamental conditions 11–14, 18–19,
    36–7, 46–7, 50, 62–4, 142–3
Fundamental interest 4 n.4, 22, 37–8,
    47–9, 53–4, 62, 89–90
Future Generations 7–8, 72 n.29, 99–122,
    101 n.3, 106 n.16, 114 n.26,
    121 n.40, 143–4, 153, 153 n.2,
    154 n.4, 155–8, 156 n.8

Garrett Cullity ix, 92–4, 94 n.26
George Sher 65 n.14, 89–92, 90 n.21
  Live effectively 81, 89–92
  Threshold of effectiveness 89–90
Gustaf Arrhenius 115–19, 115 n.28,
    116 n.31, 119 nn.35, 36
  Arrhenius' argument 115–18

Harry Frankfurt 23 nn.34, 36, 48 n.32
Hope ix, 5 n.8, 15, 31–2, 65 n.14, 90–2,
    123–5, 129–30, 136–41, 137 n.31,
    139 nn.33, 34, 140 n.35, 144
  Radical hope 139, 139 n.33, 141, 144
  Virtuous hope 139–40
Human forms of existence 2, 62 n.6, 65–7,
    67 n.18, 80–1, 91–2, 91 n.23
Human rights 2–3, 3 n.1, 6 n.10, 9, 12–13,
    34–5, 36 n.3, 40 n.14, 49–50,
    65 n.14, 68–9, 68 n.21, 72, 79–81,
    81 n.2, 88 n.17, 126, 143, 145–7
  Human rights obligations 6–7, 32 n.67,
    35, 68, 89 n.19, 142

Ideal moral code 85, 85 n.8
Ideal observer theory 12–13, 28
Ideal theory 8–9, 8 n.13, 86
Impact on generations 121 n.40, 153, 155
Individual differences 18, 53, 64
In/Feasibility 49, 60 n.4, 76 n.40, 129–30
Insecurity 15–16

INDEX

Institutional structures 14, 14 n.10, 36–7, 70–1
Institution(s) 5, 13–14, 17 n.17, 22 n.30, 30, 39 n.11, 43–4, 45 n.28, 49–52, 52 n.45, 63–4, 64 n.11, 66 n.17, 68 n.20, 69–71, 69 n.26, 72 n.30, 80–1, 86 n.10, 87–90, 88 nn.16, 17, 91 n.23, 99–100, 108 n.21, 146, 146 n.2, 149 n.5, 150
Internal/external liberty 23, 37–8, 62
International community 10–11, 68–9, 80–1, 86 n.10, 147

John Rawls 4 n.5, 22 n.30, 24 n.39, 59 n.2, 69
Justice 7 n.11, 11, 24 n.39, 32, 33 n.70, 35, 53 n.47, 54–5, 54 n.48, 59, 67 n.19, 69, 72, 74 n.35, 75–9, 81–3, 86–7, 89, 112 n.24, 135, 143 n.1, 145, 149, 150 n.7, 153
    Basic justice 6–7, 6 nn.10, 11, 12 n.5, 22 n.30, 54 n.48, 58–61, 61 n.5, 64–5, 65 n.12, 70–2, 74–85, 75 n.38, 91–3, 96–8, 97 n.32, 142–3, 143 n.1, 145, 147
    Global justice 2–3, 6–7, 9, 34, 65 n.14, 67–8, 79, 96 n.31, 142–3
Justifiable aspiration 11, 16, 18 n.18, 19–21, 20 nn.25, 26, 36–8, 50–1, 56, 62, 64–5, 76–7, 142–3

Lasse Nielsen 4 n.4, 53–5, 101 n.5
Legitimacy 3, 34, 149–50
Liam Murphy 84 n.5, 93, 151–2
Liberal neutrality 55 n.50, 69, 69 n.26
Libertarianism 58, 72, 78–9
Liberty 14, 29, 40 n.14, 51 n.38, 55, 69
Life project/plan 39–46
Life-improving goods 2, 11–13, 18–19, 36, 62–4
Lockean proviso 72–4
Longtermists 17–18, 120

Martha Nussbaum 26 n.44, 53
Matthew Liao 46–7, 65, 68, 74–5
Meaningful pursuits 11–13, 18–19, 36, 62
Minimally good/well 1–33, 3 n.1, 11 nn.2, 4, 13 nn.7, 9, 10, 14 n.12, 16 nn.14, 15, 19 n.23, 20 nn.25, 26, 21 n.27, 23 n.32, 24 nn.37, 38, 27–33, 27 n.48, 28 nn.53, 54, 57, 29 n.59, 31 n.61, 32 nn.64, 67, 33 n.70, 36–58, 39 n.11, 41 n.17, 42 n.20, 43 n.21, 44 nn.22, 23, 49 n.35, 50 n.37, 51 n.38, 44, 56 nn.51, 52, 57, 59 n.2, 60, 62–88, 63 nn.8, 9, 65 n.12, 66 n.15, 68 nn.20, 21, 69 n.26, 72 n.29, 74 nn.34–36, 75 n.38, 76 n.41, 77 nn.42, 43, 78 n.44, 81 n.2, 83 n.4, 85 n.8, 88 n.16, 91 n.22, 92 n.25, 93–5, 94 n.27, 97–101, 97 n.32, 103, 105–8, 106 n.16, 110–13, 112 n.25, 115, 119, 121, 123–34, 124 n.1, 127 n.4, 131 n.16, 136 n.27, 137–43, 138 n.32, 145–7, 149–50, 149 n.3
Well enough 1–2, 5, 7–9, 12–19, 16 nn.13, 14, 20 n.26, 21–2, 24, 24 nn.35, 38, 26 n.46, 28–32, 29 n.55, 38–9, 38 n.10, 39 n.11, 42–3, 43 n.21, 46 n.31, 48 n.33, 49 n.34, 50–2, 54–6, 55 n.50, 60–1, 63–4, 65 n.12, 66 nn.15, 17, 68–79, 68 n.20, 73 nn.32, 36, 74 nn.37, 39, 76 n.41, 78 n.45, 82, 85 n.8, 86, 86 n.10, 90–5, 91 n.22, 95 nn.28, 30, 97–8, 100–1, 107, 107 n.18, 115 n.29, 123–5, 127–34, 128 n.8, 129 n.11, 136–40, 142–7, 149 nn.3, 5, 150
Flourish(ing) 2, 9, 13, 13 n.8, 17–19, 17 n.17, 20 n.26, 21, 27 n.48, 36–7, 36 n.6, 46 n.30, 47–9, 48 nn.32, 33, 51–5, 51 n.39, 59 n.2, 60–1, 60 n.3, 64 n.11, 65–7, 66 n.15, 67 n.18, 70–2, 77–82, 81 n.2, 91–2, 94 n.27, 124–6, 132, 134–7, 134 n.23, 136 nn.26, 30, 139–41, 140 n.35, 143–6, 149–50
Minimum provision 39 n.11, 40 n.14, 47–9, 143
Model for intergenerational aid 106 n.15, 110–11, 153–8, 153 n.2, 154 n.4, 155 nn.5, 7, 156 n.8
    Principles (A and B) 153, 155–7, 156 n.8
    Diagram 103, 112 n.25, 116, 154 n.4, 155–6
    Initial situation 121 n.40, 153, 154 n.4, 155, 155 n.5, 157–8
    Present situation 153–5, 155 n.5, 157–8

INDEX

Future Situation 117–18, 153, 154 n.4, 155–7
Morality 32, 59, 67 n.19, 74 nn.35, 36, 81–3, 85 nn.7, 9, 128 n.8, 145–6, 149
 Moral Community 8 n.13, 28–9, 52 n.45, 65–7, 67 n.18, 90 n.21, 91–2, 149
 Moral equals/equality 12–13, 22, 49–52, 52 n.45, 62, 65 n.14, 89–91, 90 n.21
 Moral obligation/requirement/responsibility/duty 8 n.13, 24–5, 35, 49, 73 nn.32, 34, 86 n.11, 87, 89 n.19, 128 n.8

Necessary good 49 n.34, 102–5, 113–14, 119–20, 149, 156 n.9
Needs 2, 4 n.4, 5–9, 12–17, 16 n.15, 17 n.17, 21–3, 25–6, 28–31, 32 nn.65, 68, 36–9, 44, 47–51, 48 nn.32, 34, 53–6, 54 n.49, 56 n.51, 63–5, 65 n.14, 67–8, 77 nn.44, 45, 81 n.2, 84–5, 87–8, 90–2, 96, 100–8, 105 n.11, 107 n.19, 108 n.21, 111, 112 n.25, 116–17, 142–5, 147, 149–52, 156, 157 n.10
 Alleviating needs 101–2, 104, 105 n.11, 106, 108 n.21, 119–20, 122, 156, 156 n.9
 Fulfilling needs 28–9, 55, 65 n.14, 78 n.45, 100, 102–5, 102 n.6, 108, 110, 147, 152, 155–7
 Idiosyncratic needs 47–9, 55, 63–4
 Needs theorists 48 n.32
No mere addition 111–15, 114 n.27, 115 n.30
Non-compliance 151–2
Non-ideal world/circumstances/situations 8–9, 86, 89, 97–8, 97 n.32, 151–2
Non-identity problem 109–10

Obligation(s) 6–7, 6 n.10, 8 n.12, 24–5, 32 nn.67–69, 33 n.70, 35–6, 39 n.11, 48 n.32, 49, 51–2, 60 n.3, 61 n.5, 66 n.15, 67–72, 69 n.22, 77 n.42, 78–9, 82–4, 86–9, 86 n.10, 87 nn.13, 14, 88 n.16, 89 nn.18, 19, 91–2, 94–5, 96 n.31, 97 n.32, 103, 123, 142, 150 nn.7, 9, 151–2

Paternalism 40, 50–2, 50 nn.36, 40
Person Affecting Restriction 116–19
Person tradeoff 53–4, 100–1, 105 n.11, 114, 119–20, 121 n.40, 122, 153
Personal lives 6 n.10, 70, 70 n.27
Personal prerogatives 60 n.3, 83 n.4
Peter Singer 59–61, 59 n.2, 70–1, 70 n.27, 83, 85 n.6, 92–3, 151
Phronesis 128 n.8, 131 n.16
Pleasure 2, 5–6, 11–14, 16–19, 21, 30–1, 36–7, 46–7, 51 n.38, 55 n.50, 62–4, 100, 100 n.2, 107 n.18, 110, 142–3
Policy 11 n.2, 49, 49 n.34, 54 n.48, 77–8, 99, 105–6, 119 n.37
 Policy makers 12, 21–2, 30–1, 44–5, 49–50, 49 n.34, 65 n.12, 76–8, 120 n.39, 145, 157, 157 n.12
Political lives 2, 6–7, 58, 70, 79, 150 n.9
Political societies 6–8, 71, 86 n.10, 143, 149–50
Political and moral theories 2, 8 n.12, 24–5, 32 nn.67, 68, 33 nn.69, 70, 35–6, 49, 68, 78–9, 87
Population Axiology 108, 119 nn.36, 38
Poverty 5, 11 n.2, 15–16, 40, 42–3, 48 n.32, 77 n.42, 78 n.46, 91–2, 123, 126, 137, 145–7
 Extreme poverty 11 n.2, 40
 Global Poor 17–18, 44–5, 78–9, 120
Practical wisdom 128–9, 131 n.16
Preference-based theories of welfare 54
Present Generations 7–8, 32–3, 99–122, 106 n.16, 121 n.40, 143–4, 153, 155–8, 156 n.8, 9, 157 n.10
Principle of mutual concern 96, 97 n.32
Prioritarian 32–3, 101–6, 103 n.7, 105 n.11, 106 nn.14, 15, 121–2, 121 n.40, 156
 Prioritarian principle 41 n.16, 101–3
 Prioritization of the least well-off 7–8, 95, 100–5

Reasonable affirmation 19–20
Reasonable, free, care standard 27 n.49, 28–9, 150
 Reasonable care and concern 65, 65 n.12, 67–8, 80–1, 149–50
 Reasonable free care 4–5, 12–13, 54, 56, 59 n.2, 68, 68 n.20, 70–2, 80–1, 145–6, 150

178 INDEX

Reasonable, free, care standard (*cont.*)
   Reasonable, caring, free person 2, 5, 11–13, 13 n.7, 14 n.12, 17 n.16, 19–25, 20 nn.25, 26, 24 nn.35, 37, 39, 26 n.45, 27–8, 27 n.50, 29 n.59, 30–2, 36–8, 37 n.8, 43–4, 50–1, 56, 62–5, 63 n.8, 9, 64 n.10, 69 n.26, 76–7, 142–3, 145
Relationship(s) 2, 5–7, 11–14, 16–23, 18 nn.18–20, 29 n.57, 29–31, 34 n.1, 36–7, 40–2, 40 n.14, 41 n.17, 46–7, 51 n.38, 55, 59, 62–8, 66 nn.15, 17, 67 n.18, 69 n.26, 70–1, 72 n.29, 74–5, 80–1, 86–8, 87 n.14, 91–2, 96, 100, 112 n.25, 136 n.27, 140, 142–3, 145–7, 149–50
   Important relationships 2, 6–7, 22–3, 28–9, 34 n.1, 59, 65–8, 67 n.18, 80–1, 91–2, 149
Requirement grounding 92–4
   Requirement grounding margin 93–4
Requisite assistance 68–9, 73–4, 97 n.32, 152
Rescue cases 59–60, 70, 97–8, 151
Resource(s) 3–5, 4 n.5, 10 n.1, 13–14, 18, 21–2, 23 n.34, 24 n.35, 30–1, 34 n.2, 36–8, 39 n.11, 49, 55, 63–4, 67–8, 68 n.20, 72–6, 72 n.30, 73 nn.32, 33, 74 n.37, 89–90, 95 nn.29, 30, 100, 102, 104 n.8, 106–7, 112 n.25, 121–2, 127 n.4, 133, 137, 142–3, 145–6, 150, 153, 155
   Resource limitations 89–90, 112 n.25
   Resource theories 3–4, 39 n.11
Richard Miller ix, 96–7, 96 n.31, 97 n.32
Roger Crisp 3–5, 3 n.3, 19 n.23, 24 n.40, 102–3, 106–7, 107 n.19
Ronald Dworkin 51–2, 73–4, 73 n.31

Sacrifice(s) 1–2, 7–9, 13 n.8, 14–15, 21 n.27, 24 n.37, 26 n.44, 32, 32 n.67, 36 n.6, 43 n.21, 45 n.25, 56 n.51, 58–62, 59 n.2, 60 n.3, 64–5, 65 n.12, 67–8, 67 n.19, 68 n.20, 70–2, 74–7, 74 nn.35, 36, 76 n.41, 79–101, 85 n.6, 91 n.22, 92 n.24, 128 n.8, 129–30, 129 n.11, 132–4, 133 n.19, 134 n.23, 136 n.27, 137, 142–3, 149–52
Second person perspective 12–13, 24–5, 38–9, 54, 157–8

Security 1, 14 n.12, 15–16, 16 nn.13, 14, 31 n.61, 55 n.50, 59 n.2, 64 n.11, 83 n.3, 84–5
   Secure access 12–15, 30–1, 36–7, 49 n.34, 63–5, 77
   Sufficient security 10–11, 14 n.12, 15
Separateness of persons 32–3, 104–8, 105 nn.10, 11
Significant moral goods 8, 123, 125, 130–1, 141, 144
Slack 8 n.13, 70–1, 85 n.7, 86, 86 n.10, 87 n.13, 88 nn.15, 17, 89 nn.18, 19, 152
Social democracy 58, 77–9, 77 n.44, 96
Social safety net 1, 9, 31, 57, 73–4, 78, 78 n.45, 145–6
Stephen Darwall 19 n.23, 24–5, 25 n.42, 37 n.8, 62 n.6
Strict Comparativism 116–17
Sufficientarian(s) 11 n.2, 24 n.40, 53–4, 74 n.34, 102, 106 n.14
   Sufficiency theory 3, 10 n.1, 10–11, 39 n.12, 48 n.32, 53–4, 75–6, 76 n.40, 102
   Sufficiency theorists 3–4, 4 n.6, 10–11
   Sufficiency threshold 10–11, 24 n.36, 32–3, 35, 53–4, 75–6, 76 n.40, 102
   Positive thesis 10–11
   Negative thesis 11
Supererogatory 70
Sympathy 25–6, 25 n.42, 62 n.6

Third person perspective 12–13, 34 n.52
Tragedy(ies)/Tragic 7–9, 18 nn.20, 21, 20 nn.24, 26, 32 n.67, 49–50, 52 n.46, 65 n.12, 70–1, 73 n.33, 75–8, 82–3, 92, 120, 123–4, 127–30, 132–3, 132 n.18, 136, 139, 139 n.33, 141, 143–4, 149 n.4

United Nations' Sustainable Development Goals 1
Universal Declaration of Human rights 1

Vice 124, 128 nn.5, 8, 130, 133, 136, 138 n.32, 141
Virtue 8, 34, 34 n.52, 46–7, 65–7, 74–5, 87–8, 123–41, 124 n.1, 128 nn.6, 8, 129 n.9, 130 n.13, 131 n.16, 18, 134 nn.22, 23, 135 n.25, 136 nn.26, 27, 137 n.31, 139 n.33, 140 n.35, 144
Virtuous observer theory 19 n.23